SSU-MA CH'IEN

GRAND HISTORIAN OF CHINA

SSU-MA CH'IEN
GRAND HISTORIAN
OF CHINA

By BURTON WATSON

NEW YORK 1958

COLUMBIA UNIVERSITY PRESS

Published in Great Britain, Canada, India, and Pakistan
by the Oxford University Press
London, Toronto, Bombay, and Karachi

Library of Congress Catalog Card Number: 57-13030
Manufactured in the United States of America

CONTENTS

INTRODUCTION

Chinese history, possibly unequalled in length and continuity by that of any other nation, has witnessed the rise and decay of a seemingly endless succession of dynastic houses, native and foreign. Chinese thinkers, confronted by this spectacle of evanescent glory, might well have been led, like those of Greece or India, to turn their gaze toward higher realms of metaphysical truth beyond the transience of worldly phenomena. They have indeed at times been so tempted. But for the most part the Chinese have kept their eyes fixed upon this world, bcause they have felt that, if truth is to be discovered at all, it must be discovered in the process of change itself. For this reason the Chinese have been among the most industrious recorders of change, the most indefatigable readers and writers of history ever known.

Ssu-ma Ch'ien (145–90? B. C.) is the first major Chinese historian of whom we have any appreciable knowledge and one of the greatest. His work, the *Shih chi* or *Records of the Historian,* in 130 chapters, is a history of the Chinese and foreign peoples known to him from earliest times down to the years of his own life. For some two thousand years since its appearance it has been one of the most widely and affectionately read of all Chinese historical works. Its form became a model for most of the major historical works of later ages; its contents and style have had an incalculable influence upon the literature of China and the countries under the sway of Chinese culture. To repeat an often made analogy, what Herodotus was to the historical tradition of the Greco-Roman world, Ssu-ma Ch'ien has been to that of China, Korea, and Japan.

Ssu-ma Ch'ien's history, covering five major dynasties as well as a

countless number of smaller principalities, is a history of change par
excellence. The two thousand years which it records move with a
ceaseless rhythm of rising and falling political fortunes, a rhythm
which to the Chinese is a natural and inevitable reflection in the human realm of the larger rhythm of the seasons and the stars. It is
Ssu-ma Ch'ien's professed aim to "examine the deeds and events of
the past and investigate the principles behind their success and failure, their rise and decay." His work, like that of all major historians
of the ancient East and West, is didactic: intended, as the traditional
phrase puts it, "to censure evil and encourage good."

In the *Kung-yang Commentary* on the *Spring and Autumn Annals,*
the twentieth year of Duke Shao, we are told that Confucius, in his
historical writings, was content to let his condemnation of evil rest
with the person of the evildoer, but that his recognition of goodness
was more far-reaching, extending to the sons and grandsons of the
worthy. Likewise in the *Shih chi,* if we may find anything that ap-
proaches permanence in the midst of change, it is the lasting power
of goodness. Evil destroys the doer, but good endures, through the
sons of the father, the subjects of the ruler, the disciples of the teacher.
It is the function of the historian to prolong the memory of goodness
by preserving its record for all ages to see.

"Anecdotes," says Croce, "provide the paradigms so much required
by pedagogues." Early Chinese historians, pedagogues in the broadest sense of the word, have made full use of the anecdote, developing
it to a level of complexity and literary subtlety far above its Western
equivalent, exemplified by such stories as that of Alfred and the
cakes. The Chinese works often consist almost wholly of dramatic
episodes and scenes in which direct speech replaces narrative and
serves to reveal the character of the actors without comment from the
historian. The *Shih chi* contains a rich store of such episodes. Later
historians have produced works that are more detailed, more carefully put together, and perhaps sounder as history, but they have
never surpassed the dramatic power and imaginative appeal of the
Shih chi. It is no doubt for this reason that the *Shih chi* has had such

a deep influence upon the literature of China and Japan and has maintained its popularity to the present day.

The aim of this study is to introduce to the reader of English the figure of Ssu-ma Ch'ien, to describe the form and content of his work, and to indicate something of its importance in Chinese culture. It may be objected that the exploits of man are not so various nor his ways of thought so divergent that the historical works of one people should require lengthy explanation to be intelligible to any other. It is true that the Western reader approaching early Chinese history may for a moment be put off by the oddness of names or the allusion to beliefs and ideals with which he is unacquainted: the setting is no longer that of the Mediterranean littoral, the dress of the players is different and their voices and gestures are strange. But if he will watch the piece they play he will find it an old and familiar one. So long as history is about man himself it should be intelligible to other men regardless of the accidents of time or space. Since my purpose is to introduce Ssu-ma Ch'ien to the English reader I would, if possible, advise him to lay aside this book for the moment and turn directly to the writings of Ssu-ma Ch'ien himself. Unfortunately so little of the *Shih chi* has been translated into English that this is impossible. I am at present preparing a translation of representative sections of Ssu-ma Ch'ien's history which I believe will give the reader an opportunity to form his own judgments of the work and its author. In the meantime I hope that this study will serve to arouse his interest and prepare him for the *Shih chi* itself.

In a study of this type, dealing with a literature and culture as little known generally in the West as is that of the ancient Chinese, it has seemed desirable to make some general remarks on the history and background of the period under discussion, even though such remarks may be common knowledge to the specialist. I have therefore begun by outlining the beginnings of Chinese history as they are revealed in the *Shih chi* and describing the age in which the historian lived and wrote. In place of a biography of my subject I have presented a translation of the oldest and, for all practical purposes, the only sources for his life, the autobiography which he appended to the end of his own work, and the biography written of him by his successor Pan Ku (32–92 A. D.), principal author of the *Han shu* or *History of the Former Han Dynasty.* This is followed by a description of the beginnings of Chinese historiography and a discussion of the form and make-up of the *Shih chi.* Finally I have attempted to outline the thought of the historian and, since the *Shih chi* is a great work not only of history but of literature as well, I have tried to analyse some of the literary devices and points of style which have contributed to its popularity.

I have deliberately chosen to ignore certain aspects of the historiography of the *Shih chi,* such as the complex and difficult question of the sources upon which Ssu-ma Ch'ien based his work, or the even broader subject of the criticisms of the *Shih chi* by Chinese scholars of later centuries. I am aware that such omissions may constitute a serious defect. Yet it has seemed impossible to cover all the aspects of a work of the magnitude and importance of the *Shih chi.* I am also painfully aware of the limitations of knowledge and ability with which I have undertaken this perhaps too ambitious study. I can hope only that, in spite of errors or distortions which I may inadvertently have committed, this study will serve in a small way to suggest to the English reader something of the greatness of the *Shih chi.*

At the end of the last century the renowned French Sinologist Edouard Chavannes published a French translation of the first forty-seven chapters of the *Shih chi* with a lengthy introduction on the life, times, methods, and sources of the historian. Such is the excellence of Chavannes' work that one is tempted to ask whether there is need for another study at this time. In view of the years which have elapsed since the appearance of Chavannes' study, the breadth of the subject, and the possibility for varying interpretations which is always present in the treatment of a work of literature, I believe there is. Yet if I appear to cite Chavannes only to disagree with him, it is because it would be tedious to acknowledge at every turn the great debt I owe to his work.

I should like to take this opportunity to thank Professors L. Carrington Goodrich, Chichen Wang, and William Theodore de Bary of Columbia University, and Professor Yoshikawa Kôjirô of Kyoto University, for reading this manuscript when it was in the process of preparation and offering numerous valuable suggestions and criticisms, and also to thank the other members of the faculty and staff of both universities for their frequent help and guidance. I also wish to express to the Ford Foundation my gratitude for its generous grant which made possible several years of study in Kyoto University and the writing of this book, though the Foundation is of course in no way responsible for the contents.

June, 1957 BURTON WATSON

SSU-MA CH'IEN

GRAND HISTORIAN OF CHINA

I

THE WORLD OF
SSU-MA CH'IEN

Before proceeding to any detailed discussion of the life and thought
of Ssu-ma Ch'ien, it is well to relate something of the age in which
he lived and wrote and, since he was an historian, of the past of
China as he conceived it. Therefore, I shall try to describe briefly the
scope of his history of China, the *Shih chi,* or *Records of the Historian,*[1] and some of the main ideas which dominate it. This is no
place to attempt a condensation of the vast and complicated picture
of the first two thousand years of Chinese history presented in the
Shih chi; any such forced epitome would almost certainly be distorted
and meaningless. I shall concentrate rather upon the ideals and tem-
pers which in the eyes of the Chinese themselves characterized the
various eras of their early history. My source for this description is
mainly the *Shih chi* itself, for it is Ssu-ma Ch'ien's own view of the
Chinese past which will be most pertinent to the discussions that
follow. This view will be supplemented by a consideration of Ssu-ma
Ch'ien's own age and that of his famous successor, the historian Pan
Ku.

I have referred to the *Shih chi* as a history of China, which for practical purposes it is. Yet the fact is that Ssu-ma Ch'ien wrote a history
of the world. Most of his space he devoted to the history of the
area known to us as China, for the reason that this was, to him, the
center of the world, the highest point of human advancement and
culture, and the area about which he knew most. But he extended his
examination in all directions, including in his book accounts of the

area now known as Korea, the lands of south-east Asia, and those to the west and north of China. In other words, he seems to have taken care to describe, in as much detail as possible, all the lands outside the borders of China of which he had any reliable knowledge. The fact that he says nothing, for instance, of Japan in the east or Europe in the west, is almost certainly due not to a lack of interest but to a lack of information. In his discussions of the philosopher Tsou Yen (SC 74/7) he cites that thinker's theory that China is only one of ten great continents which exist in the world, surrounded by a vast sea that marks the limit of heaven and earth, but he neither agrees with this theory nor refutes it. It is typical of Ssu-ma Ch'ien's caution and rationalism that he himself ventures no speculations upon the size and configuration of the world. He recorded and described all of it that he could; we can only guess what he may have believed lay beyond the lands of which he knew.

A second point to be noted is that Ssu-ma Ch'ien wrote a history of the entire knowable past. In discussing both the people of China and those of other lands, he began with the earliest accounts that he considered reliable and continued his narrative down to his own day. Concerning the ultimate origins of peoples, Chinese or foreign, he had nothing to say. It was his belief that mankind had existed long before the point at which he began his story, but of these earliest men he could say nothing, for the sources he considered trustworthy told him nothing. These ancient times are too far away, he continually explains to the reader, to be known. Their history is forever lost. The men of his time had a vague metaphysical explanation of the creation of the world out of nothingness expressed in the predominantly Taoist work written when Ssu-ma Ch'ien was a young man, the *Huai-nan Tzu* (3/1). But as Ssu-ma Ch'ien is silent upon the question of the size and shape of the world, so is he silent upon its origin and the origin of mankind.

Unlike Hebrew, Christian, or Japanese historians, Ssu-ma Ch'ien and his countrymen recognize no datable beginning to human history. Their conception of time is astronomical; time is a series of cycles

based upon the movements of the planets and stars, the "Heavenly
Governors," as the Chinese call them, and such cycles may presumably
be conceived as extending indefinitely into the past or the future for
as long as the stars themselves exist. The dates of human history are
recorded in terms of the years of rulers, who are the mortal counterparts of the "Heavenly Governors." One may calculate the temporal
relationships of any series of events in Chinese history by counting the
years of the reigning monarchs. But in Chinese history, unlike that of
so many other cultures, there is no single point in time such as the
creation of the world, the birth of Christ, or the hegira, to which all
other events are temporally related.

Ssu-ma Ch'ien begins his history with an account of five ancient
rulers, the "Five Emperors," who are the paragons of Chinese political
wisdom and virtue. He then proceeds to a narrative of the history of
the first dynasty of Chinese history, the Hsia, and the second, the Yin
or Shang. In his chapters on these dynasties we note the appearance
of a pattern which is of the greatest importance in Chinese historical
writing. Each dynasty begins with a sage king of superlative wisdom
and virtue, Yü of the Hsia and Ch'eng T'ang of the Yin, resembling
closely the earlier "Five Emperors," and each dynasty closes with an
unspeakably evil and degenerate monarch, Chieh of the Hsia and Chou
of the Yin. Between these two extreme moral types we find little more
than a list of names of rulers. In the case of the Yin dynasty, however,
we note that although the dynasty gradually declined in power and
virtue, it was twice restored for a while to its original excellence by
the virtuous rulers T'ai-wu and Wu-ting.

Here we see in crude form one of the most persistent patterns of
Chinese historical writing: the rule of a new house set up by a man
of extraordinary virtue and wisdom, and the gradual decline of the
dynasty until its termination under a monarch completely incapable
or evil. The cycle begins again when a new hero-sage overthrows the
worthless tyrant of the old house and sets up a new rule. This pattern
of rise and decay is generally varied in the middle, as in the case of
the Yin dynasty, by the appearance of worthy rulers who restore for a

time the original virtue of the dynasty in an act called "revival" or "restoration." [2]

This pattern in history is regarded by the Chinese as no more than an inevitable and natural reflection of a larger, more fundamental pattern of all life. As Ssu-ma Ch'ien states: "When things flourish they shall then decay" (SC 30/45). Since human history is a part of life, it is obvious that it must follow this law of growth and decay, of waxing and waning, which characterizes the life of all heaven and earth. This concept of the cycles of history is by no means original with Ssu-ma Ch'ien, but runs through all early Chinese literature. It is already implicit, for example, in the arrangement of the poems in the various sections of the *Book of Odes,* most of which begin with songs in praise of the illustrious ancestors and the peaceful, glorious days of the early Chou and end with bitter laments and criticisms of the later days of decay and disorder. Ssu-ma Ch'ien's task, as he saw it, was simply to arrange the accounts of the early dynasties and feudal states in such a way that this pattern of growth and decay could be most readily perceived.

This stereotyped pattern of the virtuous founder and the evil or at least ineffectual terminator of the line is typical of almost every dynasty and state described in the *Shih chi.* At first glance the Ch'in Empire, set up by a cruel tyrant, seems to be an exception. But Ssu-ma Ch'ien takes special pains to point out that one must consider not merely the history of the Ch'in from the time it became master of all China, but look back to the many centuries of its history as a smaller feudal state. Thus one will see that the state of Ch'in also had its wise and virtuous rulers, while the notorious First Emperor of the Ch'in represents not the founder of the line but the final cruel and degenerate terminator.

An integral part of this accepted pattern of the virtuous founder and the evil terminator of a ruling family is the very old concept of *te* or merit. *Te* in this case has more than its later meaning of "virtue," implying rather a kind of mystical store of power set up by the sage ancestor of the family. This power, or achievement, *kung,* or blessing, *tse,* flows from the ancestor down through his heirs, bestowing upon them in turn power and good fortune in their rule. But, like all other things of creation, this ancient deposit of merit is subject to the law of decay. As the years pass, the power wears thin and the succeeding rulers sink lower and lower into evil and incompetence. As the Chinese historian describes it, the power or the "way" of the ruling family declines. At this point it is still possible for a ruler, by applying himself to the practise of wise and virtuous government, to restore the waning power of the family. The Chinese describe this act as *hsiu-te,* literally "to repair the power." But if no ruler appears who will undertake thus to replenish the original store of power and merit, the reservoir will eventually run dry and the family will be destroyed by other families who are ascending in the cycle of power. Thus the ancient Chinese historian explains the change of dynasties.

This, one may object, is too mystical and religious an interpretation to give to conventional terms which are intended merely to describe the efficiency or inefficiency of a ruler and his government. In later ages of Chinese history, they may have been used to mean no more than this. But the basically religious nature of these concepts in Ssu-ma Ch'ien's time is attested by their close association with the all-important question of the continuity of the sacrifices to the soil and the grain and to the ancestors of the ruling house. The existence of the ruling family is synonymous with the continuity of these sacrifices; the end of the sacrifices means the end of the power and blessing flowing down from the ancestors. *Chüeh-ssu,* the cutting off of the sacrifices, signifies in the *Shih chi* the destruction of the ruling house and hence of the state.

It was clearly Ssu-ma Ch'ien's conviction, as it was that of his predecessors and contemporaries, that this mystical virtue and power of the great and good ancestor was an important force in the unfolding of history. At the end of his account of the state of Yen (SC 34/25) he remarks upon the fact that, located far on the northern border and pressed by more powerful neighbors, this little state was time and again on the verge of extinction. And yet, he says, it managed to carry on its sacrifices for some eight or nine hundred years and was one of the last states to succumb to the Ch'in. This fact he attributes quite simply to the illustrious merit of the ancient founder of the state, Duke Shao. Again, in his discussion of the state of Eastern Yüeh (SC 114/11) he marvels at the great length of the life of the state and attributes it to the virtue of its early rulers and the fact that they were descendants of the sage emperor Yü, whose merit extended to his distant heirs.

Like other ancient peoples, the Chinese of this early period conceived of history as a series of great deeds by great men. These heroes of the past, in the eyes of the ancients, had an influence far-reaching and mystical, affecting by their goodness the course of countless generations that followed. Ssu-ma Ch'ien himself clearly accepted, though perhaps in a less purely religious sense, this traditional interpretation of the power of the ancestors, and it would be as great a mistake to overlook this fact as it would be to ignore the importance of divination and other similar religious beliefs in the histories of the ancient West. No matter how "modern" Ssu-ma Ch'ien or his Western counterparts may at times appear, we must not attempt to force them out of the mould in which their age cast them. Ch'ien was quick to note factors of geography, economic conditions, climate, and local custom which affect human history. And yet his discussions of history always return to the individual and the influence of the individual in history. In this he was following and giving a new expression to the ancient Chinese concept of the persistent and far-reaching power of the hero in history.

One other feature of Ssu-ma Ch'ien's picture of ancient China deserves to be noticed. From the earliest written sources on Chinese history, such as the *Book of Documents* and the *Book of Odes,* down to Han works written in the time of Ssu-ma Ch'ien himself we hear of a great many different tribes of barbarians which surrounded China, the Middle Kingdom, on almost all sides. Ssu-ma Ch'ien not only mentions these foreign tribes as they affect the course of Chinese history, but even devotes special chapters to the histories of the more important tribes.

Much of the time in these references we hear only of wars between the Chinese and the barbarians, but at other times the Chinese seem not only to have lived at peace with their neighbors but indeed to have mingled with them in complete freedom. The ancestors of the Chou dynasty lived for generations among the western barbarians (SC 4/4), while as late as the end of the Spring and Autumn period (481 B. C.) we read of Duke Chuang of the state of Wei who could look down from his castle tower upon a barbarian settlement in the midst of his territory (SC 37/26). We are often reminded that the people of the state of Ch'in were half barbarian in their ways (SC 15/2), while the state of Ch'u frankly admitted that its ancestors were barbarians (SC 40/7).

What, we may ask, distinguished the ancient Chinese from these other tribes living all about them? The answer to this we will probably never know. Herodotus may carry his descriptions of the physical characteristics of barbarian peoples to quaint extremes or compare their languages to the screeching of bats, but we will search in vain for any such information in the pages of the *Shih chi*. In the eyes of Ssu-ma Ch'ien and his countrymen there seems to have been no question of physical differences. There may, in fact, have been significant physical characteristics which distinguished the Chinese from these other peoples of ancient times. But, either through ignorance or choice, Ssu-ma Ch'ien is completely silent on the point. We are forced to conclude either that there were no significant differences or that the differences were so obvious that he felt it unnecessary to mention them.

What then of linguistic differences? Here again Ssu-ma Ch'ien is silent. We read constantly of Chinese and barbarians who speak with one another, of barbarians who settle in China, of Chinese who go to live among the barbarians, but seldom is there any suggestion of a language barrier separating the two.[3] We might even expect to find, in an area the breadth of China, divided into a number of small feudal states, evidence of considerable local variation in language. Yet we read of educated men who travel freely from one state to another, serving often in a number of different feudal courts in succession, and find no hint that they encountered even the difficulties of local dialect one would find traveling in the same area of China today. Ssu-ma Ch'ien points out that the people of Ch'u use the word *huo* to mean "numerous" instead of the usual word *to* (SC 48/19), and again mentions that, when cities were being assigned to the newly enfeoffed king of Ch'i at the beginning of the Han they were selected from cities which spoke the "language of Ch'i" (SC 52/2). But these remarks, viewed in their context, seem to indicate no more than the existence of local accents and dialect words.

It seems unlikely that any such linguistic and racial homogeneity as Ssu-ma Ch'ien's silence implies actually existed in the area of China in ancient times. The process by which the Chinese people and language as we know them spread from their small beginnings over the area which later became China must have been a long and gradual one. The point to be noted here, however, is that differences of language and physical type, if they did exist, did not seem to Ssu-ma Ch'ien to be worth noting. The Chinese apparently did not consider such differences to be of any great significance.

The *Kung-yang Commentary* on the *Spring and Autumn Annals,* under Duke Ch'eng, fifteenth year, in a cryptic passage distinguishes three divisions of mankind: the smallest unit which is the feudal state (in the case of the *Annals,* the state of Lu); the larger group known as the "people of Hsia," i.e., the Chinese states that together made up the Middle Kingdom; and beyond these the third category of barbarian tribes. The *Commentary* also implies that it is the ultimate objective of a true king to bring all of these groups under a single rule. The ancient Chinese—quite rightly, it would appear—considered themselves to be the most culturally advanced people in the world as they knew it. And at least in the Confucian tradition there was always a belief that, if a true sage-king should rule in China, the wisdom, virtue, and righteousness of his ways would be so compellingly superior and attractive that all other people of the world would come to him, "translating and retranslating their languages," as the conventional phrase has it, and beg to accept Chinese ways and become part of the Chinese hegemony. For the ancient Chinese it was not primarily race or language, but culture, which distinguished them from the barbarian tribes.

Their own Chinese-ness lay in the elaborate and stately rituals and ceremonies by which they ordered their lives and the superior moral qualities which these rites engendered and of which they were in turn the outward expression. As the Latter Han Confucianist Ho Hsiu writes in his sub-commentary to the *Kung-yang,* Duke Ch'ao, twenty-third year: "What distinguishes the people of the Middle Kingdom from the barbarian tribes is that they are capable of honoring that which should be honored."

The Chinese of the time of Ssu-ma Ch'ien still fought bitter wars with the barbarian tribes who stubbornly refused to give up their inferior ways and submit to Chinese rule. But in spite of these harsh realities, the Chinese of the Han, like the Greeks of the Hellenic age or the Romans of the Empire, had attained a degree of advancement and self confidence where they could look forward to a great day when their culture would flow beyond the borders of the old narrow kingdom to embrace in one great family all mankind. It is perhaps due to this calm self-confidence that Ssu-ma Ch'ien did not hesitate to undertake the writing of a history of all time and all people. In his history he is careful to note the degree to which various peripheral and non-Chinese peoples conform to pure Chinese ways, for this was the criterion by which their place in the hierarchy of mankind could be judged. But he took little or no notice of questions of physical appearance or language, for these were for him beside the point.

Herodotus, confronted in the temple of Thebes by the statues of some three hundred generations of high priests representing, by his calculation, 11,340 years of human history in Egypt, was shocked into a realization of the relative newness of his own people. From this experience, and others like it, he drew both humility and pride: humility as an historian before the vastly older and in many ways superior cultures of Africa and Asia, and pride as a Greek in the remarkable achievements of his own people in their more recent emergence from the darkness of prehistory. But Ssu-ma Ch'ien and his contemporaries were blessed with no such experience. Surrounded by primitive and unlettered tribes, they lacked any rival worthy of either admiration or envy. In such a situation overt national pride was unnecessary and humility out of the question. And until such a rival should appear, the Chinese had no yardstick other than their own by which they might measure the length and greatness of their culture.

This is not to say that Ssu-ma Ch'ien and his countrymen were utterly blind to the merits of all cultures other than that of China. In his description of the Hsiung-nu tribes (SC 110), Ssu-ma Ch'ien, like Tacitus in his descriptions of the Germans, appears to take an ironic delight in pointing out the simplicity of their government and the dispatch with which their legal proceedings are conducted. But whatever he thought of certain aspects of Hsiung-nu life, it is certain that he no more considered them the cultural equals of the Chinese than Tacitus considered the German tribes the equals of Rome. In the first century B. C. it is probable that only an intimate confrontation of the Chinese and Greco-Roman worlds would have been sufficient to jar the complacent conviction of superiority of either, and the vast expanse of Central Asia would not permit such a confrontation.

In a short essay at the end of *Shih chi* 8, Ssu-ma Ch'ien briefly characterizes the governments (or, in broader terms, the cultures) of the first three Chinese dynasties, the Hsia, Yin, and Chou. The Hsia, he says, was characterized by good faith, which later decayed into rusticity. Actually, we have no reliable evidence today that this so-called Hsia dynasty ever existed. Ssu-ma Ch'ien's account of it is extremely sketchy, consisting almost entirely of portraits of the virtuous founder and the degenerate tyrant who ended the line. This makes it particularly suspect, for the neatness of the pattern and the conventionalized tone of the descriptions suggest that this is nothing more than a projection backward in time of the similar pattern which marked the history of the succeeding Yin dynasty. Ssu-ma Ch'ien was himself aware of the danger involved in trying to say much about such ancient times. He relates what his sources, the Confucian Classics, told him about the period, but cautions the reader frequently that his information is fragmentary and often contradictory. His characterization of the Hsia as distinguished by good faith and later rusticity seems to be no more than a tactful way of saying that the Hsia was primitive.

Of the Yin or Shang dynasty he says that it was marked by piety, which degenerated into a concern with the spirits, i.e., superstition.[4] Fortunately, in this case we have today archeological evidence with which to check the accuracy of Ssu-ma Ch'ien's description. Excavations at the site of the capital of the Shang have brought to light a number of artifacts, bits of sculpture, and, most important, inscribed bones and tortoise shells used in divination which tell us something of the life and history of the period. Two points significant for our discussion here emerge from the results of these excavations. The inscriptions show that Ssu-ma Ch'ien's list of the Shang kings checks quite closely with Shang period lists recovered from the site of the capital; they also bear out the fact that the Shang people were deeply religious and devoted the utmost attention to matters of divination and sacrifice. Although Ssu-ma Ch'ien never mentions any basic differences of race or language which distinguished the succeeding dynasties of the Chinese past, he is careful to point out that each dynasty had its own customs and rituals, that each was marked by a different general outlook on life. In spite of the paucity of his knowledge of the Shang period he was still able, some one thousand years after its decease, to perceive that the outstanding mark of Shang culture had been at its best religious piety and at its worst superstition.

His characterization of the third of the ancient "Three Dynasties," the Chou, is equally revealing. The outstanding feature of the Chou, he says, was its refinement, *wen*, which deteriorated into hollow show. The word *wen* is one of the most troublesome in Chinese thought to define and translate. Originally it seems to have meant patterns or markings, such as the spots of a leopard. From this it came to mean that which is decorated or adorned, as opposed to that which is rough and plain; hence it acquired the sense of elegance, refinement, or culture. Again, from its meaning of patterns it came to signify writing and all the advancements associated with writing and literature. Ssu-ma

Ch'ien, I think, intended to imply all these meanings, so that in the translation above the reader must understand "refinements" to signify all kinds of order, elegance, ceremony, and culture. In particular Ssu-ma Ch'ien was referring no doubt to the *li* and *yüeh,* the rites and music which the Duke of Chou is supposed to have created and set up for the new dynasty and which are the concern of so much of Confucian literature. It is obvious, then, that this elegance and ceremony could in time degenerate into empty show.

We need not turn to archeological excavations for verification of Ssu-ma Ch'ien's description of the Chou. One of the implications of *wen,* as I have said, is literature, and we may check the *Shih chi*'s generalizations with the literature of the Chou. We will notice first of all that in the literature of the Chou, the Confucian Classics and the works of the philosophers, we find many evidences of both the piety and the superstition which Ssu-ma Ch'ien has designated as the characteristics of the Shang. Dynasties may change and we may mark off periods in history, but we must remember that customs and ways of thought observe no such precise boundaries. Worship of the spirits of nature and the ancestors and the old arts of divination continued to play a very important part in the life of the Chou people. Indeed, as has been pointed out, the continuity of the sacrifices was synonymous with the very life of the state and the family. We hear much, even in a work as late as the *Tso chuan,* of diviners and witches, prophetic dreams, baleful spirits, human sacrifices—all the superstitions which we may suppose marked the Shang at its worst. And yet, opposed to this, we find the persistent efforts of at least a group of the educated class to turn the attention of men away from supernatural things to the affairs of human society, and in particular to questions of politics and the ordering of the state. Gilbert Murray has described how the Greek philosophers of the Athenian period labored to purge from the primitive religious practices, myths, and beliefs of Greece the elements which appeared too superstitious and gross for their sensibilities.[5] Much the same thing, I believe, must have happened during the Chou period in China. Faced with the primitive fear of death and the dead, the concern for the fertility of the earth and the family that characterize all primitive peoples, the Chinese philosophers and statesmen sought, by careful and minute codes of courtesy and ritual, by high-sounding metaphysical phrases and allegories, to disguise and refine away the cruder elements of the old Shang religion. The elaborate and carefully circumscribed funeral rites of the Confucianists, for example, should be understood as a thoughtful attempt to substitute a quiet grief and reverence for the abject terror with which ancient man viewed death, and thus curb the extravagant sacrifices of possessions, animals, and even human lives that accompanied the funerals of the Shang rulers. "The subjects on which the Master [Confucius] did not talk were: extraordinary things, feats of strength, disorder, and spiritual beings" (*Analects* VII, 20). "The Master said: 'While you are not able to serve men, how can you serve the spirits?'" (*Ibid.,* XI, 11). "The people are the masters of the spirits. Therefore the sage kings first took care of the people and only after turned their efforts towards the spirits" (*Tso chuan,* Duke Huan, sixth year). "Weird occurrences arise from men. If men have no offense, then weird things will not occur of their own. It is when men abandon their constant ways that weird things occur" (*Ibid.,* Duke Chuang, fourteenth year). When we read such statements in Chou literature, we can see the best minds of the age laboring to free men from their old superstitious fear of the dead and the ghostly and turn their efforts to a constructive consideration of human society.

This process of gradually reducing the position of supernatural affairs to a place of importance secondary to human affairs continued throughout the Chou, reaching its logical conclusion in the writings of the Confucian philosopher of the third century B. C., Hsün Tzu, who interpreted all the ancient sacrificial rites of the Chinese as mere aesthetic exercises intended not for the benefit of the spirits but for the edification of the living. This tendency toward rationalism and humanism, then, was one of the points which distinguished the culturally advanced, politically minded people of the Chou from their more primitive, superstitious predecessors of the Shang, and it is for this reason no doubt that Ssu-ma Ch'ien employed the word *wen*—culture, refinement, the patterned order of society—to epitomize the Chou.

These currents of rationalism and humanism which began to develop during the Chou have had a profound influence upon all later Chinese thought. This is no place to trace their history through all the centuries of Chinese philosophy, but a few pertinent illustrations may be mentioned. Hsün Tzu, for example, one of the most eloquent exponents of rationalism, attacked both the belief in divine portents and the efficacy of the old art of physiognomy. The Han Confucianist Tung Chung-shu (179–104 B. C.), who backslid from Hsün Tzu's position to subscribe to some ideas that hardly strike us as rational today, is yet careful at times to give his views what we might call a pseudo-scientific explanation. He insists, for example, that the elaborate ceremonies which he recommended for the purpose of causing rain to fall and to cease are based upon rational laws of nature. "Thus it is not the gods that cause the rain. The reason some people mistakenly impute it to the gods is because the principle is very subtle." [6] This same desire to eradicate what they recognized as superstitions led Ssu-ma Ch'ien to refute the popular legend that at the command of Prince Tan the heavens rained grain and horses grew horns (SC 86/39), and Ch'u Shao-sun to reinterpret the ancient accounts of miraculous births in the *Book of Odes* as poetic metaphors (SC 13/29). It was this same spirit of rationalism, the scientific spirit of the Han, which inspired Wang Ch'ung of the Latter Han to write a book, the *Lun heng,* intended specifically for the refutation of superstitions.

This rationalistic spirit will help to explain much of what appears in the opening pages of the *Shih chi* as ancient history. Ssu-ma Ch'ien begins his story of the Chinese past with the account of five rulers of supreme virtue, the "Five Emperors." It is generally agreed by scholars today that these figures were originally local deities of the people of ancient China. But by the time of the compilation of the Confucian Classics two of these popular gods, Yao and Shun, had been converted into historical personages, and at some later date the other three received similar recognition by at least one branch of the Confucian school. And this is the way Ssu-ma Ch'ien has treated them in his history, carefully sifting out of the voluminous lore which surrounded their names all the elements of the supernatural and fantastic which seemed to contradict their existence as actual human monarchs. He has been criticized for this practice of trying to make what was originally myth and folktale into sober history. As the Sung scholar Li T'u remarks: "The Grand Historian (Ssu-ma Ch'ien) in his writing makes good use of facts, but he takes this factual approach and makes facts out of all the empty tales of the world." [7] The complaint is justified, but in Ch'ien's defense we must add that this practice of making rational history out of what is actually no more than myth begins a great deal earlier in Chinese historiography. It is a natural result of the desire of the educated men of the Chou, particularly those of the school of Confucius, to rationalize and humanize the accounts of their own past. We must be constantly wary of this tendency in Chinese thought, for it has led to the transformation of any number of legendary figures and events into what appears to be sober historical truth.

Nearly all the sources on ancient Chinese history which Ssu-ma Ch'ien used seem to date, at least in compilation, from the closing centuries of the Chou dynasty. Parts of this literature, such as the songs of the *Odes,* sections of the *Documents,* and the *Spring and Autumn Annals,* undoubtedly represent earlier writings. But it was probably not until the time of Confucius and his disciples that the Classics began to assume anything like their present form. Professor Naitô Torajirô has suggested that it is when a culture and a way of life is declining and seems in danger of extinction, when confusion and doubt have arisen over the old ways, that men are moved to compile canons of history and ritual and law.[8] Although as a general thesis this statement is open to some question, it would seem to apply in this case. The age of Confucius was certainly such a period of decline and chaos. From what we can see in the *Book of Documents* and the *Odes,* the early Chou was a time of considerable social and political stability. The central court was powerful and respected, the feudal lords kept peace and order in their respective domains, and the people lived a simple rustic life bound to the soil. This picture may be idealized in its air of sweetness and harmony, but there is no reason to believe that it is not true in its general contours. By the time of Confucius around the beginning of the fifth century, however, as both pre-Ch'in and Han literature never tire of pointing out, "the way of the Chou had declined." The central house of Chou, partly because of the persistent attacks of barbarian tribes, partly, no doubt, because of the natural moral decay that seems eventually to beset all courts of all ages, had declined sadly in power and prestige. The stronger and more prosperous of the feudal domains swallowed up their neighbors and grew steadily in size and might. The old hierarchical order of society and the carefully guarded rites and ceremonies that were the physical expression of that order—the *wen* of the early Chou—fell into decay. Feudal rulers assumed noble titles to which they theoretically had no right, and with them they usurped the rites appropriate to the titles. Nobles sent orders to the king, ministers assassinated their liege lords, and social disorder threatened to pervade all classes of society and undermine all traditional concepts of law and morality. It was at this crucial point that Confucius and his disciples appeared and set about to codify the old rites and ceremonies that were being abused and forgotten, to preserve the old songs and documents and legends of the bright past, and to use them to teach the rulers and men of the day where and how they had gone wrong. We must remember in reading the *Shih chi,* which is based to so large extent upon these works of the Confucian canon and considers them as the final authority on questions of historical truth, that the Classics were compiled by men living in a time of trouble and disorder, who were looking back to what they saw as an ideal age, or a series of ideal ages, in the past. We must also remember that these works were intended not primarily as objective records of the past but as guides to moral and political conduct. Like almost every major work of Chinese literature down to and possibly including the *Shih chi,* they were books of *li*—rites, or, in the broadest sense, moral principles. If so many of them are devoted to historical anecdote rather than to general moralistic pronouncements, it is because the Chinese of this age, and to a large extent of the ages that followed, believed that moral law was most faithfully embodied not in abstract codes of behavior but in the actual records of how the great, the truly moral men of the past had behaved.

But the Confucians and their canon could not stem the tide of social change. The central court and its satellites, the old feudal families, continued to grow weaker, while families that had been ministers and retainers to the feudal lords grew so powerful that they overthrew their former masters. Changes in methods of warfare, advancements in agricultural techniques, and the growth of trade all vitally affected the old feudal society. Lacking any strong central authority to which they could appeal, the various states began to form alliances to protect themselves from attack, and there began a long struggle to achieve some balance of power that would insure peace from the incessant feudal wars. These rapid social changes only hastened that decay of traditional moral values which Confucius had feared. As Ssu-ma Ch'ien writes of these diplomatic alliances: "False titles flew about and oaths and agreements could not be trusted. Although men exchanged hostages and broke tallies, they still could not enforce promises" (SC 15/3). "The world honored deceit and power and disdained benevolence and virtue. It put wealth and possessions first and modesty and humility last" (SC 30/47). In such an atmosphere it was inevitable that the old religious beliefs should also decay. Feudal lords performed sacrifices to which they were not entitled, or abolished the sacrifices of conquered states, and yet no enraged manes visited supernatural wrath upon them. Rulers repeatedly broke the oaths they had sworn before the gods and yet no angry Heaven punished them. One feudal lord, in insane defiance of the old religious ideas, went so far as to set up a leather bag filled with blood and use it as a target for his archery, declaring that he was "shooting at Heaven." [9]

One of the most important results of this breakdown of the old feudal hierarchy and its ideals was an increase in social mobility. As the old aristocracy became increasingly weak and decadent, the higher ministers and officials began to usurp the actual power and sometimes even the titles of their lords. These usurpers brought to power with them their own staffs of clerks and advisers and their own private soldiery. Men of the lowest rank of the old feudal hierarchy (the *shih*), the younger, foot-loose sons of the impoverished nobility, or even commoners, could find in these dramatic shifts of power the opportunity to rise to unprecedented heights in the social scale. The new leaders who were contending for power built up private armies and often vied with each other in making attractive offers to young men to come and join their band of retainers. A man who dreamed of a military career could choose from among these lords the one who offered the best treatment to his soldiery and who seemed most likely to do great things; if he was dissatisfied he could leave and join another household. Or if he were the clever, studious type, he might become a civil servant or political adviser to one of the new leaders. Schools of philosophy—the Confucian, the Legalist, the Mohist—arose to train young men for careers as officials and advisers. Rulers competed with each other in attracting to their local courts renowned and successful political theorists and their disciples. A new code of ideals and etiquette arose, based not upon the old rigid feudal hierarchical order, but upon the new and freer, more personal relationship between lord and retainer or, as it was significantly termed, between "host" and "guest."

Because this new code of ideals dominated the thinking of the upper classes in the late Chou and retained its vitality well into the Han, it deserves description in some detail here. What, first of all, was the incentive which, according to this code, inspired this class of "guests" or retainers in their struggles to rise in the social order? "The gentleman [*shih*]," writes Chuang Tzu, "gives himself to the pursuit of fame," [10] and this sentiment is echoed by the Han poet Chia I: "the impassioned gentleman pursues fame." [11] Mere material wealth was considered too mean an objective for the "gentleman" class, while actual rule and aristocratic title were, ostensibly at least, the prerogatives of his lord or host. He should devote himself only to making a great and admirable name for himself, as a warrior, a man of honor, an official, or a political adviser. Pre-Ch'in literature contains many tales of such men who rose from humble and obscure origins to become great military and political leaders in this period, and the *lieh-chuan* or biographical section of the *Shih chi,* written almost entirely under the influence of this code of ideals, by recording and preserving the great deeds of these men, rewards them for all time with the prize they sought, fame.

The qualities which distinguish the men of this class in many ways resemble the ideals of the chivalric codes of feudal Europe and Japan: faithfulness to one's lord, honesty in word, a sense of honor, and a concern for others in trouble and distress. And in the early, palmy days of the old Chou culture the Chinese gentleman and knight may actually have conformed to these high moral aims, though here as always we must beware of the tendency to idealize the distant past. But in the harsh world of late Chou times these resemblances to European chivalry fade. Bravery that is rash, blind loyalty, devotion to the lost cause when one knows that it is lost—these ideals which Japanese and European chivalry cherished so fondly are for the Chinese of this period the marks of mere stupidity. There is about the Chinese "knight" an individualism and cynicism which is absent, or at least disguised, in his European or Japanese equivalent. The Chinese knight is bound by no oaths of fealty or pressure of feudal society to serve one lord to the death. The first duty of the knight is to advance in life and to achieve the fame he seeks, to look out for his own interests and to seize his own opportunities. Li Ssu, a representative of the particular class known as "itinerant strategists" (*yu-shui*), emphasizes in his speeches that the man who hopes to get ahead must be ever alert to the changes of the times and quick to turn them to his own advantage (SC 87). And as he and others of his class made clear, this meant abandoning loyalties that did not appear advantageous, leaving the side that was losing and attaching oneself to the winner. If a scholar or a knight found that his talents were not being recognized and used, that he was not getting ahead as he had hoped, it was time for him to look for a new employer. Faithfulness, honesty, sacrifice were due not to just any lord, but only to the successful lord, the lord who appreciated and used his men well. This period in Chinese history abounds in stories of men who died for their lords and their friends. But they did not give their lives because of any rigid code of feudal obligation but for the much more personal reasons of friendship and gratitude to a fellow man.

This ideal of friendship is of particular importance in Chinese literature and thought. The joy of friendship, of finding a man who can recognize and appreciate one's own good qualities, and the deep debt of gratitude which is owed to such a friend, are constant themes of the stories of this age. Ssu-ma Ch'ien in his biographical section devotes great space to these tales, for the question of the loyalty of old friends was one which deeply stirred the emotions of the Han people. The second chapter of the *lieh-chuan* section relates the famous story of the loyalty of the statesman Kuan Chung to his old friend Pao Shu, who had been kind and understanding when Kuan Chung was still poor and unknown. "It was father and mother who gave me life," declares Kuan Chung, "but Pao Tzu who understood me" (SC 62/3). The question of the loyalty of old friends was for obvious reasons a vital one in these times of rapid rise and fall of personal fortunes. "If I become rich and powerful, I will not forget you" was the promise that the rebel Ch'en Shê made to his friends when he was still a laborer in the fields (SC 48/2), and the same promise was exchanged by three ladies of the late Ch'in who later became highly favored at the Han court: "She who becomes honored first shall not forget the others" (SC 49/7). Sometimes these promises were kept. Much of the success of Kao-tsu, founder of the Han dynasty, has been attributed to the faithfulness with which he remembered the men who had helped him in the early days of his struggles for power. But as often the promises were broken. Chapter 120 of the *Shih chi* is devoted to the stories of two men who were rich and powerful but who, when they fell from favor, were deserted by all their former friends. Ssu-ma Ch'ien ends his narrative with the famous words of another man who met the same fate: "When one is poor and the other rich, then the true attitude of friendship may be known; when one is high and the other low, then the true form of friendship is seen." It was this ideal of friendship, the difficult friendship of the unequal, which underlay the lord and retainer relationship of the late Chou and Han, and which gave to that relationship both its fickleness and its warmth.

If the aim of the knight was to discover a master who would appreciate and use him well, that of the lord was to attract to his court the best men of the time. The most important quality the lord must possess ✓ is the faculty of recognizing the abilities of his men. The history of this period is obsessed with the problem of how to judge men. Again and again we read of the disasters of rulers who listened to the advice of the wrong kind of men and turned the right kind away. If a lord knew how to pick good men, to perceive ability in others regardless of humble origins or circumstance, and if he treated them with respect and kindness, he could inspire a fervent and very personal loyalty which transcended all other ties of blood and country. Ssu-ma Ch'ien in *Shih chi* 75 to 78 has recorded, with care and affection, the colorful stories of four feudal lords and their bands of retainers, who exercised power in four of the feudal states at the end of the Chou. These men, the so-called "Four Heroes," particularly the Lord of Hsin-ling, are the ideal types of the lord who knows how to command the respect and loyalty of his followers, as their followers represent the ideal of the brave and crafty retainer. The whole superb and moving body of poetry which centers about the figure of the statesman Ch'ü Yüan, on the other hand, deals with the tragic fate of the truly loyal and virtuous minister who is misunderstood and rejected by a misguided lord.

With this breakdown of the old rigid feudalism which we have described came a certain air of optimism. New opportunities were opened for men, regardless of birth, to make a place for themselves in the world on the basis of their own talents and ability. One of the principles that was naturally most often insisted upon by this new class of gentlemen-retainers was that ability, not birth, distinguishes a man. This idea, though only hinted at in the *Analects,* became one of the basic tenets of Confucianism. The *Li chi* states: "There is no such thing in the world as acquiring honorable position by birth." [12] Hsün Tzu is more explicit: "Although a man be the descendant of kings and peers, of great officials or generals, if he cannot adhere to propriety and right, he should be made a commoner." [13] And Tung Chung-shu extends the principle to include even the emperor: "If the Son of Heaven cannot serve the will of Heaven, then he should be cast out and given the title of Duke." [14] This was the idea which inspired the peasant Ch'en Shê to lead a revolt against the Ch'in, boldly declaring: "Kings and generals are made, not born!" (SC 48/7). And Kao-tsu and his band of followers, by rising from the lowest ranks of society to become rulers of the empire, proved that there was no longer any such thing as a sure birthright to rule.

But if one could rise rapidly by good luck and his own efforts, he could just as rapidly fall from power when his luck changed. The schools of strategists and political advisers in particular were constantly engaged in a bitter struggle with each other for the favor of the rulers; and if the side that won gained wealth and glory, the side that lost faced exile or death. As one retainer bitterly put it: "If you are successful in your job you become a high official; if you fail you are boiled alive. That is the kind of business it is" (SC 66/22). Thus, if men were optimistic over the chances for rapid success, they were also saddened by the spectacle of the equal rapidity with which success could change to failure, honor to disgrace and execution. Having destroyed the idea that birth entitled a man to high position, the new leaders of the late Chou and early Han society found that they could no longer assure to their posterity the fruits of their own struggles. "The family that tries to be military leaders for three generations," advised one retainer at the end of the Chou, "will surely meet defeat" (SC 73/18). The men who chose a civil career found likewise that, with the vagaries of the ruler's whims and the constant machinations of rival court cliques, they could never be sure when they might fall from favor. Ssu-ma Ch'ien, who knew the inside story of the rivalries of court officials, writes: "A gentleman, regardless of whether he is wise or worthless, if he enters the court, will face suspicion" (SC 105/62).

This atmosphere of rivalry and suspicion, of dramatic rise and fall of fortunes, bred a feeling of profound doubt and despair that pervades the literature of the period. With the decay of the old religious beliefs, men lost their faith in an essentially well-ordered and benevolent universe. Like the Greeks of the Hellenic age, the Chinese came to see themselves more and more as the playthings of a blind and capricious fortune that might at any moment strike them down. As the *Huai-nan Tzu* writes: "The city of Li-yang in one night sank beneath the waves and was turned into a lake, and the brave and strong, the sage and wise suffered the same fate as the weak, the cowardly, and the unworthy. When fire breaks out and the wind sweeps it across Wu Mountain, the tall poplars and the purple iris together with the lowly sagebrush perish in the flames" (2/13a–b).

The poems of Ch'ü Yüan and his followers and of the early Han poets emphasize the capriciousness of human fortune and the pitiful shortness of human life. Some poets seek as a solution a renunciation of the world and its strifes, expounding the Taoist idea of a retreat into mystical quietude; others only counsel men to drink and make merry with their possessions while they still have the time and ability to enjoy them. Of one thing they are all certain: there is nothing constant in human life but the eternal cycle of growth and decay, nothing sure but the nearness of death.

The story of the unification of China by the Ch'in and the revolutionary measures taken by the new dynasty—the abolition of feudalism, the establishment of a strong central government, the standardization of the writing system, the completion of the Great Wall, the burning of the books—is too famous to need retelling here. One point should be emphasized, however. The Ch'in was the *bête noire* of the Han people, the personification of tyranny, oppression, arrogance, and untimeliness. Although the Han rulers availed themselves of many of the advantages of the Ch'in's labors and quietly continued to follow many of its principles and practices, they publicly declared themselves the undying opponents of all that the Ch'in stood for. They were the saviors of the nation from a reign of terror, the redeemers of the destiny of the Chou which had been untimely severed.[15] The Confucianists in particular, who had suffered most under the Ch'in's attempts at thought control, outdid themselves in heaping abuse upon the ill-fated dynasty, so that Ssu-ma Ch'ien was obliged to remind his readers that behind the demonic fury of the First Emperor of the Ch'in lay long centuries of astute and sometimes benevolent rule by the ancestors of the house of Ch'in.

The unification of the nation, the abolition of feudalism, the great shifts of population under the Ch'in, and the bitter wars and social upheaval that accompanied its downfall marked the final extinction of the old feudal aristocracy of the Chou. The world of the Han that followed was almost entirely a world of new men rising from a new class in society. Of the leaders of the new regime, one, Chang Liang, was descended from a ministerial family of one of the pre-Ch'in states, while a few others had been minor officials under the Ch'in. But the rest, including the couple who became emperor and empress of the new dynasty, were commoners of the humblest origins—several farmers, a dog butcher, an undertaker, a silk dealer, a cart puller—men who had neither birth nor learning to recommend them but who, by their vision, daring, and astute native intelligence, rose to be rulers of the world. This humble origin of the house of Han, for all we can tell, was something new and unprecedented in the history of China, and it must be constantly borne in mind if one is to understand the temperament of the new era.

We have noted above the way in which Ssu-ma Ch'ien characterized the good and bad qualities of the first three Chinese dynasties: the good faith of the Hsia and its perversion, rusticity; the piety of the Shang and its perversion, superstition; and the refinement of the Chou with its perversion, hollow show. According to Ssu-ma Ch'ien, when this cycle is completed it must begin again. The Ch'in failed because it did not sweep away the hollow show of the decadent Chou, but only added to it its own harsh and exacting laws. But the Han wisely returned to the good faith of the Hsia.

What Ssu-ma Ch'ien is referring to here, I believe, is the air of rude, hearty simplicity which characterized the early Han rulers and their administration. Kao-tsu and his followers had been commoners under the Ch'in and they knew how the common people suffered by the Ch'in laws. They were able, therefore, to do away with those laws which most offended the people, while retaining the good points of the Ch'in administrative system. They gave the nation sixty or seventy years of relative freedom from internal and external disorder and frugal, laissez-faire government, and the empire so recovered and prospered that by the time of Ssu-ma Ch'ien's birth the people were living in comparative ease and plenty and the government treasuries were overflowing.

But this negative type of government, modelled largely upon the Taoist ideal of "non-action," could not continue forever. There were many problems demanding more positive action, which the Han rulers sooner or later would have to face. One was the question of Han relations with foreign peoples, in particular with the Hsiung-nu tribes on the northern border. The Hsiung-nu posed a constant threat to the peace of the Chinese. In the early Han they often made destructive raids into the empire, riding almost to the capital itself. In addition they failed to give the proper acknowledgments of submission and fealty to the Han rulers that Chinese tradition demanded of barbarian nations; on the contrary the Han found itself in a position of having to send tribute to the Hsiung-nu in an effort to buy peace. So insensitive were these barbarians to the dignity of the Chinese court that the widower chieftain of the Hsiung-nu dared to send a letter to Empress Lü after the death of her husband, Kao-tsu, suggesting that, since they were both old and lonely, they ought to get married. The empress was livid with rage at the suggestion but powerless to do anything but send a polite note of refusal.

A second problem was the growing power of the Han peers. Kao-tsu, reviving the feudal system which the Ch'in had abolished, granted fiefs both to his followers and to his relatives. The former were ill-fated from the first. Men who had fought side by side with Kao-tsu in his rise to power, it was hard for them to realize, when Kao-tsu became emperor, that he was no longer a comrade in arms but their ruler. Some chafed at the division of spoils, some dreamed of turning the tables and replacing their old leader as monarch. Kao-tsu was suspicious of these men and doubted their loyalty. Empress Lü was even more distrustful. The doubt and fear of both sides deepened until seven of these new feudal lords, five kings and two marquises, had either revolted or fallen under suspicion of revolt. One by one they were defeated, forced to commit suicide, or to flee to the territory of the Hsiung-nu. By the time of Emperor Wen's reign, these peers who were not of the reigning Liu family—the "other-name peers," as they were called—had ceased to be of any political importance. But the peers of the Liu clan fared better. Some were degenerate and incompetent, but many of them ruled their territories wisely and well, so that their power and independence steadily grew. These men, it was soon realized, posed a constant threat to the authority of the central court.

The third problem that faced the Han administration was the direct result of its own laxity. Because the oppression and harsh rule of the Ch'in had so angered the nation, the early Han rulers were careful by contrast to keep the penal laws simple and to interfere as little as possible in the life of the people. But though this policy had many beneficial effects, it also led to a considerable amount of disorder and gangsterism, particularly in the outlying provinces. As so often in later Chinese history, local bosses appeared in the countryside and set themselves up as virtual rulers of the territory, maintaining, in the manner of the old feudal lords, their own bands of retainers to enforce their will. In addition powerful landowners and merchants, grown rich on the peace and prosperity of the nation, were constantly encroaching upon the lands and rights of the poor, forcing the small farmers into debt and servitude and seizing their fields to create great estates.

The fourth problem, unlike those enumerated above, had to do not so much with the material life of the new dynasty as with its spirit. There was a feeling among the educated class that the house of Han was lacking in dignity. The early Han rulers and their aides were, as might be expected considering their humble origins, a rowdy lot. Kaotsu was famous for his crude and disrespectful manners, the best-known illustration being the time he snatched the hat from the head of a Confucian scholar and urinated into it to demonstrate his opinion of the man, while he himself complained when he became emperor that his followers were spending all their time drinking and carousing about the palace and hacking up the pillars with their swords. Empress Lü was renowned for her inhuman cruelty; Emperor Hui died of dissipation; and Emperor Ching, when he was still heir apparent, in a fit of anger hit his distant cousin, the prince of Wu, over the head with a chessboard and killed him. Quite naturally there was a feeling among the more sensitive scholars and gentlemen at court that something should be done to give the imperial house a more dignified and exemplary tone.

It was also felt that the Han, which until now had carried over many of the institutions of the Ch'in, should make more explicit the fact that it was a new dynasty independent of preceding reigns. This individuality should be expressed, scholars believed, by the acts traditionally appropriate to a new dynasty: changing the month on which the year began, altering the color of court flags and vestments, selecting a new element of the traditional five to honor as the ruling element of the dynasty, and performing the great Feng and Shan sacrifices, symbolic of the divine election of the ruling house.

All of these problems came under discussion in the reign of the fourth ruler, Emperor Wen. But Emperor Wen was an example of a type revered in Chinese and Japanese history, the "do-nothing" ruler, who cares only for peace and economy, living in a modest palace, dressing his empress in homespun, and issuing repeated proclamations castigating himself for his errors and beseeching his subjects to show him his faults. Emperor Wen succeeded in giving peace and comparative ease to his people, and for this he has been praised by Pan Ku and later historians as the greatest of the Han rulers. But his esteem was bought at a price. He did almost nothing to solve any of the urgent problems which faced the central administration; he simply stalled them off.

Emperor Ching, who followed, attempted more positive action. He took stern measures to put down the lawlessness in the provinces, achieving considerable success. He also attempted to curb the power of the peers, but his efforts here only inspired a revolt of seven of the most powerful feudal states which, although it was quickly quelled, served dramatically to show how late the hour was.

In 140 B. C., five years after the birth of Ssu-ma Ch'ien, there came to the throne a new ruler, Emperor Wu, who set about with ever-increasing vigor and daring to cope with the problems that faced the empire. His policies were positive in the extreme, the exact opposite of the negative rule of his predecessors. His reign marks a new era in Han history. With him began many of the policies and institutions that characterize later dynasties; with him also died many of the ideals of the late Chou and early Han.

Emperor Wu realized that something must be done about Han relations with the Hsiung-nu. His solution was first to set up a strong series of defenses along the northern borders and later, not satisfied with this, to carry the warfare deep into the enemy territory. Although he never succeeded in conquering the elusive nomadic tribes, he did much to assert the power of the Han and insure at least a measure of peace for his successors. In addition he extended by warfare and exploration the borders of the empire into Korea and to the southeast, southwest and west, bringing the Chinese empire for the first time into direct contact with the lands of Central Asia.

He continued the efforts of Emperor Ching to break the power of the feudal lords. He compelled them to divide their territory among their heirs, sent spies and overseers to their courts, tripped them up on a multitude of petty crimes, forced them into bankruptcy, or seized their lands outright. His success was remarkable and in his reign the Han peers ceased to be a threat to the central government. He also increased the number and efficiency of the provincial administrators, suppressed the bandits and local bosses, greatly increased the complexity and severity of the laws, and broke the power of the wealthy merchants who had grown fat on the laissez-faire rule of his predecessors.

Finally he gave himself with spectacular energy to the task of demonstrating to the world the dignity and glory of Han rule. He changed the calendar, altered the color of the vestments, selected the element

earth as the patron element of the Han, and carried out the sacrifices of
Feng and Shan. He constructed splendid palaces, great towers, and
vast imperial parks in the capital at Ch'ang-an that dazzled the eyes of
the citizens and foreign envoys. He made frequent progresses back and
forth across the nation, showing himself to his subjects and performing
elaborate sacrifices to the gods and spirits on the way. Favoring Confucianism over the other schools of thought, he took steps to promote
the study of the Classics and to make Confucianism the official creed
of the state. To many men of his day it must have seemed that a golden
age had arrived when the ancient rites and ceremonies described in the
Classics would again flourish, the virtue and blessing of the Chinese
monarch would flow out over his people and beyond the borders to the
unenlightened barbarians, and Heaven would send down auspicious
tokens of its favor.

But a vigorous policy such as Emperor Wu pursued was bound to
arouse the opposition of many groups in society. The men of the early
Han well knew that if China was to be spared the twin curses of foreign invasion and internal strife it must be united under a single rule.
Yet they harbored a dread of the kind of ruthless totalitarianism that
had marked the brief unification of the Ch'in. The benign reign of
Emperor Wen had permitted ample scope for the exercise of individual freedom, but in doing so it had dangerously weakened the power
and unity of the state. Emperor Wu, on the other hand, in his desire
to strengthen and expand the nation and gather all power into his own
hands, showed a callous disregard for individual rights and liberty all
too reminiscent of the hated Ch'in. The principal problem engaging
thinking men of the period, such as Ssu-ma Ch'ien, was how and
where a proper balance could be struck between these apparently contradictory desires for individual freedom and national welfare. The
problem, which has plagued and continues to plague all political theorists everywhere, was more acute in their eyes because they witnessed
within the decades of Emperor Wu's rule the dramatic shift from the
imbalance of one extreme to that of the other.[16]

The court poet Ssu-ma Hsiang-ju, in a proclamation to the elders of

the district of Shu who were opposing a government plan to build a
road through Shu out of China to the west, explained that the Emperor
was an extraordinary man who was doing extraordinary things which
would necessarily be misunderstood and feared by the people.[17] That
the common people did not welcome many of Emperor Wu's policies
is plain, but they were by no means the only ones who complained.
The Confucianists, interestingly enough, clashed with their imperial
patron on a number of issues.[18] First was the question of the wars
against the Hsiung-nu. The Confucianists were in favor of spreading
the blessings of Chinese culture to foreign lands and asserting the
dignity of the throne. But the foreign wars and expansion proved to be
disastrously expensive in men and money. The burden of taxation and
military service upon the people became constantly heavier. Contact
with tribes to the west opened up a brisk new trade, but while Chinese
silk poured out of the country, all that came in return was jewels and
exotic fruits—luxury goods destined for the enjoyment of the rich
alone. Soon the Confucianists were crying for a policy of peace and
isolationism to allow the nation to recover its economic health.

Emperor Wu, in order to support the foreign wars and the increasing
lavishness of imperial life, was forced to search for new sources of
revenue. One expedient, continued from earlier times, was to grant
commutation of punishments upon payment of heavy fines. Another
was the sale of honorary ranks and titles at court. But these alone would
not suffice and the government decided to go into business. It took over
the salt, iron, and other monopolies that had been in the hands of
private businessmen or local feudal lords, and began to speculate in
grain futures and the transport of goods. In these and other actions
the government was actually following old Legalist theories, and for
the administration of these new enterprises the Emperor employed private businessmen who openly expounded Legalist doctrine. The Confucianists were horrified at the reappearance of the hated philosophy
of the Ch'in. They insisted that the government should concern itself
with higher ideals than the pursuit of profit. They complained that the
excessive government meddling in the economic life of the nation meant

only inferior goods, maladministration, and oppression for the people.

The Confucianists had recommended that the emperor set up a system of examinations for the selection and promotion of government officials, the beginnings of the famous Chinese examination system. But though the emperor put the system into effect, he used it chiefly to fill the administration with weak-willed, soft-spoken flatterers. His sale of titles threw the aristocratic hierarchy into confusion. The complexity and severity of his penal laws made it all an official could do to stay out of jail. When we read that a court official was accused of the crime of "dissent in the heart" because of "a slight curl of his lip" when hearing of a new government policy (SC 30/31), we can appreciate how far Emperor Wu's administration had departed from the old Confucian ideal of outspoken counsel and criticism by court officials.

Finally, the Confucians were dissatisfied with the way the emperor conducted religious affairs, particularly the Feng and Shan sacrifices. Emperor Wu, though he professed admiration for Confucianism, surrounded himself with a host of magicians and wonderworkers who tried to summon for him the spirits of the dead or insure him immortal life. In his execution of the Feng and Shan sacrifices, he dispensed with the confused and contradictory counsels of the Confucianists and made up his own ritual, by which the great ceremony became not an act of worship and invocation of divine blessing by the leader of the people for the sake of the nation as a whole, but a personal and secret search on the part of the ruler alone for immortality.

Ssu-ma Ch'ien, upon whose history so much of our information of this period is based, was one of the bitterest opponents of the policies of Emperor Wu. An official who spent all his life at court in the service of the emperor, he knew the true situation as few men of his period did. It has often been said that he turned against the emperor and wrote his history as a scathing condemnation of the age because of his bitterness over the punishment of castration imposed upon him by the emperor when he had become too outspoken in his criticisms. It is true that this terrible punishment did much to deepen the bitterness and anger of the unfortunate man. But it was not the motive for his history, for he had begun work on that some time before his misfortune, nor was it the sole cause of his disapproval of Emperor Wu and his rule.

Like the Confucianists, he opposed the foreign policy of the emperor and the terrible toll it was taking of the nation's health. As an enlightened and rational man, he abhorred the gross superstitions that the magicians persuaded the emperor to accept. He opposed the government monopolies and speculations for the same reasons the Confucians did—because the pursuit of profit was not a fit concern of rulers, and because these activities brought suffering to the people. As an exponent of a laissez-faire economic policy, he objected to the Legalist policies that were throwing the economy of the nation into disorder and ruining the merchant class. He was angered and saddened by the harsh penal laws that had brought fear and punishment to so many of the officials, including himself.

It has also been suggested that Ssu-ma Ch'ien was a Taoist, who therefore opposed the Confucian emperor on doctrinal grounds. This old charge of Taoist sympathies has been greatly exaggerated and misunderstood. Ssu-ma Ch'ien's father, Ssu-ma T'an, openly favored Taoism over the other schools of thought, but Ssu-ma Ch'ien himself at no point makes any such clear declaration in favor of one particular doctrine. As one of the most learned men of his day, he was familiar with all schools of thought and their literature. No doubt he saw some good in them all, but his greatest respect seems always to have been reserved for Confucius, the Confucian literature, and the Confucian doctrine at its best. It is true that he is bitterly critical of Kung-sun Hung, a Confucian scholar who became a high official at Emperor Wu's court. But this was not because Kung-sun Hung was a Confucianist, but because he was a flatterer to the emperor and an unusually stern and cruel administrator. Kung-sun Hung began his career at court by outspokenly opposing the wars against the Hsiung-nu, but when he saw which way the wind of imperial desire was blowing, he did a direct about-face and supported the wars. It was for reasons of personality, not doctrine, that Ssu-ma Ch'ien condemned Kung-sun Hung and his kind, who had become inceasingly numerous at the court of the strong-willed emperor.

But Ssu-ma Ch'ien's disillusionment with his age went much deeper than questions of specific government policies. He was an historian with an extraordinary love and sympathy for the past. And he was keen enough to discern in the changes that took place during his lifetime the death of many of the ideals of the past that he most admired. He felt a nostalgia for the days of the late Chou and early Han when men could rise by their own abilities and climb to the highest positions. He admired the rough and ready ways, the faithfulness and friendship of the lords and their bands of retainers, the outspoken frankness of the old political advisers and theorists, the willingness of the great generals to share hardships equally with their troops. He was a hero-worshipper who devoted much of his life to writing of the heroes of the past, while in his own day he saw the old freedoms, the old personal loyalties, being stifled by an ever-growing bureaucracy and a net of petty and exacting laws. His disillusionment with his own age and his nostalgia for the age that had ended appear in his history in countless wry and subtle ways. He wrote two companion chapters, *Shih chi* 119 and 122, entitled respectively "Lives of Good Officials" and "Lives of Harsh Officials." The former deals with men who distinguished themselves in the feudal states of the Chou period; the latter is devoted exclusively to officials of the reigns of emperors Ching and Wu of the Han. Thus he made his point that the men of an earlier age had known how to administer law and order without stooping to excessive sternness and cruelty. He wrote another chapter, the "Lives of the Wandering Knights," *Shih chi* 124, in which he paid tribute to some of the local "bosses" who exercised *de facto* rule in the provinces in the early Han. He freely admitted that these men had their faults, that their lives were frequently marred by lawlessness and violence, but he saw in them the last expression of the old ideal of the man of action who is loyal to old friends, sincere in his word, and ever ready to help the weak and unfortunate. Another chapter, 129, he devoted to the great financiers of the past, for he recognized that success in business was one manifestation, albeit in his eyes a not very worthy one, of human in-

genuity, imagination, and freedom. In another chapter he expressed
great admiration for the general Li Kuang who shared the hardships
of his men and who, though a rough man unable to make fine speeches,
commanded by his conduct the admiration of the nation (SC 109/10
& 21). To this portrait of Li Kuang he contrasted Emperor Wu's two
favorite generals, Wei Ch'ing, who was never admired by the people,
and Ho Ch'ü-ping, who amused himself playing football while his men
starved to death (SC 111/31). In a sense Ssu-ma Ch'ien was a romantic
and a conservative who, like many historians, lived in the past and
could not see that the old ideals of personal freedom, the old chivalric
code of personal loyalties, could not survive in a great unified empire
administered by a complex bureaucracy. A government the size of
Emperor Wu's could not tolerate the old laissez-faire policies; the nation could not afford to be weak in the face of the threat of internal
revolt or foreign invasion. The central court needed strengthening, the
local administration needed to be tightened up, and imperial dignity
had to be asserted. Emperor Wu had the vision and will to do all these
in the face of severe criticism. If it had not been for his strengthening
of the Han one cannot say what the fate of the dynasty might have
been. But for one who knew and admired the age that was coming to
an end, as Ssu-ma Ch'ien did, it was not a happy time to be alive. Under Emperor Wu much that was good was accomplished, but much
that was good was destroyed. It was the destruction, not the accomplish-
ment, that Ssu-ma Ch'ien saw.

My aim in this introduction has been to describe in brief some of the
main features of the span of history covered by the *Shih chi,* and it
would seem appropriate to end my description where the *Shih chi*
ends, with the reign of Emperor Wu. But Ssu-ma Ch'ien's work has
so often been compared to and discussed in connection with that of his
great successor, Pan Ku, author of the *Han shu* or *History of the
Former Han Dynasty,* that it is worth while to look ahead briefly to
the age of Pan Ku and note some of the ways in which it differed from
Ssu-ma Ch'ien's time.

For almost a century after the death of Emperor Wu, Han rule continued without major internal disorder or foreign involvement. But the Liu rulers grew increasingly weak and ineffective so that in 9 A. D. a high court minister, Wang Mang, was able to seize the throne without opposition and set himself up as emperor of a new dynasty, the Hsin. His success, however, was shortlived, and rebellion brought his death and the restoration of the Liu family to the throne in 25 A. D. The dynasty began a new life with its capital not at Ch'ang-an but at Lo-yang, farther to the east; the period known as the Latter or Eastern Han began. Pan Ku was born in 32 A. D. during the reign of the first emperor of this new era and spent most of his life as an official writer and historian for the government until his death in 92 A. D.

This new Han differed in many ways from the old one. The early Han rulers had had many of the manners of the *nouveaux riches*. The emperors were rough and poorly educated, the empresses occasionally ex-dancing girls who had caught the fancy of their rulers. The royal family retained many of the ideals and attitudes of the earlier disordered times when quick action, daring, and imagination, not refinement and learning, had been the qualifications for success. Particularly from the time of Emperor Wu the dynasty had had a fondness for magnificent display, grand palaces, high living. There was a rough, spirited, gaudy tone to the era.

We have noted how things began to change during the reign of Emperor Wu. The full effect of these changes can best be seen in the contrast offered by the life and spirit of the Latter Han. Emperor Wu established Confucianism as the state creed and opened the way for scholars to enter the bureaucracy by competitive examination. In the Latter Han most of the official posts were filled by men who had secured their jobs on the basis of scholastic achievement. The pursuit of learning, particularly Confucian learning, became the concern of all members of the upper class; even emperors and empresses were students of the Classics. The merchant class, that had begun to be powerful and important in the early Han, was degraded to the position almost of social pariahs and the land-owning gentry, the literati class, became the unchallenged leaders of society. These new arbiters of society disapproved of vulgarity and violence, of striving and gaudy show. They looked back to an ideal period in the early Chou when society had been perfectly ordered, when elegant rites expressing the hierarchical divisions of society had been carried out by virtuous and learned rulers, and they did all they could to recreate this ideal in their own time.

The *Han shu* clearly reflects this idealization of the ancient past and the orthodox Confucianism of Pan Ku and his age. In addition Pan Ku wrote a long poem, the *"Fu* on the Two Capitals" (*Han shu* 100 and *Wen hsüan* 1), in which he compared the vulgar magnificence of the Western Han capital of Ch'ang-an with the quiet elegance and refined frugality of Lo-yang.

In view of these differences between their respective ages, it is not surprising that Pan Ku did not wholly approve of the work of his predecessor, Ssu-ma Ch'ien. Both Pan Ku and his father Pan Piao have listed their specific criticisms of the *Shih chi*. They did not like the way Ssu-ma Ch'ien used the Confucian Classics as sources in his history, paraphrasing, chopping, and shifting around the material to suit his narrative. They objected to the importance that he gave to military upstarts like Ch'en Sheng and Hsiang Yü, who had never received official sanction for their power. They deplored Ch'ien's defense of the wandering knights, whom they saw as no more than vicious outlaws, and they found his attention to the despised merchant class inexcusable. They were also among the first to make the charge that Ssu-ma Ch'ien was a Taoist.

I have mentioned these criticisms here not only because they represent the opinions of the first major critics of the *Shih chi* but also because they represent the opinions of most of the Chinese who read the *Shih chi* for the following two thousand years. For the influence of the scholar-bureaucracy continued with little break to dominate Chinese society until the revolution in 1911, and the attitudes of the men of the Latter Han are more or less typical of the attitudes of the centuries of Chinese scholars who followed. The *Shih chi* was always read, studied, and admired by the Chinese. But it was only the exceptionally imaginative critic who could see beyond the ideals of his own age to the age of Ssu-ma Ch'ien when these ideals were not yet formed, and understand and sympathize with what Ssu-ma Ch'ien was trying to say. We have come to a time now when the ideas and assumptions of the old China, the China of the Confucian literati, no longer exercise their former dominance. It is a fit time for a new and, we may hope, less biased look at Ssu-ma Ch'ien and his work.

II

THE BIOGRAPHY OF
SSU-MA CH'IEN

The reign of Emperor Wu marked the high point of power and cultural achievement of the Former Han and has always been regarded by the Chinese as one of the golden ages of their past. Not a little of the glorious reputation of this era was due to the literary efforts of two men, the poet Ssu-ma Hsiang-ju and the historian Ssu-ma Ch'ien. The life of Ssu-ma Hsiang-ju appears from the first to have been cloaked in an aura of romance, of secret elopement and young love, music and plaintive song. By contrast the biography of Ssu-ma Ch'ien seems lean and dull, touched only by one brief, shocking moment of drama. In a way we are more fortunate than the scholars of Greek historiography, for we can say more of the life of Ssu-ma Ch'ien than they can of the lives of Herodotus or Thucydides. Yet practically all we know of Ssu-ma Ch'ien is what he himself has chosen to tell us. To the end of his history he appended a postface recounting the genealogy of his family, giving a brief summary of his father's and his own life, and discussing his aims and methods in writing his history. When Pan Ku came to compile a biography of Ssu-ma Ch'ien for his history, he simply copied out this postface of his predecessor, added to it the text of a beautiful and revealing letter written by Ssu-ma Ch'ien to a friend, inserted a few scraps of new information, and ended with the Chinese historian's customary paragraph of appraisal, in this case based upon remarks made concerning Ssu-ma Ch'ien by his father Pan Piao and the scholar Yang Hsiung.

This biography of Ssu-ma Ch'ien, compiled by Pan Ku sometime around 60–80 A. D., constitutes for all practical purposes the final word on the life of the historian. Contemporary Han sources give us no more than passing references to the man; later writers have been able to do little more than mull over, and occasionally confuse, the evidence. In the absence of startling archeological finds, we can say no more about the life of Ssu-ma Ch'ien today than Pan Ku said almost two thousand years ago. In recent years there have been a number of attempts by scholars to go over what little evidence we have and extract from it every fact and supposition possible. Of these the most reliable is the pioneer study of Wang Kuo-wei, *T'ai-shih-kung hsing-nien-k'ao,* and the longer and more detailed work based upon it by Cheng Hao-sheng.[1] These studies, however, valuable as they are for establishing the chronology of Ssu-ma Ch'ien's life and eliminating some of the misconceptions that have grown up about it, can add virtually nothing to the facts given in the original Han sources. It has seemed best, therefore, to present here a translation of these sources, supplemented in the notes by whatever other facts or suppositions seem acceptable.

A word of caution is perhaps in order at this point. In what follows, the reader unaccustomed to translations from the ancient Chinese may find himself confronted by a baffling profusion of strange names, allusions, and literary conventions. This chapter is acknowledged to be one of the most difficult of the *Shih chi,* but at the same time it is the most important and germane to our subject. Since not all of the sections into which I have divided the translation are directly related to the life of Ssu-ma Ch'ien himself, the less venturesome reader may without great loss omit the first and third sections entitled "Genealogy" and "Discussion of the Essentials of the Six Schools." For the rest I must beg the reader's indulgence for infelicities of translation and a cumbersome exegetical apparatus. This is what Ssu-ma Ch'ien has chosen to tell us of himself, and it seems only fair to let him speak in his own words.

SHIH CHI 130: THE POSTFACE OF THE GRAND HISTORIAN

Genealogy

> [Following custom, Ssu-ma Ch'ien begins his account with a genealogy
> of his family, tracing it back, as is the wont with Chinese writers, to
> the golden ages of the legendary past.]

In ancient times in the reign of Chuan Hsü, the *Nan-cheng* Chung
was ordered to take charge of the affairs of heaven, while the *Pei-
cheng*² Li took charge of those of earth.³ In the reigns of T'ang and
Yü [i.e., Yao and Shun] the descendants of Chung and Li were re-
established as the managers of the affairs of heaven and earth. During
the Hsia and Shang dynasties these same Chung and Li families continued generation after generation to manage the affairs of heaven
and earth. The Earl of Ch'eng Hsiu Fu in the Chou dynasty, was
their descendant. In the time of King Hsüan of the Chou [827–781
B. C.] the family lost its position and became the Ssu-ma family.⁴
The Ssu-ma family for generations had charge of the historical records
of the Chou.⁵

In the time of Kings Hui and Hsiang [676–618 B. C.] the Ssu-ma
family left Chou and went to Chin.⁶ When the General of the Central
Army, Sui Hui of Chin, fled to Ch'in, the Ssu-ma family moved to
Shao-liang.⁷ From the time the Ssu-ma family left Chou and went to
Chin, they became broken up and scattered, some living in Wei, some
in Chao, and some in Ch'in.

From the branch of the family in Wei came the Prime Minister of
Chung-shan.⁸ The branch of the family in Chao was famous as hereditary masters of the art of swordsmanship.⁹ K'uai-wai was a descendant
of this branch.¹⁰ In the Ch'in branch there was a Ssu-ma named Ts'o,
who argued his opinions with Chang I.¹¹ Thereupon King Hui sent
Ts'o to lead an army against Shu.¹² After subduing it, he remained to
guard his conquest. Ts'o's grandson Chin ¹³ served the Lord of Wu-an,
Po Ch'i. The name of Shao-liang was changed to Hsia-yang.¹⁴ Chin
and the Lord of Wu-an attacked the army of Chao at Ch'ang-p'ing.¹⁵

After their return to Ch'in they were both ordered to die at Tu-yu.[16] They were buried at Hua-ch'ih.

Chin's grandson was Ch'ang. Ch'ang was head of a Bureau of Iron under the Ch'in dynasty.

In the time of the First Emperor of Ch'in [221–210 B. C.] K'uai-wai's great-great-grandson Ang served as general to the Lord of Wu-hsin,[17] garrisoning Ch'ao-ko.[18] When the various feudal lords were being made kings, Hsiang Yü made Ang the king of Yin. When the Han forces attacked Ch'u [i.e., Hsiang Yü], Ang went over to the side of the Han and his territory became the Prefecture of Ho-nei.[19]

Ch'ang had a son named Wu-tse.[20] Wu-tse was a Master of the Market under the Han.[21] Wu-tse was the father of Hsi. Hsi was a Lord of the Fifth Rank.[22] All these men when they died were buried at Kao-men.[23]

The Biography of Ssu-ma T'an

Hsi was the father of T'an, who became The Grand Historian.[24] The Grand Historian studied astronomy with T'ang Tu.[25] He received instruction in the *Book of Changes* from Yang Ho.[26] With Master Huang he studied the theories of the Tao.[27] The Grand Historian held office during the eras from *Chien-yüan* to *Yüan-feng* [140–110 B. C.]. He was distressed that scholars seemed to fall short in their understanding and were misled by their teachers, and therefore he wrote a discussion of the essential teachings of the Six Schools.

The Discussion of the Essentials of the Six Schools

[It was the practice of Ssu-ma Ch'ien and later Chinese historians to insert in the biographies of great literary men the texts of their more outstanding poetry, essays, or speeches. Instead of describing in detail the life of his father, Ch'ien has here chosen to present the complete text of what he must have considered his father's most important contribution to literature.]

The Great Commentary of the *Book of Changes* says: "There is one moving force, but from it a hundred thoughts and schemes arise. All have the same objective, though their ways are different." [28] The schools of the *Yin-yang,* the Confucianists, the Mohists, the Logicians, the Legalists, and the Taoists all strive for good government. The difference among them is simply that they follow and teach different ways, and some are more penetrating than others.

It has been my observation that the theories of the *Yin-yang* School put strong emphasis upon omens and teach that a great many things are to be shunned and tabooed. Hence it causes men to feel restrained and bound by fear. But in its work of arranging correctly the all-important succession of the four seasons it fills an essential need.

The Confucianists are very broad in their interests, but do not deal with much that is essential.[29] They labor much and achieve but slight success. Therefore their discipline is difficult to carry out to the fullest. But in the way in which they order the etiquette between lord and subject and father and son, and the proper distinctions between husband and wife and elder and younger, they have something that cannot be altered.

The Mohists are too stern in their parsimony to be followed and therefore their teachings cannot be fully applied. But in their emphasis upon what is basic [i.e., agricultural production] and upon frugal usage they have a point which cannot be overlooked.

The Legalists are very strict and of small mercy. But they have correctly defined the distinctions between lord and subject and between superior and inferior, and these distinctions cannot be changed.

The Logicians cause men to be overnice in reasoning [30] and often to miss the truth. But the way in which they distinguish clearly between names and realities is something that people cannot afford not to look into.

The Taoists teach men to live a life of spiritual concentration and to act in harmony with the Unseen. Their teaching is all-sufficient and embraces all things. Its method consists in following the seasonal order of the *Yin-yang* School, selecting what is good from the Confucian and Mohist teachings, and adopting the important points of the Logical and Legalist schools. It modifies its position with the times and responds to the changes which come about in the world. In establishing customs and practices and administering affairs, it does nothing that is not appropriate to the time and place. Its principles are simple and easy to practice; it undertakes few things but achieves many successes.

It is not so with the Confucianists. They consider that the ruler of men must be the model of conduct for the world. He shall set the example, they declare, with which his ministers need only comply; he shall lead and his ministers follow. But if it were like this, then the ruler would have to labor while the ministers followed along at their ease.

The essential of the Great Tao is to discard strength and envy and to do away with intelligence and understanding; one must discard these and entrust himself to the practices of Taoism. If the spirit of a man is too much used it will become exhausted; if his bodily substance is put to much labor it will wear out. If a man has early in life exhausted his spirit and body,[31] it is unheard of that he should hope to attain the long life of heaven and earth.

The *Yin-yang* School has its teachings and ordinances which apply to each of the four seasons, the eight trigrams, the twelve signs of the zodiac, and the twenty-four divisions of the year, and it declares that anyone who follows these ordinances will meet with good fortune, while anyone who goes against them will die or at least lose his position in life. But this is not necessarily so. Therefore I say that the *Yin-yang* School causes men to feel restrained and bound by fear. Spring is the time for planting, summer for nurturing, fall for harvesting, and winter for storing away. This is the ever-constant principle of the way of Heaven and if one does not abide by this he cannot regulate and govern the world. Therefore I say that in the all-important succession of the four seasons the *Yin-yang* teaching cannot be done without.

The Confucianists consider the Six Classics as their law and model. But the books and commentaries of the Six Classics run to thousands or tens of thousands. Generations of scholars could not master their study, nor could a man in his whole lifetime thoroughly comprehend all their rules.[32] Therefore I say that the Confucianists are broad in their interests but do not deal with much that is essential, that they labor much but achieve only slight success. But as to the etiquette established by the Confucianists between ruler and subject and father and son and their distinctions between husband and wife and elder and younger, none of the other schools can change or improve upon this.

The Mohists also [33] honor the ways of the emperors Yao and Shun, and speak much of their virtuous actions, saying: "The foundations of the halls of Yao and Shun were three *ch'ih* high with three steps of earth leading up; their halls were roofed with untrimmed thatch and their timbers and rafters were untrimmed. These emperors ate from earthen plates and drank from earthen bowls. Their food was coarse grain with a soup of greens. In summer they wore clothes of coarse fiber and in winter the skins of deer." The Mohists bury their dead in coffins of *t'ung* wood three *ts'un* thick, and when they raise their voices in mourning they do not give full vent to their grief. They teach that funerals must be conducted in this way, setting this up as an example for all people. But if everyone followed their rules, then there would be no distinction between the honorable and the lowly. Ages differ and the times change, and the things people do need not always be the same. Therefore I say that the Mohists are too parsimonious to be followed. But since they emphasize what is essential and are frugal in use, theirs is the way to assure an ample supply for both individual and family. This is the point in which the Mohists excel and none of the other schools can afford to overlook it.

The Legalists do not distinguish between those who are close to oneself and those who are distant; they do not differentiate between the honorable and the lowly, but judge all men alike by their laws. If this is so, then the obligation to treat those near to oneself with special deference and to honor those who are worthy of honor is destroyed. Such laws can serve as an expedient for a particular time, but they cannot be used for long. Therefore I say that the Legalists are strict and show little mercy. But in so far as they place the ruler in a lofty position and the subject in a lowly one and make clear the division of authority between the various officers of government so that there can be no usurping of unlawful power, they have a point which the other schools cannot improve upon.

The Logicians indulge in hair splitting and tortuous reasoning, making it impossible for people to follow their meaning. They decide everything on the basis of terms and overlook the realities. Therefore I say that they cause men to be overnice and often to miss the truth. But if they can succeed in setting aside the names of things and get at their reality so that reason is not lost,[34] then they have something that one cannot afford not to look into.

The Taoist School proposes the doctrine of "doing nothing," but it insists that thereby "there is nothing that is not done." [35] Its truths are easy to practice but its words difficult to understand. Its teaching takes emptiness and inaction as its basis, and compliance and accordance [with nature and the times] as its practice. It recognizes as a fact that nothing is complete and finished, that nothing is constant in form. Therefore it is able to penetrate the spirit of all things. It does not put material things first, nor does it put them last; therefore it is able to master all things. It has laws and yet it is as though it had no laws, for it follows the times in all its undertakings. It has rules and yet it is as though it did not have them, because it follows things and accords with them. Therefore it is said that the Sage is without great skill [36] but follows the changes of the times. Emptiness is the constant law of the Tao. Accordance is the abiding principle of the ruler. Thus all the officers proceed to their business with a clear understanding of their respective duties. He who in reality comes up to what he claims to be is called upright, but he who does not actually measure up to his name is called vain. If a man pays no heed to vain words, then evil will not arise. The distinction between worthy and unworthy will become clear of itself, and white and black will become apparent. Thus one can choose the one and discard the other and thereby accomplish all things. He can be at one with the Great Tao which, formless and dark, yet lightens the whole world. Thus may one return again to the Nameless. It is spirit which gives life to all men and they assume their form in bodily substance. If the spirit be put to great use it will become exhausted. If the body be made to labor greatly it will become worn out. When substance and spirit part there is death. He who is dead cannot return to life, for that which has become separated cannot again be joined.[37] Therefore the Sage regards those things with gravity. From this we may see that the spirit is the basis of life and the substance is its vessel. If a man does not first put at rest his spirit and substance,[38] but says instead, "I can govern the world!", what reason can there be in his words?

The Early Years of Ssu-ma Ch'ien and Death of Ssu-ma T'an

Since The Grand Historian was always in charge of astronomical affairs he was not concerned with the governing of the people. He had a son named Ch'ien.[39] Ch'ien was born at Lung-men.[40] He plowed and pastured on the sunny side of the hills along the River.[41] At the age of ten he could read the old writings.[42] When he was twenty he traveled south to the Yangtse and Huai rivers [Kiangsu], he climbed Hui-chi and looked for the Cave of Yü [43] [Chekiang], and he saw the Nine Peaks [Honan].[44] He sailed down the Yüan and Hsiang rivers and in the north forded the Wen and Ssu rivers [Shantung]. He studied the learning of the cities of Ch'i and Lu.[45] He observed the customs and practices inherited from Confucius and took part in the archery contest at Mount I in Tsou.[46] He met with trouble and danger in P'o and Hsüeh and P'eng-ch'eng.[47] Then he passed through Liang and Ch'u and returned home.

After this Ch'ien entered government service as a Lang-chung.[48] He took part in the western expedition to the south of Pa and Shu, marching south as far as Ch'iung, Tse, and K'un-ming.[49] He returned and reported on his mission.

In the same year [110 B. C.] the Son of Heaven first performed the Feng Sacrifice for the house of Han.[50] But The Grand Historian [Ssu-ma T'an] was forced to stay behind at Chou-nan [51] and could not take part in the ceremony. He was filled with resentment over this and lay on the point of death.[52]

When his son Ch'ien returned from his mission, he visited his father at the place where he was staying between the Lo and Yellow rivers.[53] The Grand Historian grasped his hand and said, weeping, "Our ancestors were Grand Historians for the house of Chou. From the most ancient times they were eminent and renowned when in the days of Yü and Hsia they were in charge of astronomical affairs. In later ages our family declined. Will this tradition end with me? If you in turn become Grand Historian, you must continue the work of our ancestors. Now the Son of Heaven, following the tradition of a thousand years, will perform the Feng Sacrifice on Mount T'ai. But I shall not be able to be present. Such is my fate! Such indeed is my fate! After I die, you will become Grand Historian. When you become Grand Historian, you must not forget what I have desired to expound and write. Now filial piety begins with the serving of your parents; next you must serve your sovereign; and finally you must make something of yourself, that your name may go down through the ages for the glory of your father and mother. This is the most important part of filial piety.[54] Everyone praises the Duke of Chou, saying that he was able to set forth in word and song the virtues of King Wen and King Wu, publishing abroad the Odes of Chou and Shao; he set forth the thoughts and ideals of T'ai-wang and Wang Chi, extending his words back to Kung Liu, and paying honor to Hou Chi.[55] After the reigns of Yu and Li the way of the ancient kings fell into disuse, and rites and music declined. Confucius revived the old ways and restored what had been abandoned, expounding the *Odes* and *Documents* and making the *Spring and Autumn Annals*. From that time until today men of learning have taken these as their models. It has now been over four hundred years since the capture of the unicorn.[56] The various feudal states have merged together and the old records and chronicles have become scattered and lost. Now the house of Han has arisen and all the world is united under one rule. I have been Grand Historian, and yet I have failed to set forth a record of all the enlightened rulers and wise lords, the faithful ministers and gentlemen who were ready to die for duty. I am fearful that the historical materials will be neglected and lost. You must remember and think of this!"

Ch'ien bowed his head and wept, saying, "I, your son, am ignorant and unworthy, but I shall endeavor to set forth in full the reports of antiquity which have come down from our ancestors. I shall not dare to be remiss!"

Ssu-ma Ch'ien Becomes Grand Historian; the Revision of the Calendar

Three years after the death of his father, Ch'ien became Grand Historian.[57] He read the various historical records and the books of the stone rooms and metal caskets.[58]

Five years after this was the first year of the era *T'ai-ch'u*. At dawn on the first day of the eleventh month, the day *chia-tzu* [Dec. 25, 105], the zenith of winter, the calendar of the heavens was first corrected and set up in the Illustrious Hall.[59] All the spirits received the chronology.[60]

The Grand Historian remarks:[61] "My father used to say to me, 'Five hundred years after the Duke of Chou died Confucius appeared. It has now been five hundred years since the death of Confucius. There must be someone who can succeed to the enlightened ages of the past,[62] who can set right the transmission of the *Book of Changes,* continue the *Spring and Autumn Annals,* and search into the world of the *Odes* and *Documents,* the rites and music.'[63] Was this not his ambition? Was this not his ambition? How can I, his son, dare to neglect his will?"

A Discussion of the Spring and Autumn Annals and the Shih chi

The High Minister Hu Sui[64] once asked, "For what reason was it that Confucius in ancient times made the *Spring and Autumn Annals?*"

The Grand Historian replied, "I have heard Master Tung[65] say, 'When Confucius was Chief Minister of Justice in Lu, the ways of the Chou had declined and fallen into disuse. The feudal lords abused him and the high officials obstructed his plans. Confucius realized that his words were not being heeded, nor his doctrines put into practice. So he made a critical judgment of the rights and wrongs of a period of two hundred and forty-two years in order to provide a standard of rules and ceremonies for the world. He criticized the emperors,[66] reprimanded the feudal lords, and condemned the high officials in order to make known the business of a true ruler and that was all. Confucius said, "If I wish to set forth my theoretical judgments, nothing is as good as illustrating them through the depth and clarity of actual events." '[67]

"Above, the *Spring and Autumn* makes clear the Way of the Three Kings, and below it discusses the regulation of human affairs. It distinguishes what is suspicious and doubtful, clarifies right and wrong, and settles points which are uncertain. It calls good good and bad bad, honors the worthy, and condemns the unworthy. It preserves states which are lost and restores the perishing family. It brings to light what was neglected and restores what was abandoned. In it are embodied the most important elements of the Kingly Way.

"The *Book of Changes* makes clear heaven and earth, the *yin* and the *yang*, the four seasons and the five elements. Therefore it is most useful in matters of change. The *Rites* regulates human relations, and so is excellent in matters of conduct. The *Book of Documents* records the deeds of the former kings, and so is most useful in government. The *Odes* tells of mountains and rivers, ravines and valleys, of birds and beasts, plants and trees, and the the male and female of beasts and birds. Thus it best expresses the sentiments of the people. Through music joy is achieved, and so it excels in harmony and peace. The *Spring and Autumn* differentiates between right and wrong, and so is most helpful in ruling men. Thus the *Rites* regulates mankind, music spreads harmony, the *Documents* tells us of deeds, the *Odes* expresses the will of men, the *Changes* relates of transformation, and the *Spring and Autumn* discusses right.[68]

"Therefore, for dispersing revolt and turning the people back to the right, none of the other Classics can compare to the *Spring and Autumn*. The *Spring and Autumn* consists in all of some ten or twenty thousand words, and its ideas number several thousand. The answers to how all things join and break away are to be found in it. It records thirty-six instances of assassination of rulers, and fifty-two of kingdoms which perished,[69] and of feudal lords who were forced to flee and could not protect their altars of the soil and grain, the number is too great to be reckoned. If we reflect on how these things happened, we will find in every instance it was because they lost the True Way. Therefore the *Book of Changes* says, 'The error of a fraction of an inch can lead to a difference of a thousand miles.'[70] And it also says, 'When a minister assassinates his lord or a son murders his father, this is not something that came about in one morning or evening, but something that had built up gradually over a long period.'[71] For this reason one who rules a state cannot afford not to know the *Spring and Autumn*. If he does not, he will fail to perceive slander near about him, or will not understand the reason when rebels rise behind his back.[72] A man who is a minister must know the *Spring and Autumn,* or he will not understand what is proper in managing his regular duties, nor, when an emergency arises, will he know how to exercise independent judgment. One who is a ruler or a father and does not understand the principles of the *Spring and Autumn* will bring upon himself the infamy of chief evildoer, while one who is a minister or a son and does not understand the principles of the *Spring and Autumn* will surely fall into the sin of rebellion or regicide and suffer the judgment of death. All of this comes truly from thinking one knows the good when one does not really understand its principles. Such men will stand indicted by the moral judgments and will not dare to deny their guilt.

"Now a lack of understanding of the meaning of propriety and duty leads to lords who are not true lords, ministers who are not true ministers, fathers who are not fathers, and sons who are not sons. If a lord is not a true lord, then there will be revolt. If a minister is not a real minister, then he will suffer punishment. If a father is not a father, he will act immorally; and if a son is no son, he will be without filial piety. These four failures are the greatest faults of mankind. When one finds himself guilty of one of these great faults, he will have to accept his punishment without daring to make excuses. Therefore the *Spring and Autumn* is the basis of propriety and duty.

"Rites serve to put interdictions in advance on what has **not yet** taken place, while laws act on what is already past. Therefore the usefulness of laws is easy to perceive, while it is difficult to understand the reason for the interdictions of rites." [73]

Hu Sui replied, "In Confucius' time, there was no enlightened ruler above, and below worthy men were not employed. Therefore he made the *Spring and Autumn Annals,* handing down to posterity his theoretical judgments in order to decide on questions of propriety and duty and to serve as the model for a king.[74] But you, sir, live in a time when there is an enlightened emperor above, while all below are men fit for their positions. All affairs are handled properly, each ordered in its correct place. Now in your writings, what is it you are trying to show?"

The Grand Historian replied: "Yes, yes. What you say is quite right, but you misunderstand my purpose. I have heard my father say that Fu Hsi, purest and most virtuous of ancient men, made the eight trigrams of the *Book of Changes;* the *Book of Documents* records the glorious age of Yao and Shun, and at that time the rites and music were composed; the makers of the *Odes* celebrated the golden age of T'ang and Wu in song. The *Spring and Autumn* picks out the good and condemns the evil, exalting the virtue of the Three Dynasties and praising the house of Chou. It does not confine itself solely to criticism and ridicule.

"Since the rise of the Han we have come to the time of our enlightened Emperor. He has received auspicious omens and blessings; he has establishd the sacrifices of Feng and Shan; he has changed the beginning of the year, altered the color of the vestments, and received the Mandate in his majesty and purity; his goodness flows over our land without bound. The multitudinous tribes within the four seas, translating and retranslating their strange tongues,[75] have come knocking at our borders in submission. Those who bring tribute and beg for an audience are too numerous to be told. The ministers and hundred officials with all their might sing the praises of his holy virtue, but still they feel they have not been able sufficiently to publish it abroad.

"Now if there are scholars and worthy men of ability who are not made use of in the government, this is a shame upon the ruler of the kingdom, while if the emperor is one of shining holiness and yet his virtue is not published throughout the land, this is a fault of the men in official position. I myself have for some time held this office [of Grand Historian]. If I should cast aside this shining holiness and supreme virtue and fail to make a record of it; if I should permit the labors of the meritorious ministers, the feudal families, and the worthy officials to fall into oblivion and not be transmitted; if I should allow the words of my father to be forgotten, I could certainly be guilty of no greater sin. When I say that I 'transmitted' a record of past affairs, putting in good order the genealogies and chronicles, it does not mean that I 'made' a work such as Confucius did. Therefore when you compare my writings to the *Spring and Autumn Annals,* you mistake their true nature."

The Misfortune of Ssu-ma Ch'ien

[Here Ssu-ma Ch'ien refers to the accusation brought against him by the emperor and the punishment of emasculation imposed upon him. The letter to Jen An quoted by Pan Ku, and reproduced later in this book, describes the circumstances of this tragedy in further detail.]

For the next seven years The Grand Historian devoted himself to writing and arranging his book. Then he encountered the misfortune of the Li Ling affair and was plunged into the dark, in bonds. He sighed bitterly and said, "Such is my fault, such is my fault, that I have brought mutilation to my body and may never again serve my lord!" [76] He turned within himself and pondered deeply, saying: "The writers of the *Odes* and the *Documents* were troubled and in distress [77] and they tried to set forth the meaning of their desires and hopes. Of old when the Chief of the West, King Wen, was imprisoned at Yu-li, he spent his time expanding the *Book of Changes;* Confucius was in distress between Ch'en and Ts'ai and he made the *Spring and Autumn;* when Ch'ü Yüan was exiled, he composed his poem 'Encountering Sorrow'; after Tso Ch'iu lost his sight, he composed the *Narratives from the States;* when Sun Tzu had had his feet amputated, he set forth the

Art of War; Lü Pu-wei was banished to Shu but his *Lü-lan* has been handed down through the ages; while Han Fei Tzu was held prisoner in Ch'in, he wrote 'The Difficulties of Disputation' and 'The Sorrow of Standing Alone';[78] most of the three hundred poems of the *Book of Odes* were written when the sages poured forth their anger and dissatisfaction. All these men had a rankling in their hearts, for they were not able to accomplish what they wished. Therefore they wrote about past affairs in order to pass on their thoughts to future ages."

So at last he transmitted a record of the past from T'ao T'ang [Emperor Yao] down to the unicorn, where he stopped. (Beginning with the Yellow Emperor.)[79]

Table of Contents of the Shih chi

[Here follows a listing of the contents of the *Shih chi* chapter by chapter. In Ssu-ma Ch'ien's postface the title of each chapter is preceded by a short description of the subject. When Pan Ku copied this postface into his biography of Ssu-ma Ch'ien, he recorded only the title and number of each chapter and omitted these descriptions. The descriptions are rather meaningless without a knowledge of the contents of each chapter and so I shall omit the entire section. Ssu-ma Ch'ien then continues his narrative.]

Concluding Remarks of Ssu-ma Ch'ien

This our house of Han has succeeded the descendants of the Five Emperors[80] and has carried on the task of unification of the Three Dynasties.[81] The ways of Chou fell into disuse and the Ch'in scattered and discarded the old writings and burned and destroyed the *Odes* and the *Documents.* Therefore the plans and records of the Illustrious Hall and the stone rooms, of the metal caskets and jade tablets, became lost or confused.

Then the Han arose and Hsiao Ho[82] put in order the laws and commandments; Han Hsin[83] set forth the rules of warfare; Chang Ts'ang[84] made the regulations and standards; and Shu-sun T'ung[85] settled questions of rites and ceremonies. At this time the art of letters began again to flourish and advance and the *Odes* and *Documents* gradually reappeared. From the time when Ts'ao Ts'an [86] put into practice Master Kai's teachings of the Yellow Emperor and Lao Tzu; when Chia Sheng [87] and Ch'ao Ts'o [88] expounded the doctrines of the Legalist philosophers Shen and Shang, and Kung-sun Hung [89] achieved eminence for his Confucian learning, a period of some one hundred years, the books that survived and records of past affairs were all without exception gathered together by The Grand Historian. The Grand Historians, father and son, each in turn held and carried on the position.

Ah,[90] I remember that my ancestors once were in charge of these affairs and won fame in the time of T'ang and Yü, and in the Chou they once again managed them. So the Ssu-ma family generation after generation has been the masters of astronomical affairs. Now it has come down to me. This I remember with awe! I remember with awe!

I have sought out and gathered together the ancient traditions of the empire which were scattered and lost; of the great deeds of kings I have searched the beginnings and examined the ends; I have seen their times of prosperity and observed their decline. Of the affairs that I have discussed and examined, I have made a general survey of the Three Dynasties and a record of the Ch'in and Han, extending in all back as far as Hsien Yüan [the Yellow Emperor] and coming down to the present, set forth in the twelve "Basic Annals." After this had been put in order and completed, because there were differences in chronology for the same periods and the dates were not always clear, I made the ten "Chronological Tables." Of the changes in rites and music, the improvements and revisions of the pitch pipes and calendar, military power, mountains and rivers, spirits and gods, the relationships between heaven and man, and the faulty economic practices that were handed down and reformed age by age,[91] I have made the eight "Treatises." As the twenty-eight constellations revolve about the North Star, as the thirty spokes of a wheel come together at the hub, revolving endlessly without stop, so the ministers, assisting like arms and legs, faithful and trustworthy, in true moral spirit serve their lord and ruler; of them I made the thirty "Hereditary Houses." Upholding righteousness, masterful and sure, not allowing themselves to miss their opportunities, they made a name for themselves in the world; of such men I made the seventy "Memoirs." In all one hundred and thirty chapters, 526,500 words, this is the book of the Grand Historian,[92] compiled in order to repair omissions and amplify the Six Disciplines. It is the work of one family, designed to supplement the various interpretations of the Six Classics and to put into order the miscellaneous sayings of the Hundred Schools. I have placed one copy in the Famous Mountain [93] and another in the capital, where they shall await the sages and scholars of later ages.

The Seventieth Chapter.[94]

The Grand Historian remarks: "I have transmitted a record of the ages from the Yellow Emperor down to the era *T'ai-ch'u,* comprising a work of one hundred and thirty chapters." [95]

ADDITIONS OF PAN KU TO THE POSTFACE OF THE GRAND HISTORIAN (HAN SHU 62)

[In his biography of Ssu-ma Ch'ien in *Han shu* 62, Pan Ku has copied in the complete text of the postface translated above (with the omissions already noted). He then begins his own narrative.]

Thus says the postface written by Ch'ien himself. But ten chapters are missing, there being only the titles but no texts.[96] After Ch'ien had suffered punishment, he became *Chung-shu-ling* [Palace Secretary] and enjoyed great honor and favor in the pursuit of his duties.

His old friend Jen An, Regional Inspector [*Tz'u-shih*] of I Province, sent Ch'ien a letter urging upon him his duty to work for the advancement of older officials of worth. Ch'ien replied to it as follows:

Ssu-ma Ch'ien's Letter in Reply to Jen Shao-ch'ing [97]

Shao-ch'ing, honored sir:

In the past I had the honor of receiving a letter from you in which you advised me to be careful in my dealings with people and instructing me in my duty to recommend men of ability and work for the advancement of worthy gentlemen.[98] Your concern is indeed kind and heartfelt. Perhaps you are angry that I have not marked your words and think that I am following the counsels of worthless men. I assure you I would not dare to do such a thing. Worthless old creature that I am, I have yet heard something of the teachings handed down from the great men of old. But I remember that I am no more than a mutilated being who dwells in degradation. Anything I might try to do would only meet with censure; should I try to help others I should only succeed in doing them injury. Therefore I am "in sadness and despair with no one to speak to." [99]

There is an old saying, "Whom will you do it for, and whom will you get to listen to you?" [100] After Chung Tzu-ch'i died, Po Ya never again played upon the lute. [101] Why? "It is for a friend who understands him that a man will act, and for a lover who delights in her that a woman will make herself beautiful." [102]

But one like myself, whose very substance is marred and mutilated —though I might possess the worth of the jewels of Sui and Ho, though my conduct might be as pure as that of Yu and I, [103] in the end I could never achieve glory, but on the contrary would only succeed in arousing laughter and bringing shame upon myself.

I should have answered your letter, but at the time I had to accompany the Emperor on a trip to the east and was pressed by many petty affairs of my own. The time we had together was indeed short, and I was so busy that I could not seem to find a moment of leisure to tell you all that I really feel. Now, Shao-ch'ing, you are accused of this terrible crime. [104] The days and months have gone by and it is drawing close to the end of winter. [105] I am forced to go in attendance upon the Emperor to Yung. [106] If you should suddenly meet with that which cannot be disguised by euphemism, it would mean that I would have no opportunity to unburden to you my bitterness and anguish. Then in the long journey hereafter your spirit would forever bear me personal resentment. So I beg you to allow me to explain in brief my rude and unworthy feelings, and I pray you will not blame me too severely for having been so long in answering.

I have heard it said that to devote oneself to moral training is the

storehouse of wisdom; to delight in giving to others is the beginning
of humanity; that proper giving and taking are the mark of a man's
sense of duty; while times of shame and disgrace determine his courage; and that making a name for himself is the aim of all action.
Only when a man has shown that he possesses these five qualities may
he take a place in the world and rank among the host of superior men.
No more severe misfortune can come to a man than to be driven by
covetous desires, no sadness is so painful as the grief of the heart. No
deed is more hideous than bringing shame to one's ancestors, and no
disgrace greater than the palace punishment [castration]. That a man
who has undergone such punishment is fit no longer to be associated
with is the opinion not of one age alone but has been held since ancient
times. When Duke Ling of Wei rode in the same carriage with Yung
Ch'ü, Confucius departed for Ch'en.[107] Because Shang Yang obtained
audience with the King through the offices of Ching Chien, Chao
Liang's heart turned cold.[108] When Chao T'an rode in the Emperor's
carriage, Yüan Ssu was fired with anger.[109] So from old times men have
been ashamed to associate with eunuchs. If even ordinary men are loath
to have dealings with eunuchs, how much more so in the case of gentlemen of virtue and feeling? Although our court today may be in need
of good men, what business would I, a mere "remnant of the knife
and saw," have in trying to help and recommend the finest and most
worthy men of the world? [110]

Because of the undertakings of my father which have passed on to
me, I have been allowed for some twenty years to serve beneath the
hub of the royal carriage, always awaiting my punishment.[111] I realize
full well that first of all, in serving our enlightened Emperor, I have
not been able to pay due fidelity or inspire real confidence, nor have I
gained a name for cleverness in planning or superiority of ability. Second, I have been able to perform no service in repairing deficiencies or
supplying what was lacking in the imperial rule or in promoting and
advancing men of virtue and talent, nor have I brought to light any
gentlemen who were living in retirement. In foreign affairs I have
commanded no ranks of men, captured no castles and fought on no

field; no glories of generals slain or enemy pennants seized are mine. At the least I have not, by piling up the days and sticking to my labors, achieved any high position or large salary, or brought glory and favor to my family and friends. I have not succeeded in a single one of these four endeavors.[112] From this it is obvious that I am a worthless person who by mere chance has been tolerated at court.

Once in former times I too took my place among the lower officers and participated in the lesser deliberations in the outer court. If I could not at that time introduce any great precepts or present any of my ideas, now when I am no more than a slave who sweeps the paths, mutilated and ranked among the low and worthless—now should I try to lift up my head and look lordly and discourse upon right and wrong, would I not show contempt for the court and bring shame to the gentlemen of my time? Alas, alas! A man like myself—what can he say now? What can he say now?

It is not easy to know the beginning and end of things. When I was young I had a spirit that would not be bridled, and as I grew older I won no fine praises in my village and district. But because of my father, our Ruler graciously allowed me to offer my poor talents and to come and go in the inner parts of the Palace. Therefore I cut off my acquaintanceship with friends and visitors and neglected the business of our family.[113]

I considered then that a man who has a bowl over his head cannot hope to see the sky.[114] Day and night I thought only how to use to the fullest my poor talents and strength. I went about the duties of my office with a single mind, seeking only the favor and love of our Ruler. But, quite contrary to my hopes, things came to a terrible misunderstanding.

Li Ling and I both held office at the same time.[115] Basically we were never very close. Our likes and dislikes lay in different directions; we never so much as drank a cup of wine together or shared the joys of intimate friendship. But I observed that he was clearly a man of superior ability. He was filial to his parents and trustworthy with his associates, honest in matters of money and just in all his giving and taking.

In questions of precedence he would always yield; he was respectful and modest and gave way to others. His constant care was to sacrifice himself for his country, hastening in time of need without thought for his own safety. This was always in his mind, and I believed him to be truly one of the finest men of the nation. A subject who will go forth to face ten thousand deaths, giving not the slightest thought for his own life but hurrying only to the rescue of his lord—such a man is rare indeed! Now he has committed one act that was not right, and the officials who think only to save themselves and protect their own wives and children vie with each other in magnifying his shortcomings. Truly it makes me sick at heart!

The infantry that Li Ling commanded did not come up to five thousand. They marched deep into barbarian territory, strode up to the ruler's court and dangled the bait, as it were, right before the tiger's jaws. In fearless ranks they shouted a challenge to the powerful barbarians, gazing up at their numberless hosts. For over ten days they continued in combat with the Shan-yü.[116] The enemy fell in disproportionate numbers; those who tried to rescue their dead and wounded could not even save themselves.[117] The barbarian lords in their robes of felt trembled with fear. They summoned their Wise Kings of the Left and Right [118] and called out all the men who could use a bow. The whole nation descended together upon our men and surrounded them. They fought their way along for a thousand miles until their arrows were all gone and the road was blocked. The relief forces did not come, and our dead and injured lay heaped up. But Li Ling with one cry gave courage to his army, so that every man raised himself up and wept. Washed in blood and choked with tears, they stretched out their empty bows and warded off the bare blades of the foe. North again they turned and fought to the death with the enemy.[119]

Before Li Ling fell into the hands of the enemy, a messenger came with the report [of his attack] and the lords and ministers of the Han all raised their cups in joyous toast to the Emperor. But after a few days came word of his defeat, and because of it the Emperor could find no flavor in his food and no delight in the deliberations of the court.

The great officials were in anxiety and fear and did not know what to do. Observing His Majesty's grief and distress, I dared to forget my mean and lowly position, sincerely desiring to do what I could in my fervent ignorance. I considered that Li Ling had always shared with his officers and men their hardships and want,[120] and could command the loyalty of his troops in the face of death. In this he was unsurpassed even by the famous generals of old. And although he had fallen into captivity, I perceived that his intention was to try to seek some future opportunity to repay his debt to the Han. Though in the end he found himself in an impossible situation, yet the merit he had achieved in defeating and destroying so many of the enemy was still worthy to be proclaimed throughout the world. This is what I had in my mind to say, but I could find no opportunity to express it. Then it happened that I was summoned into council, and I took the chance to speak of Li Ling's merits in this way, hoping to broaden His Majesty's view and put a stop to the angry words of the other officials.

But I could not make myself fully understood. Our enlightened Ruler did not wholly perceive my meaning, but supposed that I was trying to disparage the Erh-shih General and plead a special case for Li Ling.[121] So I was put into prison, and I was never able to make clear my fervent loyalty. Because it was believed that I had tried to defame the Emperor,[122] I was finally forced to submit to the judgment of the law officials. My family was poor and lacked sufficient funds to buy commutation of the sentence.[123] Of my friends and associates, not one would save me; among those near the Emperor no one said so much as a word for me. My body is not made of wood or stone, yet alone I had to face the officials of the law. Hidden in the depths of prison, to whom could I plead my case? This, Shao-ch'ing, is something you must truly have seen for yourself. Was this not the way I always acted? Li Ling had already surrendered alive and destroyed the fine reputation of his family. And then I was thrown into the "silkworm chamber" [where castrations were performed]. Together we became a sight for all the world to laugh at in scorn. Alas, alas! Matters such as these it is not easy to explain in detail to ordinary people.

My father had no great deeds that entitled him to receive the split tallies or the red charter.[124] He dealt with affairs of astronomy and the calendar, which are close to divination and worship of the spirits. He was kept for the sport and amusement of the Emperor, treated the same as the musicians and jesters, and made light of by the vulgar men of his day. If I fell before the law and were executed, it would make no more difference to most people than one hair off nine oxen, for I was nothing but a mere ant to them. The world would not rank me among those men who were able to die for their ideals, but would believe simply that my wisdom was exhausted and my crime great, that I had been unable to escape penalty and in the end had gone to my death. Why? Because all my past actions had brought this on me, they would say.

A man has only one death. That death may be as weighty as Mount T'ai, or it may be as light as a goose feather. It all depends upon the way he uses it.[125] Above all, a man must bring no shame to his forbears. Next he must not shame his person, nor be shameful in his countenance, nor in his words. Below such a one is he who suffers the shame of being bound, and next he who bears the shame of marked clothing.[126] Next is the man bound and fettered who knows the shame of rod and thorn, and the man who bears the shame of the shaved head and the binding manacle. Below again is the shame of mutilated flesh and severed limbs. Lowest of all is the extreme penalty, the "punishment of rottenness!"

The Commentary says: "Punishments shall not extend to the high officials." [127] This means that a gentleman must be ever careful of proper conduct.

When the fierce tiger dwells in the deep hills, all the other beasts tremble with fear. But when he is in the trap or the cage, he wags his tail and begs for food, for he has been gradually overawed and broken. Therefore there are cases when, even though one were to draw a circle on the ground and call it a prison, a gentleman would not enter, or though one carved a wooden image and set it up as judge, a gentleman would not contend with it, but would settle the affair for himself in accordance with what is right. But when a man has been bound hand and foot with stocks and ropes, has been stripped to the skin and flogged with rods, and plunged into the depths of encircling walls, at that time when he sees the judge he strikes his head upon the ground, and when he looks at the jailers his heart gasps with fear. Why? Because he has been gradually overawed and broken by force. A man must be thick-skinned indeed if he come to this and yet say, "I am not ashamed!" What respect could people have for such a man?

Hsi-po was an earl, and yet he was imprisoned at Yu-li.[128] Li Ssu was prime minister, yet he suffered all the five punishments.[129] Huai-yin was a king, but he was put into fetters at Ch'en.[130] P'eng Yüeh and Chang Ao faced south and called themselves independent, but they were both dragged to prison and punished.[131] The Marquis of Chiang overthrew and punished all the Lü family; his power exceeded that of the Five Protectors of old, yet he was imprisoned in the Inquiry Room.[132] The Marquis of Wei-ch'i was a great general, yet he wore the red clothing and was bound with three fetters.[133] Chi Pu was a manacled slave for Chu Chia,[134] and Kuan Fu suffered shame in the prison of Chü-shih.[135] All these men achieved the positions of feudal lords, generals, or ministers, and their fame reached to neighboring lands. But when they were accused of crimes and sentence was passed upon them, there was not one who could settle the matter with his hands by committing suicide. In the dust and filth of bondage, it has ever been the same, past and present. How in such circumstances can a man avoid shame?

From this you can see that "bravery and cowardice are only a matter of circumstance; strength and weakness are only a matter of the conditions."[136] This is certain. Is there any reason to wonder at it? Furthermore, if a man does not quickly make his decision to settle things for himself outside the law, but waits until he has sunk lower and lower, till he lies beneath the whip and lash, and then decides to save his honor by suicide, is it not too late? This is probably the reason why the ancients hesitated to administer punishment to officials.

It is the nature of every man to love life and hate death, to think of his relatives and look after his wife and children. Only when a man is moved by higher principles is this not so. Then there are things which he must do. Now I have been most unfortunate, for I lost my parents very early. With no brothers or sisters or close relations, I have been left alone an orphan. And you yourself, Shao-ch'ing, have seen me with my wife and child, and know how things are.[137] Yet the brave man does not necessarily die for honor, while even the coward may fulfill his duty. Each takes a different way to exert himself. Though I might be weak and cowardly and seek shamelessly to prolong my life, yet I know full well the difference between what ought to be followed and what rejected. How could I bring myself to sink into the shame of ropes and bonds? If even the lowest slave and scullion maid can bear to commit suicide, why should not one like myself be able to do what has to be done? But the reason I have not refused to bear these ills and have continued to live, dwelling in vileness and disgrace without taking my leave, is that I grieve that I have things in my heart which I have not been able to express fully, and I am shamed to think that after I am gone my writings will not be known to posterity. Too numerous to record are the men of ancient times who were rich and noble and whose names have yet vanished away. It is only those who were masterful and sure,[138] the truly extraordinary men, who are still remembered. When the Earl of the West was imprisoned at Yu-li, he expanded the *Changes;* Confucius was in distress and he made the *Spring and Autumn;* Ch'ü Yüan was banished and he composed his poem "Encountering Sorrow"; after Tso Ch'iu lost his sight, he composed the *Narratives from the States;* when Sun Tzu had had his feet amputated, he set forth the *Art of War;* Lü Pu-wei was banished to Shu but his *Lü-lan* has been handed down through the ages; while Han Fei Tzu was held prisoner in Ch'in, he wrote "The Difficulties of Disputation" and "The Sorrow of Standing Alone"; most of the three hundred poems of the *Book of Odes* were written when the sages poured forth their anger and dissatisfaction. All these men had a rankling in their hearts, for they were not able to accomplish what they wished. Therefore they wrote about past affairs in order to pass on their thoughts to future generations. Those like Tso Ch'iu, who was blind, or Sun Tzu, who had no feet, could never hold office, so they retired to compose books in order to set forth their thoughts and indignation, handing down their theoretical writings in order to show to posterity who they were. I too have ventured not to be modest but have entrusted myself to my useless writings. I have gathered up and brought together the old traditions of the world which were scattered and lost. I have examined the deeds and events of the past and investigated the principles behind their success and failure, their rise and decay, in one hundred and thirty chapters.[139] I wished to examine into all that concerns heaven and man, to penetrate the changes of the past and present, completing all as the work of one family. But before I had finished my rough manuscript, I met with this calamity. It is because I regretted that it had not been completed that I submitted to the extreme penalty without rancor. When I have truly completed this work, I shall deposit it in the Famous Mountain. If it may be handed down to men who will appreciate it, and penetrate to the villages and great cities, then though I should suffer a thousand mutilations, what regret should I have? Such matters as these may be discussed with a wise man, but it is difficult to explain them to ordinary people.

It is not easy to dwell in poverty and lowliness while base men multiply their slanderous counsels. I met this misfortune because of the words I spoke. I have brought upon myself the scorn and mockery even of my native village and I have soiled and shamed my father's name. With what face can I again ascend and stand before the grave mound of my father and mother? Though a hundred generations pass, my defilement will only become greater. This is the thought that wrenches my bowels nine times each day. Sitting at home, I am befuddled as though I had lost something. I go out, and then realize that I do not know where I am going. Each time I think of this shame, the sweat pours from my back and soaks my robe. I am now no more than a servant in the harem. How could I leave of my own accord and hide far away in some mountain cave?[140] Therefore I follow along with the vulgar, floating and sinking, bobbing up and down with the times, sharing their delusion and madness.

Now you, Shao-ch'ing, have advised me to recommend worthy men and promote scholars. But would not such a course be at odds with my own intent? Now although I should try to add glory and fame to myself, or with fine words seek to excuse my error, it would have no effect upon the vulgar. I would not be believed, but would only take upon myself further shame. Only after the day of death shall right and wrong at last be determined.[141]

I cannot convey in writing my full meaning,[142] but I have ventured to set forth in brief my unworthy opinion.[143]

Concluding Remarks

After Ch'ien died, his book came gradually to light. In the time of Emperor Hsüan [73–48 B. C.], Ch'ien's grandson by his daughter, the Marquis of P'ing-t'ung, Yang Yün,[144] worked to transmit and make known his work, so that finally it circulated widely. In the time of Wang Mang, Ch'ien's descendant was sought out and enfeoffed with the title "Viscount Master of History."

Appraisal

From ancient times when writings and documents were first made there were historian-officials, and their records were very numerous and comprehensive. Later Confucius collected these, going back as far as Yao of T'ang and down to Mu of Ch'in. Although there are literary remains from the ages before T'ang and Yü [Yao and Shun], their words are not canonical. Therefore it is impossible to speak clearly about the affairs of the Yellow Emperor or Chüan Hsü. Then Confucius used the historical records of Lu and made the *Spring and Autumn,* and Tso Ch'iu-ming collected and discussed the events upon which it is based in order to form a commentary; he also edited those accounts which differed to form the *Narratives from the States.* There is also the *Genealogical Origins* which covers the period from the Yellow

Emperor down to the time of the *Spring and Autumn* and records the ancestors and lineage of emperors, kings, feudal lords, and great officials. After the time of the *Spring and Autumn,* the Seven States fought back and forth and Ch'in finally united the feudal lords; for this period there is the *Intrigues of the Warring States.* Then the Han arose, conquered the Ch'in and ruled the world, and we have the *Spring and Autumn of Ch'u and Han.* Therefore Ssu-ma Ch'ien followed the *Narratives from the States,* selected material from the *Genealogical Origins* and the *Intrigues of the Warring States,* incorporated the text of the *Spring and Autumn of Ch'u and Han,*[145] and added an account of recent affairs, bringing his history down to the era T'ien-Han [100–97 B. C.] His discussions of Ch'in and Han are very detailed. But when it comes to the way in which he has extracted from the Classics, selected from the commentaries, and assessed and disposed of material from the various schools of philosophy, he is often careless and sketchy and takes improper liberties with his sources. With his diligence he had browsed very widely in books, threaded his way through the Classics and commentaries, and galloped up and down from the past to the present, covering a period of several thousand years. Yet his judgments stray rather often from those of The Sage. In discussing fundamental moral law, he venerates the teachings of the Yellow Emperor and Lao Tzu and slights the Six Classics. In his introduction to the "Memoirs of the Wandering Knights" he disparages gentlemen scholars who live in retirement and speaks in favor of heroic scoundrels. In his narration on "Merchandise and Prices" he honors those who were skilled at making a profit and heaps shame on those in poverty and low station. It is these points which mar his work. Yet Liu Hsiang, Yang Hsiung, and other men of wide learning and copious letters all praise Ch'ien as a man of excellent ability as a historian and testify to his skill in setting forth events and their causes. He discourses without sounding wordy; he is simple without being rustic. His writing is direct and his facts sound. He does not falsify what is beautiful, nor does he conceal what is evil. Therefore his may be termed a "true record." Alas! Ch'ien, with all his wide knowledge and experience, yet failed to understand how to keep himself from harm. After he had suffered the extreme penalty, he was despondent and poured forth his resentment. How sincere his letter is, telling of all he suffered and felt shame for! It ranks with the "Chief Eunuch" of the Lesser Odes.[146] But what the Great Ode says, "Enlightened and wise, he keeps himself from harm" —this indeed is difficult! [147]

III

THE BEGINNINGS OF
CHINESE HISTORIOGRAPHY

The beginning of Chinese historiography, like so many problems in the ancient history of China, is considerably complicated by an accretion of later theories and rationalizations, and by the fact that some of our most important sources, such as the *Chou li* or *Rites of Chou,* are of questionable date and authenticity. Even the original meaning of the character for historian, *shih,* has long been misinterpreted because of the mistaken explanation of it given by the Latter Han lexicographer Hsü Shen.[1] Wang Kuo-wei in China and Naitô Torajirô in Japan, working independently from the oldest forms of the character found on Shang oracle bones, both reached the conclusion that it represents a hand holding a vessel used to contain tallies at archery contests, and that the official designated by this character in Shang times was originally charged with the duty of keeping track of hits at these contests.[2] From this we may surmise, though concrete evidence is lacking, that the *shih* officials later enlarged their activities to the keeping of records in general.

With the Chou dynasty we can reconstruct with greater certainty the nature and duties of the office, though again the sources are often dubious and contradictory. It is probable that the *shih* by this time had some connection with astronomical affairs, particularly the selection of lucky and unlucky days for the performance of important affairs, that they traveled with the ruler at times of important sacrifices, military expeditions or diplomatic meetings, and continued as before to

attend at archery contests. By Chou times, also, we know that the office
of *shih* was hereditary and commanded considerable prestige.

One of the important duties of the *shih,* it appears, was to memorize
and recite the interpretations of the results of divination, either by the
tortoise shell, bone, or milfoil methods. They were required to know
how to read and write, to handle various written documents and act
as secretaries to the rulers. The actual keeping of regular historical
records or annals (the so-called "spring and autumn" chronicles) seems
to have been a later development. It probably arose from the fact that
the *shih* (we may perhaps by now call them "historians") were present
at official meetings of the rulers and kept a record of these meetings for
future reference. As the various small feudal states of the early Chou
grew by conquest and absorption into larger and more powerful political units, their diplomatic relations assumed greater complexity and
importance. It was desirable, therefore, to have accurate written accounts of exchanges of envoys, transference of territory, battles, state
marriages, and the results of diplomatic conferences held among these
various states, and this led to the keeping of local chronicles. Naitô
believes that at the ceremony called *kao-shuo* or "Proclaiming the New
Year," the Chou ruler presented the calendar for the new year, marked
with dates and descriptions of important functions and duties, to the
feudal lords. This calendar was then stored in the ancestral temple of
the feudal lord, and on it the historians made notes of important events
in the state. These are the records, he thinks, which Confucius is supposed to have compiled and edited to form the *Spring and Autumn
Annals* of his native state of Lu. The fact that the *Spring and Autumn
Annals* goes back no further than Duke Yin (722 B. C.) indicates that
no such records existed in the state of Lu for earlier times, Naitô believes.[3]

This course of development—the fact that the early historian was a
semi-religious official concerned with court ceremonies, sacrifices, and
great state affairs, and only later became a keeper of detailed and day
to day chronicles—fits well with the temporal sequence of the two great
historical Classics of the Chinese, the *Book of Documents* (*Shu ching*),

or *Book of History,* and the *Spring and Autumn Annals (Ch'un ch'iu).*
The *Book of Documents* is a collection of speeches, ordinances, admonitions, and similar compositions of a hortatory nature attributed
to the ancient rulers and their advisers. As the Chinese have always
recognized, it is primarily a record of words rather than deeds. The
purpose of these documents is to provide moral lessons, to act as guides
in the conduct of political affairs; their interest is not primarily historical but moral and literary. As Professor Creel has pointed out,
many of them are actually propaganda speeches designed to justify to
the Shang people the conquest of the invading Chou armies.[4] The
Spring and Autumn Annals, on the other hand, is a bare and humdrum
record of facts, containing not a word of direct speech. Regardless of
how later commentators have labored to invest it with moral significance, it is obvious that its purpose, or at least the purpose of the original records which Confucius used as his sources, was simply the
recording of historical events. Chavannes has pointed out that in this
respect the case of China roughly parallels the development of historical writing in other countries such as Greece.[5] The earliest literature, though it relates events which often have a basis in historical
fact, is concerned primarily with the literary and ethical import of its
story. It is only after a people or culture reaches a considerable degree
of maturity that it begins to think less of its poetic, myth-embroidered
beginnings, and takes an interest in the sober and less dramatic record
of historical facts. In other words, centuries of Homer must go by in
the development of a culture before we may expect a Herodotus. The
fact that the Chinese moved beyond their early delight in the heroic
and resounding words of the *Book of Documents* and *Book of Odes*
and came to value also the day-by-day account of actual events may
well have been due almost solely to the powerful influence of Confucius and his disciples and the importance they attached to the *Spring
and Autumn Annals.* We must surely admit as we scan the dull, dry
pages of the old chronicle of Lu that nothing less than a great personality and a great tradition could ever have invested them with the

interest and life they have maintained through two thousand odd years of Chinese civilization.[6]

Such is the general picture of the beginnings of Chinese historiography as we reconstruct it today. Before proceeding to a more detailed discussion of the *Spring and Autumn Annals,* let us examine for a moment the conception of these beginnings held by Ssu-ma Ch'ien and his contemporaries in the Han.

The *Li chi* contains a statement that "When the emperor acts, the Historian of the Left records it; when he speaks, the Historian of the Right makes a record of it."[7] The *Han shu* repeats this statement (although it reverses the duties of the two historians), adding that "the record of actions became the *Spring and Autumn Annals,* that of the words became the *Book of Documents.*"[8] It has been generally agreed that this theory of the two historians who kept separate records of words and actions, and the derivation of the two Classics from them, is no more than a late rationalization of the fact that, as we have noted, the contents of these two works are so clearly divided along these lines. Ssu-ma Ch'ien does not mention this theory, and we may suppose that, if he was even familiar with it, he did not consider it of great importance. But he does make frequent mention of early historians, and his notices of them show that he conceived the office not only as one of great ritual and political significance, but viewed the historian as a sort of moral mentor and guide to the early rulers. We do not know whether the ancient historians actually wielded such moral influence upon the rulers as these later stories imply. Yet we find the beginnings of the tradition in late Chou works such as the *Tso* and *Kung-yang* commentaries of the *Spring and Autumn Annals* and continuing through Han works. The *Ta-Tai Li-chi,* for example, describes the historian who was traditionally attached to the Heir Apparent of the Chou court in these words: "When the Prince had any fault, it was the duty of the historian to record it. . . . If he failed to record these faults, he was guilty of death."[9]

Ssu-ma Ch'ien introduces this picture of the ancient historian, the stern recorder of the ruler's deeds and censor of his actions, in his description of the opening age of the Chou dynasty. At the beginning of the "Hereditary House of Chin" (SC 39/3), he tells the story of how the young prince Shu Yü, ancestor of the rulers of Chin, was one day playing with his older brother, King Ch'eng, second ruler of the Chou dynasty. The older boy picked a leaf of the *t'ung* tree and gave it to his little brother, saying, "I will enfeoff you with this." The court historian, I, asked to be allowed to select a propitious day for the ceremony, whereupon the boy ruler protested that he was only fooling. "The Son of Heaven does not speak in jest," the historian admonished. "When he speaks, the historian records his words, the rites bring them to fruition, and music celebrates them in song." The young king, we are told, was forced to go through with the enfeoffment of his brother.

But more often the historian of this early period appears as a kind of seer or prophet, an adviser who dramatizes his point with strange tales of the past. In the "Basic Annals of Chou" we read of ancient historians who presented memorials to the throne, blind singers who admonished the ruler in song, and blind historians who gave moral instruction to the king. Shortly after, in the dark reign of the evil king Yu, we meet the "Grand Historian Po Yang" who predicts the downfall of the Chou and reprimands the king for his love of the concubine Pao Ssu. He emphasizes his point by "reading from the historical records" the story of how Pao Ssu was miraculously conceived when her mother bathed in the saliva of the ancient dragons of Hsia.[10] Again in the "Basic Annals of Ch'in" (SC 5/47) appears the Grand Historian Tan of Chou with predictions of the future of the state of Ch'in.

These and similar mentions of ancient historians in the *Shih chi,* in spite of their fantastic elements, serve to bear out our earlier statement that the historian was connected with affairs of divination and the keeping of records (or perhaps we might better say legends) of the past, and was close to the ruler, acting often as adviser and moral counselor. The historians we have so far mentioned are all identified as officials of the central court, that of the Chou rulers. Let us turn now to the historians of the local feudal courts.

Ssu-ma Ch'ien mentions in the Basic Annals of Ch'in that in the thirteenth year of Duke Wen of Ch'in (753 B. C.) "they first had historians to record affairs." [11] Ch'in was traditionally late in developing as a feudal state, only receiving recognition as a vassal of the Chou dynasty in 771, so we may perhaps suppose from this that the older feudal states had had their official historians from earlier times. This assumption, as well as Naitô's theory that these early local chronicles were related to the announcements of the calendar, is borne out in a negative way by Ch'ien's statement in his "Treatise on the Calendar" (SC 26/7) that after the time of kings Li and Yu of the Chou (*ca.* 878–770) "the historians no longer recorded the seasons and the ruler did not proclaim the calendar."

There is probably little more we can say about these early chronicles of the feudal states, since so little of them survived the burning of the books carried out by the Ch'in. Yet the single major one that did survive, the *Spring and Autumn Annals* of Lu, with its commentaries, has had such a tremendous and lasting influence upon Chinese historical thought that it largely overshadows the ancient historian-prophets of the early Chou central court and the Classic associated with the central court, the *Book of Documents.* It, not the *Book of Documents,* became the prototype, in concept and often in form, of later historical works. It was not, indeed, until the composition of the *Sui History's* "Treatise on Literature" (*Ching-chi-chih*) in the seventh century A. D. that the Chinese even recognized a separate category of "history" in their literature. The earlier writers of the Han dynasty "Treatise on Literature" had simply classified all historical works, including the *Shih chi,* under the category of the *Spring and Autumn Annals.*

THE SPRING AND AUTUMN ANNALS

The *Ch'un-ch'iu* or *Spring and Autumn* is a chronicle of the reigns of twelve dukes of the state of Lu covering the period from 722 to 481 B. C. It contains, in barest outline, notations of the internal affairs of Lu, of diplomatic conferences, feudal wars, and Lu's other relations with neighboring states, and occasional records of eclipses, floods, earthquakes, and prodigies of nature. The account is entirely impersonal, with no trace, at least to the untutored eye, of the personality or attitude of the recorder or recorders.

Mencius has the following remarks to make about the *Annals:*

The traces of imperial rule were extinguished and the imperial odes ceased to be made. When these odes ceased to be made, then the *Ch'un-ch'iu* was produced. The *Ch'eng* of Chin, the *T'ao-wu* of Ch'u, and the *Ch'un-ch'iu* of Lu were books of the same character. The subject of the *Ch'un-ch'iu* was the affairs of Huan of Ch'i and Wen of Chin, and its style was that of the historians. Confucius said, "Its righteous decisions I venture to make" (IVB, 21). The world fell into decay and principles faded away. Perverse speakings and oppressive deeds waxed rife again. There were instances of ministers who murdered their sovereigns, and of sons who murdered their fathers. Confucius was afraid and made the *Spring and Autumn*. What the *Spring and Autumn* contains are matters proper to the emperor. On this account Confucius said, "Yes! It is the *Spring and Autumn* which will make men know me, and it is the *Spring and Autumn* which will make men condemn me" (IIIB, 9). Confucius completed the *Spring and Autumn* and rebellious ministers and villainous sons were struck with terror (*Ibid.*).

It will be seen that these statements, the earliest we have on the *Annals,* attest to a belief in two facts: that Confucius himself wrote or compiled the *Spring and Autumn Annals* as it was handed down in Mencius' time, and that it contained matters of profound political and moral significance. It is difficult indeed, without the aid of commentaries, to discern any such moral lessons or principles in the bare narrative of the chronicle. For this reason scholars of recent years have sometimes tried to dismiss this idea, the so-called "praise and blame" theory, denying that the text is anything more than it appears to be, a brief, dull record of a small feudal state. Yet we know that Confucius in his teaching often used the texts of older works to illustrate moral lessons, sometimes taking considerable liberty with the meaning of the original to make his point. There is admittedly nothing in our present text of the *Annals* to prove that it *has* any abstruse moral significance. But neither is there anything to deny the possibility that Confucius and his disciples formulated and passed on interpretations of the events and notations of the chronicle which attempted to give the text such significance, and that these are the interpretations which were later collected and written down to form the various commentaries on the *Spring and Autumn Annals* we have today. Modern scholars have also questioned the other assumption of Mencius, that Confucius himself in any way wrote, edited, or compiled the chronicle. Here again, since there is nothing in the way of definitive proof either for or against this assertion, which appears as early as the time of Mencius, only two centuries after the death of Confucius, there seems to be no advantage to be gained in denying it simply for the sake of denial.

As is generally known, there are three principal commentaries on the *Annals*, the *Kung-yang*, the *Ku-liang*, and the *Tso* or *Tso-shih*. Of these the *Kung-yang* seems to be the oldest as a ritual commentary directly connected with the text of the *Annals*. It preserves no divisions between the text of the Classic itself and that of the commentary and it is assumed that the two texts were combined from the time the commentary was first written. In thought, the *Kung-yang* interpretation exactly parallels the assertions of Mencius quoted above. We may assume, therefore, that Mencius was referring to the *Kung-yang* or *Kung-yang* school of interpretation of the *Annals*, indeed that he probably was familiar with no other interpretation.[12] The *Ku-liang Commentary*, because of the way it borrows and elaborates upon the *Kung-yang* and because of the more advanced knowledge of astronomy it displays, appears to be a later work, probably of the early Han. The *Tso-chuan* or *Tso Commentary* is a genuine text of the Warring States period and was probably written, or compiled from earlier sources, around the third century B. C. to fill in the historical background of the events mentioned in the *Annals*, and to present its own interpretation of their moral significance. Its material falls into two categories: historical narrative of events related to notations in the *Annals*, much like the similar narratives found in the *Kung-yang* but more extensive and detailed, and a ritual commentary upon the moral significance of the Classic and the judgments of praise or blame which Confucius was conveying. Both types of material are mingled together in our present text and the fact that Ssu-ma Ch'ien quotes frequently from both types suggests that the two were combined from early times. But just what the exact form of the original text was, and when it was broken up and appended to the dated entries of the *Annals* as it is today, is still a matter of dispute.[13]

Since it is apparent from the *Shih chi* that it was the interpretation of the *Annals* set forth in the *Kung-yang* and *Tso* commentaries that influenced Ssu-ma Ch'ien, let us examine some of the main ideas of these works. The basic premise of the *Kung-yang* school, and to a lesser extent of the *Tso school,* is that Confucius compiled the *Spring and Autumn Annals* to act, not as an impartial record of historical facts, but as a work displaying in subtle and abstruse form his moral and political principles. As such it is a book primarily not of history but of philosophy or, as the Chinese term it, a book of rites (*li*) where this word has its broadest connotation of moral principles. Confucius set forth his ideas, not in generalized codes of behavior such as are found in the *Li chi* and other Confucian works on ritual, but by passing judgment upon the events of the past, showing what he approved or disapproved of in the conduct of rulers and statesmen by his choice of material, the order of presentation, or the particular way it was worded.[14] His work was written for the ages, and in it he laid down the principles upon which he believed a just ruler of the future must base his government. Therefore the *Annals* is a work of government; it relates, as Mencius has said, the business of the emperor, and Confucius who wrote it assumes the position of an "uncrowned king" of this new ideal dynasty. Han commentators carried this idea even further, declaring that the Han represented the realization of this ideal dynasty, and even in some cases attributing to the sage a foreknowledge of the house of Han.[15]

No matter how fanciful and forced this interpretation may seem, no matter how far removed from the reality of the text, we must keep it constantly in mind if we are to understand the statements of later scholars concerning the *Spring and Autumn Annals,* the profound significance which they so lavishly attribute to it, and the influence which it has had upon Chinese thought. We must remember, in short,

that when Chinese scholars talk about the *Spring and Autumn Annals*
they do not mean simply the brief, dull text of the Lu chronicle, but
the text as interpreted in the light of this tradition.

The *Kung-yang Commentary* is largely in the form of a catechism,
containing one sentence of the basic text followed by questions and
answers upon the meaning of the sentence, the moral point which Confucius is supposedly making, and occasionally the historical background
of the events mentioned. The commentary tries valiantly to discover a
series of basic principles to explain this moral significance, the praise
or blame which Confucius is implying by the wording, order, inclusion
or omission of material, etc. The impartial reader will soon discover,
however, that it postulates so many different principles of interpretation, often quite contradictory, that by juggling them around one might
make the basic text imply almost anything he wished. Yet in spite of
the crudity of its application, we must not lose patience with the general
idea behind this theory of interpretation, for it is of far-reaching significance.

In this welter of forced and anomalous interpretations we may, I believe, discern three basic ideas which are being attributed to the chronicle. The first two, characteristically enough, are absolutely antithetical
—namely, that the historian must make a completely objective, realistic record of the facts, and that he must *not* make a record of the facts
but must "doctor them up" to accord with preconceived ideas. The
third is that unusual occurrences in the natural world such as drought,
flood, comets, eclipses, etc., are directly related to human affairs and
have an important bearing upon history. I shall attempt to explain these
three ideas more clearly by concrete illustration.

Under Duke Yin, seventh year, we read in the *Annals:* "The Marquis of Teng died." The *Kung-yang Commentary* says of this: "Why
does it not record his name? Because Teng is a minor state. If it is a
minor state, then why does it call him 'Marquis'? There is no objection
to this. In the cases of both noble and lowly the *Annals* does not object
to using the same terminology." Ho Hsiu (A. D. 129–182), the Latter
Han commentator on the *Kung-yang,* adds that "rulers who succeeded

their fathers are said to 'ascend the throne,' while those who assassinated their lords are also said to 'ascend the throne.'" In other words
the *Annals* is a straightforward record which does not hesitate to state
facts whether it approves of them or not.

A little further on we find how important it is for the historian to
record no more than he knows to be absolutely true. Under Duke
Huan, fifth year, we find two days recorded for the death date of Marquis Pao of Ch'en. "Why two death dates?" the *Kung-yang* asks itself
and replies: "The Scholar [i.e., Confucius] was in doubt and so he recorded both days." Tung Chung-shu, the most important exponent of
the *Kung-yang* school in the early Han, remarks on this: "He copied
down what he saw but did not speak about what was unclear." [16] In this
connection we may notice a saying of Confucius recorded in the *Analects* (XV, 25): "The Master said, 'Even in my early days a historiog-
rapher would leave a blank in his text.'" The passage, obscure as it is,
has been interpreted to mean that the ancient historians were in the
habit of leaving unrecorded anything they were in doubt about, but
that this commendable practice was being violated in Confucius' later
years.

Even more impressive evidence for the care, accuracy, and integrity
of the ancient Chinese historians is found in the *Tso Commentary*
under the twenty-fifth year of Duke Hsiang, where we read: "Ts'ui
Shu assassinated his lord Kuang." In this year, according to the *Tso*,
Ts'ui Shu, minister of the state of Ch'i, assassinated Duke Chuang of
Ch'i and set up his own brother in his place as Duke Ching. The Grand
Historian of Ch'i recorded: "Ts'ui Shu assassinated his lord," whereupon Ts'ui murdered him. The historian's brother succeeded him,
wrote the same thing, and was also murdered, but another younger
brother came forward to write the same, and with this the evil man
finally desisted and let the record stand. In the meantime, another
historian, hearing that the Grand Historian had been murdered,
grasped his writing tablets and hastened to court, retiring only after he
had been assured that the deed of assassination had been truthfully

recorded. Ssu-ma Ch'ien reports this story of sacrifice in his "Hereditary House of Ch'i" (SC 32/45), and no doubt its model of honest and fearless recording stirred him as it has later readers. These then—recording the facts carefully, fearlessly, and without personal bias—were some of the ideals of historiography which one might learn from the *Spring and Autumn Annals* as interpreted by its commentaries.

It is now my unhappy duty to destroy this enlightened picture of the historiography of the *Annals* by describing the opposite set of ideals. We find in the commentaries, for example, the invocation of a principle called *hui,* "avoidance" or "taboo." Under Duke Yin, tenth year, the *Kung-yang* states: "The *Spring and Autumn* records internal affairs and abbreviates external affairs. In the case of other states it records great faults but does not bother with minor ones. But with regard to internal affairs [i.e., within the state of Lu] it 'avoids' mention of great faults and only records minor ones." Again, under Duke Min, first year, the *Kung-yang* clearly states that the *Annals* observes this kind of "avoidance" of the truth for the sake of "those who deserve to be honored, those who are closely related to one, and those who are virtuous."

Lest one suppose that this concept represents a delusion of the *Kung-yang* alone, I hasten to add that the *Tso* agrees fully. Under Duke Hsi, first year, it states that the reason the chronicle does not state that the duke ascended the throne is because he violated propriety by fleeing from the country and then reentering. "The Classic does not record it because it wishes to conceal the fact. It is proper to conceal the evils of the state." The *Tso,* under Duke Wen, fourteenth year, elaborates this principle of what it is proper to record. "All deaths of emperors, high lords and ministers, unless formally announced to the court of Lu, are not recorded. Likewise rulers who go into exile or who are restored to their rule after exile are not recorded unless the fact is formally reported. This is done to reprimand the lack of respect implied."

Here we see the commentaries making of the chronicle not a record of fact, but a book of moral principles, a work designed not to impart information but to pass judgment upon the events and persons described. I shall illustrate this a little further with two famous incidents from the *Annals*.

In 631 Duke Wen of the state of Chin summoned the weak king Hsiang of the Chou to a meeting with the other feudal lords at a place north of the Yellow River. But the *Spring and Autumn Annals* simply records that "The King of Heaven went on a hunt north of the River" (Duke Hsi 28). This is because a vassal is not permitted to summon the Son of Heaven, says the *Kung-yang,* and the *Tso* agrees. "In recording events," Tung Chung-shu explains, "the *Spring and Autumn* sometimes perverts the truth in order to avoid certain things. . . . Thus it perverts the fact that Wen of Chin got his way and thereby avoids showing that he made the king come to him." [17] Ssu-ma Ch'ien apparently considered the incident, and the fact that Confucius could not bear to record the truth, of great importance, for he tells the story three times, in the "Basic Annals of Chou" (SC 4/73), the "Hereditary House of Chin" (SC 39/61), and the "Hereditary House of Confucius" (SC 47/84).

Duke Ling of Chin, I Kao, was a very evil ruler who used to amuse himself by shooting at his courtiers with a sling-shot from his royal terrace and watching them flee. He was anxious to get rid of his chief minister, Chao Tun, whom he very nearly succeeded in murdering before the latter fled from the court into hiding. Shortly after, in 606, Chao Tun's younger brother, Chao Ch'uan, assassinated the duke. But the *Annals,* under Duke Hsüan, second year, records that "Chao Tun assassinated his lord I Kao." The *Tso* explains that when Chao Ch'uan assassinated the duke, his brother returned to the court without having gone beyond the borders of the state of Chin. The Grand Historian thereupon wrote: "Chao Tun assassinated his Lord," and showed the document to the court. When Chao Tun protested his innocence, the historian replied, "You are the chief minister. When you fled you did not go beyond the border [to absolve yourself of allegiance]. Now when you return you do not punish the offender. If you are not responsible, then who is?" Confucius, the commentary adds, though he sympa-

thized with the difficult position of Chao Tun, also praised the historian. "He was a good historian of ancient times. In his way of recording
things he did not hide anything." Ssu-ma Ch'ien repeats the story, with
Confucius' comment, in his "Hereditary House of Chin" (SC 39/71).

These stories and others like them will serve to show that in the
Annals moral or didactic principles, according to the commentaries,
often take precedence over a simple, honest recording of facts. The
historian must conceal facts out of deference for the reputation of his
own ruler or state or for other ritualistic considerations, while at times
he may deliberately falsify the account in order to make some ethical
point. Sometimes we are told that Confucius went out of his way to
record certain events ordinarily beyond the scope of his chronicle "because he was grieved by them." [18] Again we are informed that Confucius recorded in different ways what he had personally seen, what he
had heard about, and what was told to him as hearsay by others.[19] We
are further warned that in the latter years of the chronicle which
covered living rulers, Confucius was forced to be particularly obscure
in his criticisms to avoid danger to himself.[20]

This brief discussion of the *Spring and Autumn Annals* as it was
traditionally interpreted will show, I think, that in spite of the fact that
it was supposedly a record of ancient affairs written by the greatest of
sages, it was a very poor model for actual historical writing. Indeed, as
we have seen, it was in spirit often emphatically anti-historical. For
this reason, and because it would be presumptuous even to attempt to
imitate the moralizing of the sage, few Chinese historians have ever
considered directly and openly modeling their work upon the principles
of the *Spring and Autumn,* at least to the point of obviously altering
the facts. Yet, as I hope to show, the spirit of the *Annals* has not been
without its influence, especially in the case of Ssu-ma Ch'ien.

Before passing on to a discussion of the *Shih chi,* however, we must
notice one more characteristic of the *Spring and Autumn Annals* as
interpreted by its commentaries, namely its attention to weird and unusual occurrences in nature. The chronicle makes frequent mention of
these occurrences, which, according to the commentaries, are all

brought about by misrule or disorder in human society. "When men abandon their constant ways," the *Tso Commentary* explains (Duke Chuang 14), commenting on a strange battle of snakes in the state of Cheng, "then weird things appear." These unnatural events, according to the *Kung-yang*, were deliberately recorded by Confucius "for the sake of the heirs of the king" (Duke Wen 3) or "for the sake of the world" (Duke Shao 18), so that they might serve as warnings against future errors.

Tung Chung-shu elaborated this idea into an important part of his political philosophy. At times he explained these prodigies and portents as direct signs from a benevolent Heaven that wished thereby to inform men of their errors; at other times he interpreted them mechanistically as the natural and inevitable results of dislocation in the order of human society which occasioned reactions in the natural world. Pan Ku copied into his *Han shu* a long essay by Liu Hsiang and Liu Hsin, the "Treatise on the Five Elements" (HS 27), which discusses each one of the portents mentioned in the *Annals* and the various interpretations of them, attempting to assign to each some definite cause in the history of human affairs.

Most of these accounts of disasters and prodigies need not concern us here, but something must be said of the last and most famous of them, the capture of the unicorn.

The last entry in the *Annals,* in the fourteenth year of Duke Ai, reads: "Spring. At the western hunt a unicorn was captured."

The *Kung-yang* comments:

Why did Confucius record this? Because he recorded unusual things. Why was this unusual? Because the unicorn is not a beast of the Middle Kingdom. . . . The unicorn is a beast of virtue. When there is a true king, it appears, but when there is no true king, it does not appear. Someone reported that there was a small deer with a horn. Confucius said, "Ah! For whom did it come? For whom did it come?" and, turning back his sleeve, he brushed his face and his tears wet his robe. When Yen Yüan died, the Master said, "Alas! Heaven is destroying me!" When Tzu Lu died, the Master said, "Alas! Heaven is cutting me off!" At the western hunt a unicorn was captured. Confucius said, "My way is ended!" [21]

The commentary then passes immediately to the reasons why Confucius wrote the *Spring and Autumn,* concluding, "He ordered the principles of the *Spring and Autumn* in order to await the sages of later years, for he considered that other gentlemen would also take delight in them."

What is the significance of the unicorn? As commentators have pointed out, the beast should never have appeared when it did, for at this time the world was in chaos and there was no true king. Therefore Confucius asked "For whom did it come?" and wept that, born like himself into an evil and benighted age, it suffered only misfortune. The sad spectacle of the untimely arrival of the beast of virtue portended, in his eyes, his own fate and approaching death, and thus he said, "My way is ended." The *Kung-yang* implies by the order of its narrative that the portentous appearance of the unicorn was connected with the composition of the *Annals.* Ssu-ma Ch'ien certainly interpreted it in this way. In his biography of Confucius (SC 47), though he mentions the sage's literary labors on the other Classics earlier in his narrative, his description of the composition of the *Spring and Autumn Annals* appears only after the capture of the unicorn, and in his chapter on eminent Confucianists (SC 121/3) he explicitly relates the events causally: "At the western hunt a unicorn was captured. Confucius said, 'My way is ended!' Therefore he used the historical records to make the *Spring and Autumn."*

THE INFLUENCE OF THE SPRING AND AUTUMN ANNALS ON THE SHIH CHI

Fortunately, as I have said, Ssu-ma Ch'ien did not attempt to imitate the perversions, the suppressions, the deliberate distortions of fact, that the commentaries attribute to the labors of Confucius. Such an effort would have been both presumptuous and absurd. For Ssu-ma Ch'ien felt that the facts of history, recorded just as he found them, told a story sufficiently interesting and instructive. It is the first principle I have noted in the *Spring and Autumn Annals,* the tradition of Confucius' care and honesty in the handling of his sources, that Ssu-ma Ch'ien set himself to emulate. In the introduction to his "Chronological Table of the Three Dynasties" (SC 13/3) he remarks:

When Confucius arranged the *Spring and Autumn* from the old historical texts, he noted the first year of a reign, the time when the year began, and the day and month for each entry; such was his exactitude. However, when he wrote his prefaces to the *Book of Documents,* he made only general references and did not mention year and month. Perhaps he had some material, but in many cases it was lacking, and so he could not record things exactly. Therefore, where there was a question of doubt he recorded it as doubtful; such was his circumspection. . . .

Many examples of Ssu-ma Ch'ien's circumspection, his rejection of doubtful material, and his attempts to correct errors of fact or supplement his sources by personal experience or interviews with men who had first hand knowledge of the events he is describing, may be found in his notes at the end of each chapter and I shall not bother to cite them all here. Criticism may be made here and there of the way in which Ssu-ma Ch'ien applied his methods of historiography or the degree of success to which he realized his aims. But these methods and aims themselves, as he explains them, would do credit to a historian of any age. The worth and integrity of Ssu-ma Ch'ien's work was quickly recognized by his countrymen. Yang Hsiung (53 B. C.–18 A. D.) called his history a "true record"[22] and Pan Ku, in praise of Ch'ien, repeated the phrase: "His writing is direct and his facts are sound. He does not falsify what is beautiful nor does he conceal what is evil. Therefore his may be termed a 'true record.'" Even the philosopher and critic Wang Ch'ung (27–97 A. D.), who found little to praise in the works of his predecessors, made an exception of Ssu-ma Ch'ien, holding up his common sense and realism as examples of the true scientific spirit.[23]

But the opposite principle of the *Annals,* that history is not the mere recording of events but a moral and didactic labor, could not but have its effect upon Ssu-ma Ch'ien, living as he did at a time when the greatest work of history, in so far as history was recognized at all as a category of literature, was the *Spring and Autumn Annals* and its commentaries. Ssu-ma Ch'ien's own description of his work in his autobiography, translated in the preceding chapter, amply bears this out.

As we have seen there, it had been the intention of Ssu-ma Ch'ien's father, Ssu-ma T'an, to compile a history, perhaps only of the Han, perhaps of all ages, and he had already begun work on it, it appears, by collecting material and possibly beginning the writing. On his death bed, he reminded his son that their family had from most ancient times been in charge of historical matters, exhorting him with the memory of the great writers of the past, particularly Confucius.

My father used to say to me [Ssu-ma Ch'ien reports]: "Five hundred years after the Duke of Chou died Confucius appeared. It has now been five hundred years since the death of Confucius. There must be someone who can succeed to the enlightened ages of the past, who can set right the transmission of the *Book of Changes*, continue the *Spring and Autumn Annals*, and search into the world of the *Odes* and *Documents*, the rites and music!"

Here Ssu-ma T'an is paraphrasing the theory of Mencius that in the course of every five hundred years a true sovereign will arise. Mencius traces the line from Yao, Shun, and Yü, most ancient of the sage-emperors, to T'ang, founder of the Shang, to King Wen, founder of the Chou, and finally to Confucius. Ssu-ma T'an, however, adapts the theory in a special way to apply not to rulers but to writers, that is, from the Duke of Chou, author of many of the *Odes*, to Confucius, author of the *Spring and Autumn Annals*, to (he hopes) himself and his son. This passage reveals the extent to which Ssu-ma T'an and his son regarded themselves as peculiarly the heirs of Confucius and his model of historical writing.

Ssu-ma Ch'ien follows immediately with a lengthy exposition of the significance of the *Spring and Autumn Annals* according to the teachings of Tung Chung-shu in which he quotes Confucius as saying: "If I wish to set forth my theoretical judgments, nothing is as good as illustrating them through the depth and clarity of past affairs."

Here we must give some attention to the phrase *k'ung-yen*, which

I have translated as "theoretical judgments." The original meaning of this phrase seems to be the one that appears obvious at first glance, "empty words." We find it in this sense, for example, in the *Lü-shih ch'un-ch'iu:* "empty words and vain phrases." [24] It appears frequently in the *Shih chi* in the same sense: "with empty words seek the jewel"; [25] "empty words and vain speeches"; [26] "this is no empty saying." [27]

But there is another special meaning which dates, so far as I know, from the writings of Tung Chung-shu. In his exposition of the *Spring and Autumn Annals* upon which Ssu-ma Ch'ien based this passage, he writes: "Confucius said, 'I have used the facts of the past and added to them the mind of a king. I believe that in illustrating theoretical judgments [*k'ung-yen*] nothing is as good as the depth and clarity of past affairs.'" [28] Here *k'ung-yen* clearly has no meaning of vain or false words, but means general moral principles which can be used to guide all men. It is this special use of the phrase which Ssu-ma Ch'ien repeats in his autobiography. He makes this clearer farther on when he says, "Such men will stand indicted by the theoretical judgments [*k'ung-yen*], and will not dare to deny their guilt." He also uses a second phrase, *k'ung-wen,* meaning apparently the same thing, for he says, "Therefore he [Confucius] wrote the *Spring and Autumn Annals,* handing down his theoretical writings [*k'ung-wen*] in order to decide on matters of ritual principles." In his letter to Jen An, Ssu-ma Ch'ien once more uses this second phrase to refer, not to the *Annals,* but to the writings of Tso Ch'iu-ming, reputed author of the *Tso Commentary,* and Sun Tzu, who "retired and wrote their books and stratagems, . . . handing down their theoretical writings in order to make themselves known."

This peculiar usage of the phrase *k'ung-yen* or *k'ung-wen* appears to be a part of the thought of the *Kung-yang* school as interpreted by Tung Chung-shu, who wished to emphasize the moral significance of the *Annals* at the expense of its value as a record of historical fact. But the other schools, or at least that of the *Tso Commentary,* did not, it seems, accept this use of the phrase. Liu Hsin, for example, an exponent of the *Tso* school, says in his work on literature, used by Pan Ku as the basis for his "Treatise on Literature" (HS 30/19a) : "Tso Ch'iu-ming discussed the original affairs and wrote his commentary in order to show that Confucius did not use 'theoretical judgments' [perhaps better translated here as "empty moralizing"] in explaining the Classic." Here, if I understand the passage correctly, Liu Hsin is trying to steer the interpretation of the *Annals* away from the highly theoretical and sometimes far-fetched ideas of the *Kung-yang* school and emphasize instead the historical background which the *Tso Commentary* supplies for the events mentioned in the *Annals*. He is using *k'ung-yen*, which in the writings of Tung Chung-shu and Ssu-ma Ch'ien was a technical phrase, with a suggestion of the old meaning of "empty or vain words."

In later years the phrase seems to have reverted to its original deroga-tory meaning, for it almost entirely drops out of discussion of the *An-nals*. It is not used once, for example, in any of the prefaces to the three commentaries on the *Annals*, that of Ho Hsiu to the *Kung-yang*, of Tu Yü (A. D. 222–284) to the *Tso*, and of Fan Ning (A. D. 339–401) to the *Ku-liang*. Much later, it was revived by Ch'ing scholars such as Ku Yen-wu and Chang Hsüeh-ch'eng to characterize the abstract metaphysical theorizing of the Wang Yang-ming school to which these scholars were so bitterly opposed. They cited this same passage of Ssu-ma Ch'ien's exposition of the *Annals*, interpreting it, however, to mean that Confucius did *not* indulge in "empty words" but confined himself rather to a recital of historical facts.

When Ssu-ma Ch'ien has completed his exposition of the meaning and value of the *Annals*, his questioner, Hu Sui, points out that in Confucius' time the world was in chaos and hence there was a real need for such a guide to political and moral principles. But why, he asks, should Ch'ien, living in the present age of peace and enlightened government, undertake to write such a work?

In answer Ch'ien denies that his own history is related to the *Annals*, explaining that his own reason for writing the *Shih chi* was simply to glorify Emperor Wu and his age. There are two things obviously pe-culiar about this explanation. If his purpose was merely to praise Em-peror Wu and record the virtues of that sovereign's reign, he should naturally have confined himself to a history of that period, or at most to a history of the house of Han. But instead Ch'ien began his story some two thousand years earlier, relating the history of four other dynasties before he reached the Han. We must therefore not take his professed aims too seriously, it seems. Faced with the question of why, in an age of a sage ruler and benevolent government, he should yet be composing a work of history—at a time when history, and in fact most literature of any kind, was considered to be a vehicle for satire or moral instruction—he could hardly have said less without incurring the suspicion of lèse majesté. The second odd point is why Ssu-ma Ch'ien (who for all we know may have invented this whole dialogue between himself and Hu Sui), should go to such lengths to expound his interpretation of the *Spring and Autumn Annals,* only to tell us at the end that his own work has nothing to do with this theory. Is the whole passage a long-winded literary joke? I hardly think so. He wishes to imply, it would seem, that his own work is *related* to the *Annals,* but at the same time different. It is related because they are both works which record the affairs of the past, are both works of history. He has tried to approach the writing of his record of the past with all the care, gravity, and moral awareness of the sage. He recognizes Confucius as the greatest recorder and transmitter of the past, the historian par excellence. But he is searching for a new definition of history, a new category of writing that will exclude the willful distortions and falsifications which were traditionally attributed to the *Annals.* So he is quick to point out where his own work differs from that of Confucius. His purpose has not been to set up any eternal moral principles, to pass judgments of a sage upon his material. From any such elevated object he excuses himself with a reference to the famous words of Confucius himself, "I am a transmitter and not a maker." [29]

Ssu-ma Ch'ien's reference to this saying demands special attention, for there was much controversy in the Han over the use of these terms "transmit" (*shu*), and "make" (*tso*). The *Li chi* states: "He who makes is called a Sage; he who transmits is called an Enlightened Man." [30] But if Ssu-ma Ch'ien was aware of this technical distinction, he did not try very hard to observe it. In replying to Hu Sui he specifically denies that he "made" the *Shih chi,* yet in his table of contents and general description of his history which follows he invariably uses the word "made"—"I made the 'Basic Annals of the Five Emperors,'" "I made the thirty 'Hereditary Houses,'" etc. Either he did not bother with such fine points of terminology, or he did not mean what he said to Hu Sui when he insisted that his history was a work of "transmitting" and not "making." [31]

As we read on in Ssu-ma Ch'ien's autobiography, the suspicion grows that, in spite of his demurrer, he believed that his history was more closely related to the *Spring and Autumn Annals* than he would openly admit. After a reference to his punishment and a description of how men of ancient times poured forth their anger and bitterness in writing, he says: "So at last I have transmitted a record of the past from T'ao T'ang [Emperor Yao] down to the unicorn, where I stopped." Now obviously either there is something wrong with our present text of the *Shih chi,* or Ssu-ma Ch'ien is deliberately lying. Emperor Yao is the *fourth* of the five emperors whom Ssu-ma Ch'ien describes in the first chapter of his history; he began, as anyone who turns to the beginning of the *Shih chi* can see, not with Emperor Yao, but with the Yellow Emperor. Therefore the first part of his statement is inaccurate. At the end of 123 B. C., a white unicorn was captured when Emperor Wu was in residence at Yung, and this is the event which some commentators have taken as the meaning of Ch'ien's terminal date. But in 123 Ssu-ma T'an was still alive and Ch'ien had not even become Grand Historian. And if we take the statement to mean that he wrote only about the period up to 123, then we must regard as spurious the large and important sections of the *Shih chi* which relate affairs occurring after that date. However, almost all commentators have readily agreed that Ch'ien's use of the unicorn here is purely metaphorical.[32] He is adopting the purest Confucian terms in this description of the scope of his history, marking the beginning not with the Yellow Emperor, the account of whom he recognized to be of questionable reliability, but with the universally accepted account of the emperor Yao, and ending it at the point where the *Spring and Autumn Annals* ends, with the unicorn. It will also be noted that although, as I have said, Ch'ien consistently uses the term *tso,* "I made," in the table of contents which follows, in this one sentence he bows to prescribed Confucian modesty by employing the term *shu,* "I transmitted," to describe his labors.

But Ch'ien's imitation of the *Annals* does not end with this statement. At the very end of the chapter, he says:

This is the book of The Grand Historian, compiled in order to repair omissions and amplify the Six Disciplines. It comprises the work of one family, designed to supplement the various interpretations of the Six Classics and to put in order the sayings of the Hundred Schools. I have placed one copy in the Famous Mountain and another at the capital, where they shall await the sages and gentlemen of later times.

The end of this last sentence, "await the sages and gentlemen of later ages," we recognize at once as an allusion to the closing words of the *Kung-yang Commentary*'s description of the *Annals* which was written "to await the sages of later times."

Unless we are prepared to regard such resemblances as purely coincidental, we must admit that, though he denied the full moral and didactic significance of the *Annals* to his own work, Ssu-ma Ch'ien considered his history as a direct successor to the labors of Confucius. This is not surprising when we remember, as I have pointed out, that there was in Ssu-ma Ch'ien's time no such thing as historical writing as distinct from philosophical writing. All the Confucian Classics, as Ssu-ma Ch'ien shows by his use of them as sources, were in a sense works of history, and Confucius, who edited, arranged, or wrote them, was the father of Chinese history. But at the same time not only the Classics, but also such works as the *Tso Commentary,* the *Narratives from the States,* and the *Intrigues of the Warring States,* were works of philosophy, expositions of a particular school of thought. In the quotation above, I have translated the sentence *"ch'eng i chia chih yen"* as "it comprises the work of one family." Ssu-ma Ch'ien certainly intended this meaning, for the *Shih chi* was the work of his father and himself, who were themselves descendants of a long line of historians.[33]

But if we take the word *chia,* "family," in its other meaning of a "school of thought," we may interpret Ch'ien's words to mean that he is, in his work, setting forth his own school of thought.[34] I do not think there is any reason to choose between the two interpretations. The sentence means both. It was inconceivable to Ssu-ma Ch'ien that he could write a work of history without at the same time conveying his own thought, his own interpretation of the material he treated. He had no concept of history as a mechanical process, a "science" which exists independent of the personality of the historian; if he had he would hardly have added his highly personal comments to the end of each chapter. He did not presume to say that his work should rank beside the *Spring and Autumn Annals* as the eternal moral judgments of a sage. But he felt, we may surmise, that it was of the same essential nature, a spiritual descendant of the *Annals.* Both Confucius and he himself, according to Ch'ien, wrote out of the same impulse of despair and disillusionment and it is therefore entirely appropriate that both their works should end with the symbol of the unicorn, the beast of virtue untimely come. Critics have justified the boast of Ssu-ma T'an and his son that they would fulfill the destiny of the great writers who appear every five hundred years, that their work would succeed to the labors of Confucius. As the great Sung historian Cheng Ch'iao remarks of the *Shih chi:* "After the Six Classics there is only this work." [35]

If Ssu-ma Ch'ien meant these allusions, these covert insinuations that his own work was somehow related to the *Spring and Autumn Annals,* we should be able to find evidence of this relationship in places other than this one chapter, the statement of the writer's aims and methods. For example, one of the characteristics of the *Annals,* according to its commentaries, is the fine shades of meaning which Confucius conveyed by his precise choice of words. The exact term he used to refer to a person or describe an action was what, in many cases, conveyed his praise or blame. But we will be disappointed, I believe, if we attempt to discover any such preciseness in Ssu-ma Ch'ien's use of words and terms. Like any great writer he was undoubtedly a seeker of the *mot juste.* But his history is far too large and sprawling, too vigorous and colorful, to permit the nicety of terminology which the commentators find (with what justice may be questioned) in the brief entries of the Lu chronicle. To cite a glaring example, in his frequent references to the murder of King Yu, Ch'ien usually says (as in SC 38/23): "King Yu of the Chou was killed [*sha*] by the Ch'üan Barbarians." But in *Shih chi* 40/9, he suddenly changes to "King Yu of the Chou was assassinated [*shih*] by the Ch'üan Barbarians." Anyone familiar with late Chou political thought knows that the difference between these two words *sha* and *shih* is the difference between the simple murder of one person by another, and the murder of a sovereign by his subject. To one seeking in the *Shih chi* the subtle verbal judgments of the *Annals,* this inconsistency in the use of such key terms must suggest either a shocking lack of sensitivity upon Ch'ien's part, or an attempt to convey through apparent inconsistency some even more subtle meaning. I do not think we need torture the text for any such subtleties. Shocking or not, Ssu-ma Ch'ien seems in such cases to have made no attempt to imitate in detail the delicate terminology traditionally attributed to the *Annals.*

But though his use of terms does not come up to the preciseness attributed to the *Annals,* Ssu-ma Ch'ien was well aware of the tradition which discovered in Confucius' writing a wealth of veiled satire and concealed utterance. We have already mentioned above that, according to the *Kung-yang Commentary,* Confucius was forced when writing about the reigns of dukes still living to use a great many "veiled words" (*wei-tz'u*). Ssu-ma Ch'ien makes striking use of this tradition at the end of his chapter on the Hsiung-nu (SC 110/68), where he remarks: "When Confucius wrote the *Spring and Autumn,* he was very open about the times of Yin and Huan, but when he came to those of Ting and Ai, he was very obscure [*wei*]. In the passages which dealt with his own time, he did not praise, but used words of 'avoidance' [*chi-hui*]." The subject of Chinese relations with the Hsiung-nu was, in Ssu-ma Ch'ien's time, an extremely controversial and dangerous one and, although he undoubtedly had strong opinions, he was forced to express them with care and indirection. There is nothing surprising about the fact that Ch'ien, writing under the eyes of Emperor Wu, never ventures a clear statement of his position on this vital question of the day; the surprising thing is that he has the boldness to tell the reader why. "My hands are tied," he says in effect, "and if you wish to know what I think you must pay very close attention to what I say." Faced with the same difficulty as Confucius in his attempts to write of his own times, Ssu-ma Ch'ien demands of his readers the same attention and sensitivity that they would give to the works of the sage.[36]

We have noted above that, according to the commentaries, Confucius occasionally distorted or even falsified the facts of history because he wished to avoid the recording of things which did not agree with his moral principles, or at other times made a special note of events that moved or grieved him. This dilemma, the distressing discrepancy between what we would like history to say and what it actually says, was solved by Ssu-ma Ch'ien in a unique way. He did not dare, like Confucius, deliberately to suppress or alter the facts. Indeed such a procedure would have been inimical to the new conception of historical writing he was striving to create. He was bound to tell all that his sources told him. But he was not bound to tell it all in the same place. The various large sections and one-hundred-and-thirty chapters of the *Shih chi* represent no merely arbitrary divisions of Ch'ien's material. Each one is a significant formal unit whose contents have been selected and disposed with care and intention.

One thing that has often struck readers of the *Shih chi* is the fact that material relating to one person or one event is frequently broken up and scattered through a number of chapters. A modern critic of the *Shih chi,* Chi Chen-huai, has pointed out two principles which seem to have governed Ch'ien in his disposition of material relating to a single person or incident. The first is the obvious one: that the historian wished to avoid relating in detail the same incident in two or three places. Although a story might concern several people, he told it only once simply to save time, sometimes inserting a cross-reference to it in the appropriate place in the biography of the other principal character or characters concerned.[37] From this follows directly the second principle: that he chose to relate the incident in the biography of the person to whom it was most closely related and upon whose life it had the deepest bearing. Chi cites for example the tale of how Chu Chia concealed in his home the ex-general Chi Pu who was hiding from the wrath of Kao-tsu. Ch'ien tells the story in detail in the biography of Chi Pu (SC 100/3), but gives only a passing reference to it in that of Chu Chia (SC 124/8). This is because the incident was of only temporary importance to the benefactor, Chu Chia, but a matter of life and death to Chi Pu.[38]

These two principles may serve to explain many of the ways in which Ssu-ma Ch'ien has disposed of his material, but I do not believe they can account for them all. The Sung scholar Su Hsün, in his brilliant little essay entitled "A Discussion of History," distinguishes two other principles in the writing of Ssu-ma Ch'ien which must be taken into account.[39] The first of these he calls the principle of "concealing and yet revealing." This means, he explains, that if a man had ten good points and one fault, Ch'ien did not record the one fault in the chapter or section devoted to the man, but mentioned it in a chapter devoted to someone else. "He concealed the fault in the biography of the subject, but disclosed it in the biography of someone else." The second principle he designates as that of being "honest and yet generous." In this case, if a person had ten faults and only one merit, Ch'ien took special care to record the one merit in the biography of the subject.

Su Hsün gives two examples of the way in which Ssu-ma Ch'ien "conceals and yet reveals." Ch'ien's short biography of Lien P'o (SC 81) is devoted to the great deeds of this general of Chao. But it is the biography of another Chao general, Chao She (SC 81/13), which reveals that, when the king of Chao asked his generals whether the armies of Ch'in might profitably be attacked at O-yü, Lien P'o advised against the campaign, while Chao She urged it and, after receiving the king's consent, accomplished a smashing victory. Thus Lien P'o's error in judgment is concealed from the reader while he is admiring the good points of the man, and only revealed to him when he has passed on to another subject. The second example which Su Hsün mentions is the biography of the Confucian adviser to Kao-tsu, Li I-ch'i (SC 97), which says nothing about his great error of judgment, the fact that he counselled Kao-tsu to reestablish the heirs of the rulers of the extinct Six States. This untimely move, which might well have delayed the unification of the empire for years, was fortunately blocked by Chang Liang, and it is in the chapter devoted to Chang Liang (SC 55/13) that the story is related.

Su Hsün's second principle, the mention of the one merit to help balance the ten faults, is well illustrated by the case of Su Ch'in. Ssu-ma Ch'ien, concerned at the overwhelmingly bad reputations of some of the famous men of history he described, sometimes used the essay at the end of the chapter to try to correct this impression, to plead for a more generous judgment of his subject. At the end of his biography of Su Ch'in (SC 69/62) he remarks:

Because Su Ch'in met death as a traitor, the world has united in scoffing at him and has been loath to study his policies. . . . Su Ch'in arose from the humblest beginnings to lead the Six States in the Vertical Alliance, and this is evidence that he possessed an intelligence surpassing the ordinary person. For that reason I have set forth this account of his deeds . . . so that he may not forever suffer from an evil reputation and be known for nothing else.

Again, in his "Basic Annals of Empress Lü" (SC 9/37), after a hair-raising account of this lady's lurid crimes, Ch'ien is careful at the end to point out that, regardless of what her personal life may have been, her rule brought peace and prosperity to the nation.

But perhaps the most striking example of this delicate arrangement of material may be found in the companion portraits of the two rival heroes, Hsiang Yü and Kao-tsu (SC 7 and 8). The unsavory fact, for instance, that when pursued in desperate chase by Hsiang Yü's men, Kao-tsu tried to throw his own children out of his carriage to lighten it, is reported in the "Annals of Hsiang Yü" (SC 7/52), and in the biography of Kao-tsu's aide, Hsia-hou Ying (SC 95/35), but *not* in the "Annals of Kao-tsu." Again, in the "Annals of Hsiang Yü," when the two contending armies are drawn up face to face at Kuang-wu, we read only of Hsiang Yü's brave and laudable suggestion that he and Kao-tsu settle the affair by personal combat rather than dragging the whole country into their quarrel, and Kao-tsu's hardly admirable reply, "Since I cannot fight you with strength, I prefer to fight you with wisdom" (SC 7/60). But in the "Annals of Kao-tsu" at this point we are not told the words of Hsiang Yü nor Kao-tsu's reply, but instead are treated to a long and stirring speech by Kao-tsu on the "ten crimes" of Hsiang Yü (SC 8/57). In other words, the bad points of each man are revealed only in the chapter devoted to his rival, while his own chapter is designed to present him in the most favorable light. This is also apparent when we compare the bright picture of Kao-tsu built up in his Annals with the rude, short-tempered, ill-bred Kao-tsu who appears so often in the chapters on his ministers and associates.[40]

These two phenomena, the attempts by the historian to suppress the minor faults of his heroes and to apologize for his villains, derive directly, I believe, from the ideal expressed in the *Spring and Autumn Annals* that there are certain things the historian must scruple to record, that out of consideration or sympathy for his subject he must somehow alter or soften the harshness of reality. The reader in search of all the facts may well complain of such sleight-of-hand with the materials of history. But, as I have stressed, Ssu-ma Ch'ien has no concept of history as a cold, objective recital of facts. He was writing inevitably under the influence of the *Spring and Autumn Annals,* and the remarkable thing is that he managed to free himself as far as he did from its more inimical precepts. He concealed the facts, as the work of Confucius had taught him to do, but he also revealed them.

The last of the three principles of the *Annals* which I have mentioned above, the theory of portents, had the most direct and obvious effect upon Ssu-ma Ch'ien's work. This theory was an integral part of Han thought, accepted to one degree or another, it seems, by rulers, bureaucrats, and philosophers alike. Empress Lü, for example, troubled, as well she might have been, by an uneasy conscience, remarked of an eclipse that occurred toward the end of her reign: "This has hap-

pened because of me!" (SC 9/19). Tung Chung-shu made the theory
of portents a basic tenet of Confucian doctrine, and though there were
a few scholars such as Yang Hsiung who objected to this inordinate
attention to natural disasters and prodigies, their view represented the
minority.[41] Even had Ssu-ma Ch'ien not believed in the theory himself, his sources would almost have forced him to record the numerous
occurrences which the Han people considered portentous.

But the theory gave Ch'ien an unusually fine opportunity to drama-
tize and emphasize the flow of his narrative, and it seems to be this
aspect of it, its potentialities as a means of vivid and often ironic comment, that interested him. At the end of SC 50, for example, he states:
"When a state is about to rise there will always be omens of fortune
and good luck." [42] Thus the stories of the dragons, the mysterious
clouds which hovered in the air over the young Kao-tsu (stories surely
not original with Ssu-ma Ch'ien) dramatized for the reader better than
could any rhetoric the heavenly blessing and glorious future of the
founder of the Han. But if portents could signify blessing, they could
also signify the opposite. Through Ssu-ma Ch'ien's narrative of the
struggles and eventual triumph of Prince Cheng who became the
First Emperor of the Ch'in are scattered the accounts of the omens
which accompanied *his* rise to imperial ruler—not benevolent dragons,
but comets, earthquakes, droughts, locusts, and plague. This fact alone
was quite sufficient to make the reader of the Han understand that the
Ch'in was an evil and untimely rule, for it not only failed to receive the
good omens due an ordained and virtuous dynasty, but called forth
the very opposite, the signs of cosmic disorder. Ch'ien's notices of portentous happenings, instead of breaking into the narrative, serve to un-
derline his meaning. The eclipse in the reign of Empress Lü, the great
wind that blew from the heavens the night the Lü family was massacred (SC 9/32), the carriage axle that broke when Prince Jung was
on the way to his fateful trial (SC 59/5)—such occurrences, often not
in themselves miraculous, were darkly significant to the Han people.[43]
They were reflections of the human condition in the natural world, and
as such were as much a part of history as all the facts of economic and

social life that fill our histories today. Ssu-ma Ch'ien's concept of history was essentially poetic and these omens and wonders where often his symbols. Their use was a lesson he had learned from the *Spring and Autumn Annals,* as he acknowledged by his adoption of the *Annals'* most trenchant symbol, the unicorn.

IV

THE FORM OF
THE *SHIH CHI*

Western historians from Herodotus on have for the most part been content with simple chronological order for the form of their narrative. In recent years a minor variation, in which social, economic, and cultural developments in each period are dealt with in succeeding chapters or sections, has become popular as the concept of history broadens to include more than the narration of political events that was the core of older histories.

The earliest Chinese histories likewise followed this seemingly most natural of forms. The various speeches, ordinances, and other documents which make up the *Book of Documents* conform to chronological order, while the *Spring and Autumn Annals,* being a year-by-year, sometimes month-by-month, record of events, is the prototype of Chinese *pien-nien* or "chronological" histories.

But the two historical works which by traditional dating follow the *Spring and Autumn Annals,* the *Narratives from the States (Kuo-yü)* and the *Intrigues of the Warring States (Chan-kuo-ts'e),* at least in their present form, depart from overall chronological order by arranging their material in chapters devoted to the histories of single feudal states, though within these chapters the order is chronological. It was already realized, it would seem, that the complex affairs of a number of political units existing simultaneously could not be dealt with satisfactorily in the framework of a single overall chronological order. We do not know enough about the original form of the *Tso Commentary* on the *Spring and Autumn Annals* to state definitely how it fits into this course of development. But the reader who attempts to read through it in its present form, in which all the events of the various states have been broken up and appended to dated entries of the Lu chronicle, will realize the disadvantages of the chronological form in dealing with the history of this period. The narrative jumps back and forth with baffling suddenness from the events of one state to another, while the recital of a single chain of events in one state is broken up and scattered by the overriding dictates of the Lu chronology. If the Chinese historian were not, like Herodotus, to allow himself long digressions to fill in background and considerable freedom in disposition of material, it was obvious that he must find some more suitable form to deal with the complex history of a broad and disunited China.

This was one of the major problems confronting Ssu-ma Ch'ien in the writing of his history of the entire past of his country. His solution was hailed as a masterpiece of creation, and quickly became the model for the main tradition of later Chinese historical writing.

To the Chinese, particularly to the men of the Han with their hierarchical concept of society and the natural world, form is synonymous with meaning. The extent to which this idea has been applied to the forms of literature in China is hard for the Western mind to imagine. Much of the Chinese search for meaning in the form and order of their ancient literature strikes us as fanciful and forced. But it must be remembered that this concept did exist, at least by the time of the Han dynasty and that, if attempts to read meaning into the form of pre-Han works seem questionable, such attempts applied to the works of writers who were themselves believers in the concept cannot so easily be dismissed.

This practice of descrying meaning in form was given full expression in the interpretations of the *Spring and Autumn Annals*. The *Kung-yang Commentary,* for example, considers significant not only the points of beginning and end of the chronicle, but the exact order of the wording throughout. Under the first entry in the *Annals,* for instance, "First year. Spring. The King's first month," it comments in its usual catechizing form: "Why does it say 'First year'? Because this is the first year of the Lord [i.e., Duke Yin of Lu]. Why does it say 'Spring'? Because this is the beginning of the year. Who is meant by 'The King'? This means King Wen [ancestral founder of the Chou dynasty]. Why does it first mention the King and after that the first month? Because it is the first month of the King. What is meant by the first month of the King? The Great Single Beginning [i.e., the unity and continuity of the ruling house of Chou which proclaims the calendar for all the feudal states]." This sort of minute attention to the wording, order, and form of the chronicle continues through the entire commentary. Later commentaries have carried this search for meaning in the form of the *Annals* to absurd lengths, even attempting to relate the twelve dukes of Lu treated in the *Annals* to the twelve months of the year. Similar attempts have been made to discover symbolic meaning in the form of the *Odes* and *Documents*.

The next important work which by its form lends itself to this type of symbolic interpretation is the *Lü-shih ch'un-ch'iu,* a collection of moral and political essays written by a group of itinerant scholars under the patronage of Lü Pu-wei, the powerful prime minister of the First Emperor of the Ch'in. The title, *ch'un-ch'iu,* "Spring and Autumn," an abbreviation of "spring, summer, autumn, winter," i.e., years, originally designated a court chronicle of one of the feudal states. Here, however, it is being used in a metaphorical sense. Since the work is in no sense a chronicle of historical events, we must assume that it was named "Spring and Autumn" to mark it as a work of moral and political principles such as the *Spring and Autumn Annals* of Confucius was by this time interpreted to be. The form of the book further bears out this supposition. It is in three large sections. The first section is divided into twelve chapters, each of which begins with a description of the rites and functions of government appropriate to one month of the year. Therefore this section has been taken to represent the first member of the Chinese trinity, heaven, whose number is twelve. The twelve chapters are further divided into five subsections each, suggesting the five elements which govern the workings of heaven. The second large section is divided into eight chapters with eight subsections each; eight being the number assigned to the second member of the trinity, this section has been taken to represent the affairs of earth. The third section is in six chapters of six subsections, six being the number of the third member of the trinity, man.

Such an arrangement seems too ordered to be accidental, and we must admit that there the Chinese symbolists are sound in their interpretation. Similar attempts which have been made to relate the sections of the *Shih chi* either to those of this work or to astrology and numerology appear less than convincing.[1] But if Ssu-ma Ch'ien did not actually adopt the number symbolism of the *Lü-shih ch'un-ch'iu,* its precedent of significant form undoubtedly influenced the plan of his own work. However, whereas the form of the *Lü-shih ch'un-ch'iu* represents symbolic concepts, the actual contents of its various divisions, with a few exceptions, seem to be quite arbitrarily distributed. Its form is superficially imposed and does not spring internally from the nature of its material. Ssu-ma Ch'ien, on the other hand, by sacrificing superficial symbolism to the demands of his material managed, by careful arrangement of the content of his various divisions, to give inner significance to his form.

The *Shih chi* is divided into five sections:

"Basic Annals" (*pen-chi*)	12 chapters	
"Chronological Tables" (*piao*)	10	"
"Treatises" (*shu*)	8	"
"Hereditary Houses" (*shih-chia*)	30	"
"Memoirs" (*lieh-chuan*)	70	"

This form is so radically different from the general Western concept of the form of a history that it demands considerable explanation. The significance of the various sections, and the effect which this form has upon the organization and usefulness of the work as a whole, may best be conveyed, I believe, by imagining a history of America composed in this way. If the reader will bear with the fancifulness of this idea and the obvious discrepancies between the history of China and America, I shall try to outline what such a work might be like.

The "Basic Annals" would be devoted to the lives of men who exercised authority over a large section of the country. If England were considered as the dominant power of colonial times, we would expect an "Annals of English Rulers" arranged in chronological order and ending with a biting portrait of George III, weak, degenerate, and the victim of evil counselors. There would follow the "Annals of the Presidents." For the less important men this would be hardly more than a list of names with dates of office. But in the case of more important figures, men who had captured the imagination of their age, such as Washington, Lincoln, and the two Roosevelts, we should have fairly complete biographies beginning with their childhood (the cherry tree, the log cabin, recorded in order to indicate the unusual character and determination of these men even in their youth) and concentrating on a few dramatic and significant scenes in their lives.

The "Annals" section would be followed by the "Chronological Tables," each introduced by a short essay on the history of the period covered in the table. One table, arranged with dates along the top, would record in parallel cross-sections the founding of the various colonies, with brief notations of the various governors and rulers of the colonies and the important events of their history. Another table would do the same thing for the various states created from the old territories. A third would list vice-presidents and important cabinet ministers with dates of office in relation to the various presidents. Others, divided month by month instead of year by year, would note in the form of graphs the major battles and events of the Revolutionary and Civil wars.

Next would follow a series of treatises on political, economic, social, and cultural themes. These would include sections on the economic history of America, the development of canals and railroads (recording for purposes of illustration folk songs such as "Erie Canal" or "I've Been Workin' on the Railroad"), the religious history of the colonies and the nation, science, warfare, music (here would appear the text of "Yankee Doodle," "The Star Spangled Banner," "My Country, 'Tis of Thee," etc.), and any other subjects that the historian felt needed to be discussed separately. As in other sections, however, the emphasis would be upon the men who did most for the advancement of the nation in each field, rather than on abstract discussions of the subject itself.

The next section, "Colonies and Territories" (the *Shih chi*'s "Hereditary Houses"), would be devoted to brief histories of the various colonies on the American continent. These would relate the founding of each colony, with special attention to the life and personality of the founders (the Pilgrim Fathers, William Penn, etc.) and would follow the history of the colony up to its incorporation into the Union. While most of these would end with the Revolutionary War, some, such as those dealing with the Louisiana Territory, Alaska, and Hawaii, would continue into later times and even down to the present. Included would be a chapter relating the unhappy story of Jefferson Davis and his Confederacy.

Finally would follow a series of short chapters devoted for the most part to individuals. The first chapter would relate the story of Leif Ericson, with speculations upon the reliability of his legend and general remarks on the difficulties of writing history. Then would come short biographies of outstanding statesmen of the colonies, early explorers, generals of the Revolutionary War, etc., some already mentioned in previous sections, some appearing for the first time, arranged more or less in chronological order. Other chapters (chronological order goes to pieces here) would discuss important statesmen—Franklin, Paine, Seward; men of letters—Emerson, Hawthorne, Poe (with quotations from their works); thinkers—Cotton Mather, Emerson, Dewey; generals—Jackson, Lee, Pershing, MacArthur; patriots—Paul Revere, Betsy Ross, Barbara Frietchie. One chapter would discuss the influence upon history of presidents' wives, with sketches of Martha Washington, Dolly Madison, and Eleanor Roosevelt; another would be devoted to great financiers—Vanderbilt, Carnegie, Gould, Ford, Rockefeller. Several chapters would describe Indian tribes, Mexico, and Canada, and the relations between the American government and these peoples and lands. Others might be devoted to famous inventors—Morse, Edison, the Wright brothers; to the movie industry, with lives of outstanding actors; to western pioneers and outlaws, etc. The work would end with an autobiography of the historian and a brief exposition of his aims and methods in composing his work.

I shall not attempt to elaborate this fantasy any further. I hope I have indicated, however, something of the peculiar arrangement which such a form imposes upon the material of history. The arrangement has obvious advantages from the historian's point of view. He may shuffle his material around so that, in the midst of a discussion of railroads, for example, he need not explain in detail who Jay Gould is, since Gould has a biography in another section of his work; in a narrative of the Revolutionary War he need not bother with the dubious tales of Paul Revere or Betsy Ross, which he has treated elsewhere; in a discussion of the opening of the west, he may refer to Indian tribes without explanation, since they are the subject of special treatment. Whereas Herodotus must digress from his main narrative when he wishes to relate the tale of Arion and the dolphin or outline the ancient history of Egypt, Ssu-ma Ch'ien can simply shift such material to other sections of his work, and in doing so convey, by the place in which he puts it, something of his opinion of its importance and reliability.

But the *Shih chi* is provided with no index and, although a few simple cross-references are found, the unwary reader who tries to dip into it for a particular set of facts is apt, if he is not careful, to be led woefully astray. Let us suppose that, with our hypothetical history of America in the *Shih chi* form as a source, we wish to make a study of the Civil War. In the annals of Lincoln and Grant we get a good start from the point of view of the Federal government, but to learn the southern side of the question we must turn at once to the chapter on Jefferson Davis (where we discover that this was not a "civil war" at all but a "war of secession"). Furthermore, the "Annals of Grant" records only his career as president, while his military exploits are to be found in the biographies of Lee and other important generals of the war. While other biographies give us vital information on the statesmen of the period, we must consult the treatises for an understanding of the economic background of the war and the question of slavery. A reading of the "Colonies and Territories" is necessary to understand the question of admission of free and slave states into the Union. Finally, the "Chronological Tables" on the war will give us an outline of the progress of the war and occasional information we could not find elsewhere.

Chinese critics have described the *Shih chi* form as one of the greatest creations of historiography. The scholar trying to get at all the relative facts on a particular subject might be more inclined to describe it as a monstrosity which deliberately obscures the flow and relationships of history. But the *Shih chi* was not designed to be dipped into or thumbed through for facts. It is a unified work constructed on a grand plan that does not, in the opinion of the Chinese, disrupt or confuse the materials of history but, on the contrary, brings to them a hierarchical order that in the simple chronicle form they lack. Through its form the history passes judgment upon its material. It is worthwhile therefore to examine in detail the elements of this masterpiece of form and see how they work.

BASIC ANNALS

[Of the affairs that I have discussed and examined, I have made a general survey of the Three Dynasties and a record of the Ch'in and Han, extending in all back as far as the Yellow Emperor and coming down to the present, set forth in the twelve "Basic Annals."]

Like some of the other formal divisions of the *Shih chi,* this, or at least its name, "basic annals," does not seem to have been original with Ssu-ma Ch'ien, for at the end of SC 123/43, we find mention of an old "Basic Annals of Yü." As pointed out by commentators, *pen* or "basic" indicates that these chapters deal with the rulers and ruling families of the nation as a whole, and *chi* or "annals" calls attention to the fact that, more than in other sections of the *Shih chi,* the narrative follows strict chronological form, though in the earlier chapters it is by no means a year-by-year account.

The first chapter, the "Basic Annals of the Five Emperors," has been the subject of much controversy. Ssu-ma Ch'ien was well aware of the controversial nature of his material, for at the end of the chapter he went to lengths to explain why he began his history with the first of the Five Emperors, the Yellow Emperor, when the Confucian Classic, the *Book of Documents,* went back no farther than the fourth of the Five Emperors, Emperor Yao.

Why did Ssu-ma Ch'ien extend the scope of his history beyond classical sources? Several reasons have been suggested. The first is that Ssu-ma Ch'ien, like his father, was a Taoist and as such honored the Yellow Emperor as the founder of his creed.[2] But this whole charge of Taoist sympathies, as I shall show later, has been greatly exaggerated. Chavannes quite rightly rejects this explanation, but remarks instead that the *Shih chi* begins with the Yellow Emperor because of the theory of the five elements [3] (yellow being the color of earth, the first of the five elements). It is clear that, at the time of the great calendar reform of 104 B. C., the Han dynasty chose the element earth, with its color yellow, as the element which it should honor.[4] But there seems to have been no attempt to relate this decision to the figure of the Yellow Emperor. There is, for example, no suggestion that the Liu family was descended from the Yellow Emperor, as it was later declared that it was descended from Emperor Yao (the Fire Emperor), when the Han rulers changed their mind and chose fire as their patron element. If Chavannes intended by his statement to imply a direct relationship between the adoption of the element earth by the early Han and the fact that the *Shih chi* begins with the Yellow Emperor, it is hard to go along with his opinion.

As a matter of fact, Ssu-ma Ch'ien, as I have said, explains at the end of his chapter exactly why he recorded the reigns of these early emperors, namely, because he found them recorded thus in his sources, which he considered reliable. He might have begun his account even earlier with the vague figures of Fu Hsi and Shen Nung, which were obviously known to him.[5] But he either doubted their existence as historical figures or felt he did not have enough reliable material to say anything about them.[6]

Ssu-ma Ch'ien, as he himself says, based his chapter on two early texts, "The Virtues of the Five Emperors," and the "Successions of the Emperors." These two texts were apparently part of the ritual expounded by Master Hsü, a Confucian scholar of the time of Emperor Wen, which later, in the time of Emperor Hsüan (after Ch'ien's death), took form as the *Ta-Tai li-chi* or *Collected Ritual of Tai the Elder*. This collection of ritual texts, however, was soon replaced in favor by a similar one, the *Li chi* or *Collected Ritual* as we know it today. The *Li chi* did not include the two texts used by Ssu-ma Ch'ien as the basis for his account of the early rulers, and later writers have accordingly criticized Ch'ien for using texts which were not "canonical." [7] There is no indication, however, that in Ch'ien's time these texts were either more or less canonical than others, since the question of what was canonical had not yet been decided. As Ch'ien states, some scholars of his day did not accept these two texts. But these men were merely following a different tradition of the ritual texts from the one Ch'ien accepted. One may question Ch'ien's judgment as a historian in utilizing such texts, but it is both irrelevant and unfair to introduce the question of canonicity. After comparing these texts with others of undisputed authority and with oral traditions as he knew them, Ssu-ma Ch'ien accepted the texts as reliable and that was all that interested him.[8]

There was a special reason why Ch'ien, with his usual interest in genealogy, should desire to begin his history with the Yellow Emperor. According to tradition, most of the rulers of later dynasties were descended from the Yellow Emperor. Emperor Yü, founder of the Hsia dynasty, was a great-great-grandson of the Yellow Emperor, while the rulers of the Ch'in dynasty were descended from Emperor Chüan Hsü, a grandson of the Yellow Emperor. Although the ancestors of both the Yin and Chou are in the Annals reportedly born of miraculous conceptions (the ancestress of the Yin conceived after eating a swallow's egg, that of the Chou after stepping into the traces of a giant), both ladies were consorts of Emperor K'u, a great-grandson of the Yellow Emperor. As Ch'u Shao-sun [9] ponderously explains in an addition to *Shih chi* 13, the progeny of these miraculous births were actually the natural descendants of the Yellow Emperor, being only "spiritually" born of the gods. Ch'ien had already indicated he attached no literal meaning to the miraculous conceptions by listing both men as descendants of the Yellow Emperor in his "Chronological Table of the Three Dynasties," *Shih chi* 13.[10] So it was of special importance that Ssu-ma Ch'ien should begin with the earliest historical personage, in his judgment, from whom all these illustrious families of later history had sprung.

The "Annals of the Five Emperors" are followed by those of the Hsia, Yin, and Chou dynasties and those of the state of Ch'in in two parts, the first part covering the history of the rulers of Ch'in up to the time they became masters of all China, the second part relating their fortunes as emperors. Some commentators have criticized the fact that, in these "Basic Annals" chapters, Ssu-ma Ch'ien relates the history of the Chou and Ch'in ancestors before they became rulers of the empire.[11] There are, I think, two reasons why he chose to place this material here. First, he was interested in genealogy, in the fortunes of one family. It was therefore important, in his view, to trace a ruling family not from the time it acquired actual power, but from the time it first manifested signs of worth and eminence, to emphasize the continuity of the heritage of virtue. Second, in the hierarchical order of the various sections of the *Shih chi,* the "Annals" naturally occupy the highest place. In this conception of history it would be unseemly to have to search for the account of the beginnings of a dynastic family among the pages of the "Hereditary Houses" or "Memoirs."

The "Annals of Ch'in" are followed by those of the Ch'u general Hsiang Yü. This chapter, also, has been the source of much dispute. Hsiang Yü was a military dictator, but never an ordained emperor, and critics contend that his story has no place among the "Annals," which they believe should be reserved for emperors. But Ssu-ma Ch'ien had no such definition in mind when he compiled his "Annals." He called them "Basic Annals"; it was later historians who changed the name, and hence the interpretation, to "Imperial Annals," *ti-chi,* and critics have been led by this interpretation to berate Ssu-ma Ch'ien for failing to conform to a rule he never recognized. Hsiang Yü was for a period the *de facto* ruler of most of China, and Ch'ien, with his customary realism, recognized this fact by placing his story in the section of actual rulers, the "Annals." [12]

He further demonstrated the fact that his "Basic Annals" were not synonymous with "Imperial Annals" by omitting the record of two emperors, the rulers Emperor I of Ch'u and Emperor Hui of the Han. Emperor I was a puppet created, and later destroyed, by Hsiang Yü, while Emperor Hui was a powerless figurehead set up by Empress Lü, who continued to exercise actual rule. Therefore Ch'ien realistically ignored the *de jure* monarchs and included the accounts of their brief reigns in the chapters of the persons who wielded the real power, Hsiang Yü and Empress Lü.

But such realism is a rare thing in historical writing. Pan Ku, more concerned, it seems, with the name and form of imperial rule than the reality, created a separate "Annals" for the Han emperor Hui. The ingenious formal plan which Ssu-ma Ch'ien designed to express and emphasize the realities of history was more often used by his successors as a façade to conceal reality. One has only to glance at the great Japanese work patterned on the *Shih chi,* the *Dainihonshi,* with its long, dreary succession of annals of emperors who were in actual fact powerless nonentities, while the real rulers, the shoguns, are crowded off into a corner of the memoirs, to realize what an imposture the *Shi chi* form can become when it is not used honestly.

CHRONOLOGICAL TABLES

[After this had been put in order and completed, because there were differences in chronology for the same periods and the dates were not always clear, I made the ten "Chronological Tables."]

The "Chronological Tables" of the *Shih chi* have been justly praised as a masterful idea. In the form of graphs the "Tables" record the important events of pre-Han and Han political history. Most of them consist of a series of dated columns which list the important accessions, battles, depositions, and deaths that occurred in the various feudal states. Others, such as those of the Han peers, reverse the form by listing at the top of the columns the names of the various fiefs while noting below in chronological order the men who held them.[13]

Later historians have admired the patience and efficiency with which Ssu-ma Ch'ien unscrambled the confused chronologies of the feudal states and arranged them in terms of the chronology of the ruling Chou house. As Ch'ien himself remarks, the chronological records of these feudal states were never, like the Classics and philosophical writings, the possession of private families, but were kept in the archives of the Chou capital. When the Ch'in assumed full control of the nation, it destroyed all these chronicles because they contained deprecatory references, preserving only its own chronicle of Ch'in.[14] Ssu-ma Ch'ien therefore had at his disposal only this "Ch'in Chronicle" (which has been appended by Ch'ien or later editors to the end of *Shih chi* 6), and that of Lu, the *Spring and Autumn Annals,* with its commentaries. He was thus forced to chase back and forth among these and other scattered materials at hand to try to reduce his narrative to some sort of unified chronological order. When we remember that these materials were usually recorded in terms of varying local chronologies, we can appreciate some of the difficulties which confronted him in his labors.[15]

As might be expected, there are still discrepancies to be found between dates in the "Chronological Tables" and those recorded in other chapters of the *Shih chi*. But, as Professor Okazaki has suggested, these may not represent actual errors or oversights on the historian's part. Rather they may be due to the fact that, with typical Chinese respect for sources, Ssu-ma Ch'ien did not presume to alter errors in the texts which he was copying verbatim into his "Annals" and "Hereditary Houses," but reserved his corrections for the chapters of his own composition, the "Chronological Tables." [16] If this theory is true, it is but another indication of the care and thoroughness with which the scholar must approach a work so far removed from the traditions of Western historiography as the *Shih chi*.

The many brief entries in these "Chronological Tables" sometimes contain facts not to be found anywhere else in the *Shih chi*. The Ch'ing scholar Chao I has singled out this aspect for special praise. "In the

case of important officials who were without either great merit or fault,"
he writes, "Ssu-ma Ch'ien did not feel they warranted separate biographies, and yet he was unwilling to ignore them completely, so he recorded them in the 'Chronological Tables.' In the form created by the
Historian, nothing is more admirable than this!" [17]

As Chavannes has remarked, the form of the "Chronological Tables"
was the creation of Ch'ien himself.[18] Although this form may have been
suggested to him by the genealogical tables of the Chou period, nothing
to compare with these chapters in design and elaborateness is known to
have existed before the *Shih chi*. It is customary to praise the concept of
time which the historian displayed in arranging all the events of history in terms of a single chronology. But, as Takeda Taijun has pointed
out, it is not merely the temporal order of events that the tables illustrate,
but their spatial relationships.[19] The *Spring and Autumn Annals* with
its commentaries, for example, achieves a fine temporal unity by sub-
jecting all events of the various feudal states to the Lu chronology, but
achieves this by destroying the continuity of the narrative for events
relating to all other parts of China. By creating separate lines for the
events of each state, the *Shih chi* tables allow us not only to read down
the columns to see what each state was doing in any given year, but
also to read across and see the course of development within any given
state. Many pre-Han works had shown great competence in dealing
with the history of single political units. It was Ssu-ma Ch'ien who, by
frequent cross-references and particularly by his tables, attempted to
bring these histories of individual states into spatial as well as temporal
relationship with each other.

Special mention should be made of the brief introductions which
precede most of these tables. In these little essays Ssu-ma Ch'ien often
displays his most interesting and original thinking. Some are concerned
with problems of the completeness and accuracy of his sources; others
are short philosophical treatises on such historical themes as the downfall
of the Chou, the rise and fall of Ch'in, the sudden rise of the Han, the
feudal system of the Chou and the Han, or relations with the Hsiung-nu.
For a rare moment he breaks away from his sources, steps back, and

contemplates the broad panorama of history. Sometimes he chides men of his time who jump to superficial conclusions on the course of history (*Shih chi* 15/6), or throws out a novel theory, such as that new dynasties arise from the west (15/4). As is his custom, he does not labor over or develop his ideas, but moves with frustrating rapidity from point to point, correcting misconceptions, lamenting the lack of reliable sources, or sighing over the pattern of rise and decay that dominates all history.

A glance at the *Han shu* tables will help to show by contrast the liveliness and originality of Ch'ien's writing. Though Pan Ku borrowed an occasional phrase from his predecessor, the introductions to his tables are for the most part original. Like Ch'ien he begins his discussions with the most ancient times, tracing the development of feudal institutions down through the ages. In places he achieves a clear, moving rhetoric that is in its majestic effect superior to Ch'ien's rapid, laconic style (e.g., *Han shu* 16/3b, the fine passage on the downfall of the peers). But by Latter Han times the Chinese concept of the past had become hardened into conventional Confucian molds. Pan Ku's essays are classical, stately, and dull. There is no longer any suggestion that there may be controversy over the interpretation of history or that new interpretations are possible. The past is a closed story and all that remains for the historian is to summarize it in fine, stereotyped phrases.[20]

TREATISES

[Of the changes in rites and music, the improvements and revisions of the pitch pipes and calendar, military power, mountains and rivers, spirits and gods, the relationships of heaven and man, and the faulty economic practices handed down and reformed through the years, I have made the eight "Treatises."]

The "Treatises" have also been praised as an invaluable contribution to historical form. Ch'ien had as the model for these a number of short texts, or chapters of longer works, devoted to similar subjects, such as Hsün Tzu's essays on rites and music. Unfortunately some of the *Shih chi* essays are in a rather confused and obviously unfinished state, but a reading of at least the last three, those on the Feng and Shan sacrifices, rivers and canals, and economics ["The Balanced Standard"], serve to give an idea of what he intended the form to be. In these, the historian traces briefly the historical background of his subject and then proceeds to be a detailed account of Han affairs relating to it. In many ways the subjects of these chapters were closer to Ch'ien himself than those of any other sections of his history. The "Feng and Shan Sacrifices" deals with the sacrifices and religious affairs of the Emperor Wu, which Ch'ien and his father knew personally from their long attendance upon the Emperor. The chapter on rivers and canals reaches its climax in the description of how the emperor himself, with his ministers, among them Ch'ien, labored to repair the break in the dikes of the Yellow River at Hu-tzu. The "Treatise on the Calendar" relates matters which were the official concern of Ch'ien and his father in their capacity as Grand Historian. Ssu-ma Ch'ien's decision to deal with such important subjects, and subjects in which he possessed more than ordinary knowledge and experience, was indeed a happy one, and it is regrettable that at least the first three treatises seem to be in incomplete form.

Pan Ku changed the title of the treatises from *shu* to *chih,* combined some of the subjects Ch'ien had treated in separate chapters, and added new ones. His treatises, in finished form and having the advantage, as he did throughout his work, of Ch'ien's models to draw upon, are much more useful as historical sources. But it should be noted that he was indebted for his material not only to the *Shih chi,* but also to Liu Hsiang and Liu Hsin, whose extensive writings he drew upon in his treatises on "The Five Elements," "Geography," "Literature," "Rites and Music," and "The Musical Tubes and the Calendar." His only entirely original work seems to be the rather short treatise on the penal code. Another difference between the treatises of the two historians has often been noted. While Ch'ien confines himself largely to the affairs of the Han, with only an occasional reference to the history of ancient times in order to illustrate a point, Pan Ku, in true Confucian style, insists upon beginning the discussion of every subject with a dubious and idealized description of "ancient times" before he gets down to actual Han history.

HEREDITARY HOUSES

[As the twenty-eight constellations revolve about the North Star, as the thirty spokes of a wheel come together at the hub, revolving endlessly without stop, so the ministers, assisting like arms and legs, faithful and trustworthy, in true moral spirit serve their lord and ruler. Of them I made the thirty "Hereditary Houses."]

The term "hereditary house" (*shih-chia*), was not original with Ssu-ma Ch'ien, but appears in the *Mencius,* designating a family which holds hereditary rights to some office or benefice in the state.[21] It is possible therefore that there were already in existence histories of such hereditary officeholding families before Ch'ien compiled the thirty chapters of his history under this title.

In form these chapters differ little from the "Basic Annals." Most of them describe the fortunes of eminent feudal families of pre-Ch'in times. Like the "Annals," they begin with a fairly detailed portrait of the illustrious founder of the line who, because of military merit, outstanding service, or, in the case of descendants of earlier dynasties, the mere fact of noble birth, was enfeoffed under the early Chou. There follows a brief outline of successive holders of the fief, sometimes no more than a bare list of accessions and deaths. As the centuries pass, the virtue and merit which originally distinguished the family wear thin, unworthy descendants misuse the power inherited from their eminent ancestor, and at last the state, weak and decadent, succumbs to the attack of some more virile neighbor. This pattern is occasionally elaborated, like that of the "Annals," by a restoration of power and moral eminence through the efforts of some exceptionally worthy heir. But often Ch'ien's sources allowed him to give a detailed picture only of the two extremes of the cycle of rise and decay, the illustrious founder and the decadent terminator of the line.

The histories of the various feudal states, beginning for the most part with the founding of the Chou dynasty and continuing until the conquest of Ch'in, run in parallel lines through the same area of time. Ch'ien was concerned, as we have already noted, that the reader, as he followed the narrative of each individual state, should be aware of the relationship of its development to simultaneous developments in other parts of the country. For this reason he has employed a kind of framework of cross-references to important events in the history of the period, which serves to relate each individual history to the others. Brief notations of the move of the Chou capital to the east, the beginning of the ascendency of Ch'in, the death of Confucius, or the destruction of Wu, serve to punctuate the history of each little principality and remind one of the progress of greater changes beyond its borders that will eventually affect its whole existence. In a similar way, the personality of the itinerant nobleman of Wu, Chi Cha, runs like a thread through the histories of the various feudalities, as he wanders from state to state, advising its leaders and predicting its future.[22]

With the end of the histories of the pre-Ch'in states, we come to two chapters which have been the subject of much controversy, the "Hereditary House" of Confucius and that of Ch'en Shê (SC 47 & 48). Commentators have generally assumed that Ssu-ma Ch'ien meant his "Hereditary Houses" to be the histories of men and their families who were formally enfeoffed as feudal lords. By this definition neither Confucius, according to tradition a minor official of Lu, not Ch'en Shê, a peasant upstart who led a rebellion against the Ch'in and set himself up as a self-styled king, have any place in this category. Some commentators have tried to interpret the fact that Confucius and his descendants appear among the feudal lords as a token of the honor that Ssu-ma Ch'ien paid to the sage, referring for support of their interpretation to the theory popular in the Han that Confucius, by the mandate of Heaven if not of the men of his time, was an "uncrowned king." Others have pointed out, however, that according to this interpretation Ssu-ma Ch'ien should rightly have put Confucius in the "Annals" among the rulers of the nation, not among the lesser peers. Such explanations seem to me to be unconvincing and to contradict the realism with which Ch'ien customarily treated history.

Much more pertinent, I believe, is the suggestion of Liao Teng-t'ing, that "Those who achieved dominance by grasping power were designated for the 'Basic Annals'; those who lasted through a long period of time were designated for the 'Hereditary Houses.' " [23] In other words, power is the outstanding characteristic of the men and families of the "Annals," duration that of those of the "Hereditary Houses." How does this suggestion apply to the two problematical chapters under discussion here? The biography of Confucius ends with a genealogy of his descendants, showing that his family endured through the ages to the writer's own time. (In fact, Ssu-ma Ch'ien studied with a descendant of Confucius, K'ung An-kuo.) Furthermore it not only endured as a private family, continuing through the generations to perform sacrifices to its illustrious ancestor; as the ages passed, Confucius came to receive the sacrifices and homage of important officials, nobles, and even emperors as well. Ritualistically Confucius continued through the ages to receive all due religious obeisance, while culturally he was honored by an increasingly wider group as the father of learning and the final authority in questions of the Classics. All the powerful and famous aristocratic families of the Chou had perished in the great social upheavals of the Ch'in and early Han. Only the descendants and teachings of this humble official of Lu seemed, in Ssu-ma Ch'ien's time, to grow more honored with each passing year. The "Hereditary House of Confucius" comes after all the chapters dealing with these pre-Ch'in families who perished; it marks the emergence of a new group in history, the men whose influence would extend through their heirs and followers into the Han.

But if the principle governing the inclusion of families in the "Hereditary Houses" is persistence in time, how are we to account for the presence of Ch'en Shê, who did not even live out his natural life, but was defeated by Ch'in and murdered by his carriage driver? In this case Ssu-ma Ch'ien, as though anticipating the question, has taken pains to explain his reasons at the end of the chapter. "Although Ch'en Shê was killed, the nobles and kings, generals and officials, whom he set up and employed eventually overthrew the Ch'in, because Shê had opened the way for them. In the time of Kao-tsu thirty families were established for Ch'en Shê as guardians of his grave at Tang, and down to this day he continues to enjoy the blood and flesh [of sacrifices]." The spirit of Ch'en Shê, then, continued to receive the sacrifices due the ancestor of a noble family; in this most important ritualistic aspect his line was preserved. And through the men he raised to power, the task which he began in his rebellion was carried on and brought to eventual completion. This was not the work, of course, of his actual descendants. Ch'ien is here thinking beyond strict lines of blood to the spiritual kinship of men engaged in the same great undertaking, the destruction of Ch'in. In this respect the entire house of Han was an heir of the military achievements of Ch'en Shê, as it was a spiritual heir of Confucius. It is probably with these considerations in mind that Ssu-ma Ch'ien placed the biographies of these two men at the head of the "Hereditary Houses" of the Han.

Ssu-ma Ch'ien completed his set of "Hereditary Houses" with histories of the statesmen, generals, and imperial relatives who were enfeoffed in the early days of the new dynasty. But, though he perhaps did not fully realize it, the old feudal forms were by this time rapidly becoming empty and meaningless. Emperors Ching and Wu worked ceaselessly to whittle away territory and power from these Han peers and their descendants until, by the time of Ssu-ma Ch'ien's death, feudalism was in spirit, if not in form, a thing of the past. In his *Han shu,* Pan Ku eliminated this category of "Hereditary Houses" and shifted the Han peers to the "Memoirs" and, with a few exceptions, this form was never again used in Chinese histories.

MEMOIRS

[Upholding righteousness, masterful and sure, not allowing themselves to miss their opportunities, they made a name for themselves in the world. Of such men I made the "Seventy Memoirs."]

Let us turn now to the last and longest section of the *Shih chi,* the *lieh-chuan* or "Memoirs." As with the other forms of the *Shih chi,* there has been much discussion among scholars as to just what Ssu-ma Ch'ien meant by his designation *lieh-chuan* and what he conceived as the unifying characteristic of these chapters. It is generally agreed that *lieh* means "arranged," "set forth," but the interpretation of the second character presents greater difficulties.

The term *chuan,* "transmission," or, in its verbal form, *ch'uan,* "to transmit," was from early times used by the Confucian school to designate oral or written exegeses of a Classical text. Thus, in the case of the *Spring and Autumn Annals,* the early Confucian school possessed two types of texts, the original Classic or *ching,* in this case the chronicle of Lu and the commentaries or *chuan,* explaining the background and exact meaning of entries in the Classic. As demonstrated by Professor Naitô, this same two-fold division of texts was also used, perhaps in imitation of the Confucianists, in the writings of other schools of philosophy.[24] Our present *Lao Tzu* is, he believes, a somewhat confused combination of a set of ancient philosophical admonitions and a later exegesis by someone called Lao Tzu, and this same pattern of basic text and later exposition may be seen in the *Mo Tzu, Kuan Tzu,* and *Han Fei Tzu.*

In a recent article, Professor Chen Shih-hsiang reviews this early meaning of the word *chuan* as an exegesis of an older and loftier text, or tradition, and then continues to a discussion of the *Shih chi,* remarking, "We know that in naming his 'biographies' *chuan,* Ssu-ma Ch'ien was holding fast to the earlier sense of the word, that the individual lives he depicted were mere illustrations of the greater events and ideals of the times; and his *lieh-chuan* therefore stands in a subservient position to his 'imperial annals' [sic] (*pen-chi*) in a sense not too different from that of the *Kung-yang chuan* to the *Spring and Autumn Annals.*"[25]

The division of material into five sections in the *Shih chi* undoubtedly represents a certain judgment upon its relative importance, a hierarchical order established by the historian among the personalities of history. Ssu-ma Ch'ien's conception of history is basically political and therefore men who dictated the fate of the empire can hardly stand side by side with obscure philosophers and country ruffians who wielded negligible political influence. In this sense the *lieh-chuan* are without doubt "subservient" to the *pen-chi.* But I think Professor Chen's statement, by emphasizing the earlier meaning of the word *chuan,* implies that Ssu-ma Ch'ien made a qualitative, a basic moral, distinction between the characters and events of his "Annals" and those of his "Memoirs," or biographies. "The personalities of the sketches," Professor Chen continues, describing the *lieh-chuan,* "look oblique and lopsided, the focal interest being elsewhere on a much larger panel overhead, which is the whole corpus of a general history of several millennia." The biographies do indeed appear oblique and lopsided, not because the historian's interest is elsewhere, I believe, but for other very definite reasons. Ch'ien often writes with greater interest, personal feeling, and even passion, in his "Memoirs" than he does in his "Annals." There was, for him, no such thing as "a general history" outside the lives of the individual men of history. The core of all his writing, "Annals," "Treatises," "Hereditary Houses," and "Memoirs" alike, is the life of the individual. In the course of these many lives he discerned a few overall patterns such as the ceaseless cycle of rise and decay. But he is happily free of "trends," "tendencies," "movements," and similar vague concepts, which so often today threaten to drive the individual out of the pages of history.

In Ssu-ma Ch'ien's time, the word *chuan* was often used very loosely to designate any book not already designated as a Classic, whether it had to do directly with the exegesis of a Classical text or not. It meant, in other words, the teachings or traditions of a man or group of men. It was Ssu-ma Ch'ien, as has been clearly recognized, who first made the word mean "biography" by calling his biographical chapters *chuan.* But he also wrote chapters on the history of foreign peoples and lands which he called *chuan.* In these cases we cannot, of course, speak of "The Biography of Korea," and therefore the English word "biography" represents only a partial translation of *chuan.* We must, it appears, look somewhere between the old meaning of "exegesis" and the later meaning of "biography" to discover what Ssu-ma Ch'ien had in mind when he adopted this term. Most pertinent, I believe, is Professor Hightower's suggestion that what Ssu-ma Ch'ien meant by *chuan* was the tales or stories handed down to him and his age concerning the lives of individuals and peoples.[26] By adopting this meaning of "tale," we may further suggest something of Ssu-ma Ch'ien's own attitude toward the material contained in these chapters.

In the first of his *lieh-chuan,* which serves as a general introduction to the whole section, Ssu-ma Ch'ien again warns the reader, as he did in the first chapter of his history, that the writing of history is not a cut and dried affair but a matter of doubt, danger, and choice.[27] He first discusses several ancient legends of virtuous men who were supposedly offered the throne of the empire but declined it. He himself, he remarks, has seen what is said to be the grave of one of these men. Yet these stories, he notes, not only are not authenticated by the Confucian Classics, the final judge of reliability, but are inconsistent with reason and good sense. Here he raises the first great dilemma of the historian, the lack of sufficient reliable sources. He proceeds to the story of Po I and Shu Ch'i, two men of ancient times praised by Confucius for the fact that they did not bear grudges. But, he continues, "their story [*chuan*] relates that . . ." and he proceeds to tell their tale as he found it in his sources,[28] which shows clearly that they bore long and bitter grudges indeed. He here points out the second great dilemma of the historian, the contradiction of sources. It is clear from his use of the word *chuan* here that Ch'ien had in mind the tales or legends told about men of ancient times, and in addition that he was well aware that these old tales were sometimes of questionable authority.

It is further clear from a reading of the *lieh-chuan* themselves that Ssu-ma Ch'ien did not regard his chapters as full-length "biographies" in our sense of the word. Many of the most important aspects of the subjects' lives are dealt with in other sections of his history and not mentioned at all in the *lieh-chuan.* The classic examples of this are the stories of the famous ministers of Ch'i, Kuan Chung and Yen Ying (SC 62), in which most of the important aspects of their official careers and their teachings are ignored in favor of a few ancedotes illustrating their personalities. Ch'ien did not believe it his duty to tell all he knew about the subject of his chapter, but only those incidents and ancedotes which would most clearly indicate the person's character and worth, the things that people had remembered and repeated about him. Since his stated aim was to rescue from oblivion the memory of great men of old, he felt it was sufficient if he recorded only their most outstanding and memorable points. In the case of persons of lesser importance, if he thought there was no danger they would be forgotten, he did not even bother to mention more than their names.[29] Ssu-ma Ch'ien was creating an entirely new literary form by writing chapters devoted specifically to the lives of individuals. If we are not to misjudge the success of his efforts, we must not be misled, I think, either by the old term *chuan* to which he was trying to give new meaning, nor by what the *chuan* or "biographical" form became in the hands of later writers. We can only decide what Ch'ien intended the new form to be by examining what he himself did with it.

If, as has been generally conceded, the biographical form was a creation of Ssu-ma Ch'ien, what, if any, were the sources and precedents for this new form? As Professor Chen points out, the editors of the *Ssu-k'u ch'üan-shu tsung-mu* (ch. 57) trace the origin of the biographical form to a work probably of the 4th century B. C., the *Yen-tzu ch'un-ch'iu* or *Spring and Autumn of Master Yen*.[30] But this work, though containing a number of speeches and admonitions supposedly by the famous minister of Ch'i, Yen Ying, is actually a philosophical work expounding policies associated with his name and anecdotes in which he figures; it cannot be regarded as a life of the man himself. If we are to consider it as a prototype of biographical writing (and it is certainly one step in that direction), we might go farther back and consider the *Mencius* and *Analects,* which do not differ basically from it in form, as similar prototypes. But these early works are all characterized by a single objective; their purpose is not to record the life of an individual, but to present his teachings, to set forth the doctrines of a school of thought.

While we are indulging in this game of tracing things beyond their actual beginnings, however, we should take note of another possible ancestor of the biographical form and the concern for the life of the individual which it represents. This is the brief tale of Princess Po of Lu recorded in the *Spring and Autumn Annals* and its commentaries.

In 582 B. C., at the age of about twenty, Princess Po, daughter of Duke Hsüan of Lu, was married to Duke Kung, who had succeeded to the rule of Sung some seven years before. In 576, six years after their marriage, Kung died and was succeeded by his son Ch'eng, who became Duke P'ing. According to Tung Chung-shu, the princess, like a proper widow, went into retirement for the rest of her life.[31] One night in 543, when she was around sixty, the house where she was living caught fire. Her attendants urged her to flee, but the old woman, insisting that it was improper for a lady to venture out of her dwelling at night without a duenna, adamantly stayed where she was and burned to death. Although a few commentators have opined that, under the unusual and pressing circumstances, the princess might have disregarded the ordinary demands of propriety, most have agreed in naming her, because of her noble act of sacrifice, a paragon of virtue. The important point in this tragi-comic tale is that the *Spring and Autumn Annals,* in its brief chronicle, makes a total of eight entries concerning the life of the princess, and although this may simply be because she was a native of Lu, both the *Kung-yang* and the *Ku-liang* commentaries, as well as Tung Chung-shu,[32] all agree that the reason for the amount of space devoted to her affairs is that Confucius, and the sources he followed, wished to emphasize her virtue by recording her life in some detail. As a later commentator has remarked, "In historiographical practice there is detailed and abbreviated recording. Although we cannot examine today the most ancient histories, from the time of Ssu-ma Ch'ien and Pan Ku on, the comparative moral worth of various individuals determined the length and brevity of the narrative devoted to them. Princess Po displayed worthy action, and therefore the ancient historians made an especially detailed record of her life, and the Sage followed this without change." [33]

Ssu-ma Ch'ien had, of course, fairly detailed accounts of the lives of heroes and famous men already at hand in his early sources. Some of these, like the tale of the famous Ch'ung-erh in the *Tso Commentary* or that of Su Ch'in in the *Intrigues of the Warring States,* were probably based upon early historical romances that had been handed down and added to through the centuries.[34] It required no great labor to compile these early stories in the form of separate biographies. But, as Ch'ien makes clear in his chapter on Po I and elsewhere, he did not see himself simply as a teller of old tales; he believed he had a much more profound moral obligation to preserve for posterity the merits of the men of the past and to reward them for their trials and sorrows by conferring upon them, when they deserve it, the immortality of history. It is this deep-felt moral aspect of Ssu-ma Ch'ien's biographies that must, I think, lead us back to the brief, sad story of the princess of Lu and her moment of glory.

The influence which the tale of Princess Po and its interpretation in the *Kung-yang Commentary* had upon Ssu-ma Ch'ien must be purely a matter of conjecture. Yet it is certain that somehow, for some reason, Ch'ien created in his writing a new place for the individual in history. Works prior to his time had been content to treat only the great and outstanding deeds of the individual, or weave his story into a larger narrative or an exposition of a particular school of thought. It was Ssu-ma Ch'ien who first saw that the life story of the individual could be given independent existence and could reveal in its form and development a meaning larger than that of single deeds and different from schools of thought. Some of his *lieh-chuan* are, it is true, hardly more than recitals of a single great act of a man, but this may often have been due to a lack of other material. Certainly the nearer to his own time his subjects come, the more complex and detailed are their stories. Again, his chapters dealing with philosophers are necessarily concerned largely with their ideas, as, for example, his biography of Tsou Yen (SC 74). But many of the *lieh-chuan* fit neither of these traditional patterns. They tell the story of the man of action not only in his moment of glory, but from his youth, when he first dreamed of great deeds, to his death, when success was a memory of the past. Some century and a half before Plutarch in the West, Ch'ien conceived the idea, so natural to us today that we can hardly believe that it had to be thought of, that the life of the individual as well as that of the state or the age is a fit subject for the concentrated attention of the historian. We may point to the

interest in lineages and genealogies that characterized the late Chou
as a reason for Ch'ien's attention to biography. We may recall the great
social upheavals of the late Chou and early Han, and the opportunities
they afforded for the man of ability, regardless of birth, to rise in the
world, as a source of interest in and respect for the individual. But
these are only factors contributing to a favorable atmosphere for Ssu-ma
Ch'ien's creation, not causes which made it inevitable. The art of creation is Ssu-ma Ch'ien's, and we can attribute it only to that same mysterious leap of the imagination that is responsible for all true artistic
innovations. The historian, as Ssu-ma Ch'ien saw him, had two aims:
to console the dead for their sorrows by handing on their story, and to
instruct the living and unborn, by means of these same stories, in the
ways of human life. He had learned from Confucius' own *Spring and
Autumn Annals* that the most profound and meaningful lessons of
life were best conveyed in the stuff of human history. Parables were
sometimes used in China, as they were later to be used in the teachings of Jesus. But Confucius, Ssu-ma Ch'ien believed, had shown that a
judicial arrangement of the facts of the past taught men better and
more truthfully. It was this method which Ssu-ma Ch'ien, in his own
search for the principles that govern human life, adopted. But, in his
lieh-chuan chapters, and indeed in his history as a whole, he focused
not upon the history of the state, but upon the will and actions of
the individual.

It is hardly necessary to remark at this point that his interest was
not in just any individual. The idea of the worth of the common man
was as foreign to him as it was to his contemporaries in the West. To
the thinker of the ancient world, East or West, the life of the common
man told only what it is to be common, a thing which interested few
people. It was not the mean of human capabilities but the extreme
which excited the interest of the historian and the philosopher, and it
was for this reason that Ssu-ma Ch'ien, as he himself explains, chose
for his subjects only extraordinary men who accomplished extraordinary things.

As we read his lives of these extraordinary figures of the Chinese past, we may ask what, if any, are the lessons that Ch'ien would teach by them. The lesson seems to be only this: that the world is a fickle place in which virtue must be its own reward, for it may assuredly look in this life for reward from no other quarter. This is what he hints in his introductory chapter of the *lieh-chuan,* and what the following chapters substantiate with painful monotony. And yet there is one thing that rescues the *lieh-chuan* from futile pessimism, and that is the sympathy of Ssu-ma Ch'ien himself. As he takes up each gloomy tale of the past, the love and understanding of the historian, in an act resembling religious salvation, rights all the injustices, assuages all the sorrow, and sets down in imperishable words the true form of the individual's life where it may await the understanding of all sympathetic men of the future.

One may object at this point that not all of Ssu-ma Ch'ien's portraits are by any means kindly and lovable. This is of course true. He was no sentimentalist but an historian with the historian's fearless gaze. He saw and recorded, even in the men he most admired, each flaw of character and error and judgment. For, fickle though the world might be, he recognized that neither success nor failure is completely the fault of environment. Had he, in his sympathy, white-washed his heroes and idealized them into flawless paragons, he would have falsified his whole picture of life and deprived the reader of one of the most important keys to the hero's downfall, his own faults. But in every man he treated he found merits, and it was these with which he sympathized, these which he felt made the story worth relating to future ages. On the other hand, no matter how important a man might be in actual history, if he were wholly without good points, Ssu-ma Ch'ien chose as much as possible to ignore him. The eunuch Chao Kao wielded tremendous power at the end of the Ch'in, and Ssu-ma Ch'ien was forced to devote much space to his evil deeds and their influence in the biographies of other men. But he wrote no biography for Chao Kao. If good was to be rewarded by the perpetuation of its name, then the reward for evil was oblivion. Actually Chao Kao appears in the pages of the *Shih chi,* but formally, and symbolically, he is condemned to this oblivion.

In his biographies, Ssu-ma Ch'ien did not simply string out a series of individual lives, nor did he always, as one might expect, group his subjects by chronological or geographical affinities. He held strongly to the conviction, derived from the classics and philosophical writings of his past, that there are profound and unchanging moral patterns that underlie the course of human events. He followed chronological order where it was convenient, but he subordinated it to these patterns that he perceived in the lives of the men of the past. He classified his subjects into groups by the contour of their lives and the ambitions that motivated them, placing men of the same category in one chapter. Some of these categories were clearly enough defined to warrant a label, and so he wrote chapters entitled "Assassin-Retainers," "Wandering Knights," "Good Officials," "Harsh Officials," etc. Others fell into groups by their similarity of interest—the philosophers, the doctors, the tragic poets. In other cases the pattern is less obvious, the bond more subtle (or, as some critics have objected, farfetched). Whatever we may think of these groupings of lives, we must recognize that in this very search for a pattern the basic philosophy of history which motivated Ssu-ma Ch'ien and his countrymen is revealed. The ages before Ch'ien had created in history the "types" of the evil and the virtuous ruler, the upright and the wicked minister. The idea of patterns, the patterns themselves, were old in Ssu-ma Ch'ien's day. It was he who perceived that they could be applied not only to the men of ancient history but also to those of his own day. He took the old cardboard stereotypes of the past and made of them portraits of living men of flesh and blood; he discovered subtleties of shading that the old black and white caricatures had ignored. But he never abandoned the idea that there is a basic moral pattern to all human life which determines its real meaning, the only meaning it has in history. Later Chinese historiographical writing, when it became the creation not of an individual but of committees of bureaucrats, disregarded this ancient meaning, writing biographies for all men who achieved a sufficiently high official rank, regardless of the true worth or interest of their life stories. But the *Shih chi* tradition of writing biographies not merely of men who were important in their own times but of men whose lives exemplified a transcendent moral greatness continued to exercise its influence in Chinese literature. Shortly after Ssu-ma Ch'ien, and probably due to his example, there began to appear a number of biographical works, such as Liu Hsiang's *Stories of Outstanding Women* (*Lieh-nü-chuan*) or Huang-fu Mi's (215–282) *Stories of Eminent Men* (*Kao-shih-chuan*), which were devoted to groups of individuals whose lives displayed the same moral pattern. This new genre, derived from the categorized "types" of the *Shih chi* and *Han shu* biographies, has continued to occupy a major position in Chinese biographical writing down to the present.

Fortunately for us, however, Ssu-ma Ch'ien did not in his *lieh-chuan* section confine himself solely to the writing of individual lives. From his biographies of men of similar professions and interests it was only a step to chapters relating the lives of men associated with foreign regions—native rulers, Chinese explorers, generals, and envoys who brought these lands into contact with China. So we have his invaluable accounts of non-Chinese peoples which became the model for similar monographs in later Chinese histories.

It had become the custom in pre-Ch'in and early Han philosophical works to place at the end a chapter summing up the principles of the work as a whole and outlining the aims and makeup of the book. Ssu-ma Ch'ien followed this practice by ending his history with a chapter setting forth his objectives in writing his work, listing its contents, and giving brief biographies of his ancestors, his father, and himself. This not only serves the valuable purpose of introducing the structure and purpose of his book much as does the preface in a modern western book, but aids our comprehension of the work by explaining, as modern prefaces generally fail to do, who the author himself is. This practice was fortunately adopted by many later historians, providing one of our most valuable sources for the history of Chinese historiographical thought. [35]

One more characteristic of the form of the *Shih chi* demands discussion. This is the "judgment" or "appraisal" with which Ssu-ma Ch'ien ends most chapters of his history. Chinese historians have always attempted to achieve what Francis Bacon calls "a naked delivery of facts, with but a sparing use of private judgment." [36] One may object that it is nothing but private judgment which tells the historian what the facts are and the way they are related; without private judgment he would have no facts to deliver. Yet beyond this critical judgment which we may assume underlies all historical writing we find many historians, ancient and modern, interrupting their narrative to indulge in caustic comment or sighs of melancholy, or to draw for the reader some pious moral. Interruptions of this kind have generally been condemned by the Chinese. Yet, realizing the value of such comments when aptly and appropriately made, Chinese historiography has dictated that they should be set aside by some conventional phrase or word which will warn the reader of their private nature, and placed customarily at the end of a chapter.

Numerous examples of such short passages of judgment and appraisal may be found in the *Tso Commentary* and the *Narratives from the States,* introduced by the conventional phrase *"Chün-tzu yüeh,* "The gentleman remarks." [37] These supplied the model for Ssu-ma Ch'ien's passages of personal opinion which he used at the end, or occasionally the beginning, of his chapters to comment upon his subject. At present these passages are all introduced by the words *T'ai-shih-kung yüeh,* "The Grand Historian remarks." There have been a number of theories put forward to explain the use of this phrase. Some commentators believe that Ssu-ma Ch'ien used it to honor his father, the Grand Historian Ssu-ma T'an, who may possibly have written some of these sections. Yet we know from internal evidence that in many cases they must have been written by Ch'ien himself, and it would have been presumptuous of him, critics claim, to use the honorary appellation *T'ai-shih-kung* when referring to himself. To avoid this difficulty it has been suggested that the phrase "The Grand Historian remarks" was in all cases added by a later editor, either Tung-fang So or Ch'ien's grandson Yang Yün. Still another theory is that the phrase *T'ai-shih-kung* is no more than an official title having no particular honorary connotation and so Ch'ien is within the bounds of modesty in referring to himself in this way.[38]

Whatever may be the explanation for the way the present *Shih chi* text introduces them, the means to which Ssu-ma Ch'ien put these little essays should be noted. At times he follows the older convention of the *Tso Commentary* in introducing in these sections moral judgments upon the characters and events of his narrative, quoting sometimes from the Classics to emphasize his point. But he did not confine himself to this practice. At other times he supplements the narrative with new facts, discusses the reliability of his sources, explains his reasons for writing the chapter, or describes his own personal emotions and experiences as they relate to his subject. In other words, he uses the "judgment" form freely to make any type of comment he feels necessary or desirable. By setting these comments off clearly from the rest of the text, he allows himself to be as subjective and emotional as he likes without violating the historical objectivity demanded by Chinese custom.

When Pan Ku adopted this form of the *Shih chi* for his own work, he of course eliminated the words "The Grand Historian," even when he was quoting verbatim from the *Shih chi,* and substituted the word *tsan.* His choice of this word was unfortunate. He may in fact have intended it to mean a section which assists or supplements the narrative.[39] But the term has generally been interpreted in its more common meaning of "praise" or "eulogy," an inaccurate description of Pan Ku's judgments, which, while they sometimes praise, as often condemn. Later historians set up two categories, the *p'ing* or *lun,* which they used, like Ssu-ma Ch'ien, to discuss the reliability of their narrative, add new material, and judge the persons and events of the chapter, and the *tsan* of Pan Ku, which they used for a brief summary or epitome of the subject. Following the tendency already evident in the Table of Contents of the *Shih chi,* these epitomes were composed in four-character rhymed phrases.[40]

The exact form of the *Shih chi* in all its aspects has seldom been imitated by later historians. Although Pan Ku adopted most of the formal divisions of the work of his predecessor, he made one vital change in its scope by limiting the range of his history to the span of one dynasty, the Former Han. In doing so, Pan Ku became the father of the *tuan-tai-shih* or "single dynasty history" form. The *Han shu,* employing four of the five formal divisions of the *Shih chi,* but with this important temporal limitation in the scope of its narrative, became the model for the later *cheng-shih* or "dynastic histories," also known as *chi-chuan* or "annal and memoir" histories, because they invariably contained at least these two sections. Although there was at least one earlier attempt to write a comprehensive history on the scale of the *Shih chi,* it was not until the Sung that any major work of history was produced that did not follow the "single dynasty" pattern laid down by the *Han shu.*

It is readily understandable why historians preferred to imitate the more amiable dimensions of Pan Ku's history rather than attempt anything on the awesome scale of the *Shih chi.* But the "single dynasty" form has one great fault which has long distressed Chinese philosophers of history. At least from Han times the essence of human history, as of the whole natural world, was regarded by the Chinese as the phenomenon of change. All creation, whether in the heavenly, terrestrial, or human spheres, is constantly in a process of growth, waxing and waning, flourishing and dying, rising and falling. Therefore, to understand the world, and human history, one must understand this process of change and know its direction at any given point in time. In human history the greatest and most significant change is the fall of an old ruling house and the rise of a new one, and the greatest lesson that history teaches is how and why dynasties rise and fall, and how a ruler may preserve the health of his state. Thus it is said of the *Spring and Autumn Annals* that it "preserves states which are perishing" because it imparts just this knowledge. But the "dynastic history" form, though it traces the rise and fall of one ruling house, does not fully encompass this all-important process of change from the first signs of decay in an old dynasty to the final victory of a new. It begins its story when the old rule is already doomed and tottering, and looks only far enough ahead into the history of the following dynasty to record the last dying gasps of its original subject. Many Chinese historians have rightly felt that this arbitrary temporal division into dynastic periods does violence to the dynamic spirit of change, rending the living fabric of history and thereby obscuring the significant pattern written thereon.

It was to preserve this significant continuity of history that the Sung historian Ssu-ma Kuang (1019–1086) and his associates undertook the writing of a mammoth account of the past from the year 403 B. C. to 959 A. D. Their work, the *Tzu-chih t'ung-chien* or *Comprehensive Mirror for the Aid of Government,* has been considered the finest example of the *t'ung-shih* or "continuous history" and is probably the best known and read of all Chinese histories after the *Shih chi.* Cheng Ch'iao (1108–1166), another Sung historian who produced a monumental history of the past modeled on the *Shih chi* form, argues in the preface to his work that the history of a single dynasty is meaningless and without value unless it is seen in terms of the eras which preceded and produced it. He berates later historians for ignoring in this respect the excellent example of Ssu-ma Ch'ien to follow that of Pan Ku, likening Ch'ien to a dragon and Pan Ku to a pig.[41] The same point is also made, without recourse to scurrility, by the last of the great Sung historians, Ma Tuan-lin (13th century), who argues that, although the "single dynasty" form may be acceptable for accounts of purely political history, because of its arbitrary divisions it renders institutional and cultural history incomprehensible.[42] The Chinese have thus not been blind to the theoretical advantages of the "continuous history" over the "single dynasty" form. That most historians after the Han modeled their work on the *Han shu* rather than the *Shih chi* is more probably proof that all but the hardiest found themselves intimidated by the staggering scope and demands of the *Shih chi* form.

V

THE THOUGHT OF
SSU-MA CH'IEN

SSU-MA CH'IEN'S THEORY OF HISTORY

In a previous chapter I have examined the historiographical principles of the *Spring and Autumn Annals* and their influence upon the *Shih chi*. I should like here to consider some other aspects of Ssu-ma Ch'ien's thought and its relation to the main currents of Chinese philosophy.

It is impossible to say definitely when, in the course of the development of Chinese culture, a true historical consciousness appeared. The *Book of Documents* of the early Chou, we might argue, already displays the respect for the past and interest in past events that is the essential quality of the historical consciousness. Yet in another sense even the *Shih chi* is still too embroiled with ancient ritualistic considerations to meet the test of straightforwardness and true objectivity we demand of historical writing today. It is certain, however, that somewhere between the composition of these two works there was growing slowly and tentatively in the Chinese mind a concept of history and a feeling for historical writing that was to father the great histories of later ages.

This historical consciousness grew quite naturally (though not inevitably) from the humanism of the Chou people. Little by little they worked to remake their old myths, to refine their crude superstitions and religious ideas into conformity with the rationalism and humanism that were growing ever stronger in Chinese thought. At the same time that the idea of historical writing, and of history itself, was slowly developing, the raw materials of history, and the methods and objectives

of historical literature, were being shaped by these concepts of rationalism and humanism.

For the most part the course of this development in Chinese thought
is hardly more than a vague impression that comes from the writings
of this period. But there are a few scattered pronouncements that may
serve to pinpoint the main direction of this process. One is the statement in *Mo Tzu,* quoted in *Shih chi* 79/47: "I have heard it said that
he who looks into the water will see the form of his face, but he who
looks at men will know fortune and misfortune." [1] There are two important points to be noted in this statement. First are the words "fortune" (*chi*) and "misfortune" (*hsiung*). These two words we will
recognize as part of the terminology of the ancient art of divination.
It was precisely for the purpose of knowing "fortune and misfortune"
that the Shang people divined with their tortoise shells and sheep bones,
and that the Chou people consulted the milfoil stalks and the *Book of
Changes.* But among the men of the Chou there had come a realization
that there was another, more subtle and difficult, and yet somehow
more reliable way to foretell the future of men, and that was by the
careful and thoughtful observation of men themselves. This idea represents the stirring of a humanism that was to give to historical writing
its *raison d'être.* The second point is the use of the word *chien,* "to
look at," "to observe." In its nominal form the word means "a mirror"
and in this sense it has been traditionally associated with the Chinese
concept of history from earliest times. History is a mirror of mankind
in which the reader may look at the men of the past and observe their
fortunes and misfortunes, and from this observation come to understand the fortunes of his own age. It is for this reason that the Sung
emperor Ying-tsung conferred upon Ssu-ma Kuang's great history of
the past the title *T'ung-chien,* or "Comprehensive Mirror."

This embryonic concept of the function of history becomes more ar-
ticulate in a saying which appears in the *Kuan Tzu* and is repeated by
Tung Chung-shu: "He who is in doubt about the present, let him
examine ancient times. He who does not understand the future, let
him look to the past." [2] History, then, is a teacher, instructing men in

the ways of the world and bringing them to an understanding of human society. It is no mere intellectual comprehension that history conveys, however, but judgments of moral worth. Of the *Spring and Autumn Annals* the *Tso Commentary* writes: "Its words censure evil and encourage good" (Duke Ch'eng 14). Here we have a clear expression of the didactic function of history so familiar to us in classical Western historiography, a concept that has been an essential part of Chinese historical thought from ancient times to the present. Ssu-ma Ch'ien at the end of his chapter on "Harsh Officials" (SC 122/45) remarks: "Among these ten men those who were pure may serve as a model for conduct, while those who were vile may serve as a warning." Chang Fu, fourth-century author of a comparative study of the *Shih chi* and *Han shu,* praises the work of Ssu-ma Ch'ien because of its didactic excellence: "Its good men serve to encourage the diligent; its evil men serve to exhibit warnings." [3]

Simultaneous with the development of this concept of the didactic function of history was the actual use of historical figures and events in persuasive speaking. Perhaps the strongest impetus to the growth of historical writing and the historical consciousness in China was the rise of the various schools of philosophy in Chou times. In the hands of these early thinkers, expounding their particular theories and panaceas, history became the handmaiden of rhetoric.

It has often been noted that, in comparison to Greece or other countries of the West, China is strangely lacking in ancient myths. Whether, as some have supposed, the Chinese mind was never disposed to the creation of such myths or, as seems more likely, a later development of that mind led to the neglect and obliteration of earlier myths that had once existed, it is now difficult to decide. But it seems to be an incontrovertible fact that in mid-Chou times, when our literary sources begin in earnest, there was no rich mythology of the past, such as the Greeks possessed, for the Chinese philosophers and poets to draw upon. Furthermore, such legends and myths as did exist were for the most part regarded not as myth but as sober historical truth. [4]

The ancient Greek rhetoricians and orators of the time of Pericles, when they wished to stir the minds of their hearers, invoked the great principles and ideals of the state, or referred to the gods and heroes of Greek mythology. But they did not appeal to the memory of historical events in Greek history or evoke the names of historical personages. The reason, as has been pointed out, was that the Greek people of this time had no clear idea of historical events and persons, and allusions to them called forth no image and no emotional response as did references to the ancient myths. The Greek orator, in search of a set of symbols to illustrate his point, could more readily draw them from the corpus of ancient myths and legends, already known to all his listeners, than try to create them from the stuff of Greek history.[5]

But the case of the Chinese rhetorician of the late Chou was different. He might appeal to the names of Yao, Shun, and Yü, figures quite as remote for the Chinese of his time as Herakles or Jason for the Greeks of the age of Pericles. But he could not embroider the stories of these men at will, nor could he too openly impute to them ideas and institutions that he wished to expound. For there was already a feeling that these men were historical, and that the remoteness of their age made it difficult to say more about them than was already recorded in the old texts, such as the *Book of Documents*. From the time of Confucius and on, men were already beginning to question how many of the stories of ancient times could be accepted as true, and how many had to be rejected as "vulgar," that is, fantastic and unreasonable. If men could no longer maneuver the old legends in any way they pleased to illustrate their ideas—as their contemporaries, the Greek dramatists, could do with their own myths—then they had to search for their symbols elsewhere.

One solution to the problem was to invent pseudo-historical personages that could be made to represent anything the speaker desired. This was the literary technique used to such good effect by Chuang Tzu, who created not only his own "historical" figures, but fabulous birds and beasts as well, to convey his ideas. But this solution, with what loss to Chinese literature we can only wonder, was never accepted by the main tradition of Chinese thought. Ssu-ma Ch'ien remarks of Chuang Tzu's writings (SC 63/10): "His sayings are for the most part allegorical. . . . They are empty tales without basis in fact," and it is clear that for this reason he considers them inferior.

To the Chinese, these "empty tales," products of the imagination, have never had the same value as writings which are based upon the actual facts of human life and history. This is one reason why fiction in China was so slow in developing and why for so long it held an inferior place in Chinese letters. It also explains why so much early fiction took the form of historical romance, at times even attempting to masquerade as actual history. The Chinese rhetorician could not really move his audience by reference to persons and events which were products of his own mind, no matter how trenchant or ingeniously conceived. He had to draw his symbols from the common experience of the nation, from the records of things which all men believed to be historical truth. He might assert that such-and-such had been true of the ancient emperors Yao, Shun, and Yü. But these figures were remote and dim. How much more effective if he could assert that the same thing was true of King T'ang, founder of the Shang dynasty, and kings Wen and Wu, founders of the Chou! He might wish for a symbol of the evil tyrant. There was an ideal one in Chou, the last ruler of the Shang. But how much more effective to have two, going back to Chieh, the evil ruler of the Hsia, or more, adding the evil Chou rulers Li, Hsüan, and Yu! In the sayings of Confucius and Mencius, the writings of Han Fei Tzu and Hsün Tzu, the speeches of Su Ch'in and Chang I, we find time and again these allusions to persons and events of Chinese history, both of the distant past and the time of the speaker. Names come to have a symbolic meaning, like the figures of a morality play; battles, conferences, palaces, become metaphors for victory, defeat, wasteful luxury, or oppression.

This use of historical allusion as a tool of rhetoric has had a profound effect upon the materials of early Chinese history. It has imposed upon them, by repeated use and modification, a number of literary patterns.[6] The search for types of personages to illustrate virtue and vice, wisdom and folly, has led to the development of supremely virtuous sovereigns such as Yü, T'ang, Wen, and Wu, or arch villains like Chieh, Chou, and the First Emperor of the Ch'in. Images of ideal men of the past have been forced upon figures of later times, and the moral patterns of later history read back into the past. Professor Pearson has noted that the characters in Herodotus inevitably tend to resemble in their personalities and the course of their lives the patterns of Greek mythology.[7] Exactly the same is true of the *Shih chi.* The patterns of the virtuous founder of a dynasty, the wise ruler who revives the waning fortunes of his family, the evil and decadent terminator of the line with his just and unjust counselors—these stereotypes, the symbols created by the rhetoricians—are inevitably repeated in the narrative of the historian and even imposed upon his account of contemporary times. The mind of the Chinese historian continued to seek for the same configurations in contemporary history that it had been taught to find in the history of the past.

It was the business of the educated Chinese to know these ancient figures and events and to understand their significance, as it was the business of the learned man of the west until recently to know the great names of the Bible and classical mythology and the moral concepts and values they represented. This meant the study of the ancient texts, such as the *Book of Documents,* and later, after Confucius and his school had made the figures of the chronicle of Lu the symbols of moral judgment par excellence, the study of the *Spring and Autumn Annals* and its commentaries. Fan Chü, one of the most famous of the itinerant rhetoricians who made their living by traveling from one feudal court to another expounding their political theories and seeking employment, boasted: "All the affairs of the Five Emperors and the Three Dynasties and the theories of the Hundred Schools of Philosophy are known to me" (SC 79/36). Although this class of wandering theorists gradually disappeared in Han times, the custom of employing historical examples in rhetoric continued without change. The early Han poet and statesman, Chia I, for example, could utilize historical figures from the most ancient times down to the Ch'in, with the assurance that his readers would immediately respond to their symbolism in such lines as:

> Wu was powerful and great;
> Under Fu Ch'a she sank in defeat.
> Yüeh was besieged at K'uai-chi.
> But Chu Chien made her lordly.
> Ssu, who went forth to greatness, at last
> Suffered the direst penalty.
> Fu Yüeh was sent into exile,
> Yet Wu Ting made him his aide.[8]

Chinese argumentation at this time did not depend for its effectiveness so much upon logical development as upon rhetoric, and among rhetorical devices the historical allusion was the most frequently used, and apparently the most compelling. The debates on the salt and iron monopolies between the Confucianists and the government officials held shortly after the time of Ssu-ma Ch'ien, for example, were conducted almost entirely in terms of rival historical allusions and examples. This intimate connection between history and rhetoric has had a profound effect upon the nature of historical writing and has helped to keep history in a place of prominence in Chinese letters and thought. Almost every major Chinese philosopher from the Han to the present has leaned heavily both upon examples from history and the historical essay form to expound his ideas.

This relationship between rhetoric and history, as we have seen, helps to account for the recurrence of certain patterns and of particular, well-developed "types" in history. Ssu-ma Ch'ien gave full recognition to these recurrent patterns in history. First of all there was the pattern of rise and decline, based upon the growth and decay of the natural world and the constant revolution of the seasons which was a natural and inevitable part of human history. Ssu-ma Ch'ien makes two attempts to describe, in moral terms, this cycle of rise and decay. First is the theory of the alternation of *chih,* "solid qualities," and *wen,* "refinements." [9] "One period of solid qualities, one of refinements; they alternate one after the other," he remarks in SC 30/45, and in his biography of Confucius he attributes the theory to the sage: "One period of refinements, one of solid qualities. Therefore Chou surveyed the two past dynasties. How complete and elegant are its accomplishments! I follow Chou." [10]

The second theory of Ssu-ma Ch'ien, which we have noted in Chapter I, is very much like this one. It is that each of the dynasties of the past was characterized by a particular dominant virtue, good faith for the Hsia, piety for the Shang, and refinement for the Chou, and that as each dynasty declined this virtue devolved into a fault—good faith into rusticity, piety into superstition, and refinement into hollow show —requiring for its correction the next virtue in the cycle. Ch'ien employs this theory in an attempt to explain and rationalize the development of the past so that men may understand the course of action necessary to correct their faults. When the virtue of refinement has declined, for example, it cannot be restored simply by adhering to its outward forms. Thus he remarks in his "Hereditary House of Lu" (SC 33/57): "As for the ceremonies of bowing and giving way, people still observed them, yet how contrary to them were all their actions!" Again, when the cycle demanded a return to simple good faith to repair the fault of hollow show, a complex system of exacting laws and regulations such as that instituted by the Ch'in could only lead to disaster.

Croce writes of the somewhat similar cyclical theories of ancient Greek historiography: ". . . the psychological attitude of the ancients toward history must be described as pessimistic. They saw much greatness fall, but they never discovered the greatness that does not fall and that rises up greater after every fall." [11] This illustrates one basic difference between the ancient Western and Chinese (or at least Confucian) concepts of the cycles of history. The Chinese state was not struck down by a jealous god or gods, but decayed from quite natural causes as its virtue and moral stamina declined. But if states and dynasties rotted and fell to pieces from moral decay, it was apparent that only a reform of policy, a rebirth of virtuous rule, was needed to restore

them to health.[12] The Taoists spoke of the ancient times of simplicity
and nature which had been destroyed by man and his civilization; the
Huai-nan Tzu in particular makes much of this golden age of the far
distant past, now lost almost beyond hope of recovery. But Ssu-ma
Ch'ien made fun of this idea.[13] History to him was a constant process of
growth, and it was impossible to think of returning to some static
golden age of the past. What was possible, however, was the creation
of a new golden age in the present by a wise application of the moral
values appropriate to the times.

Hsün Tzu had emphasized in his teachings that any man has the
potentiality to become as good or as bad as the most virtuous or most
evil men of the past.[14] There is for him no barrier of time separating
the golden ages of the past from the present. "The beginning of heaven
and earth, that is today. The ways of the hundred kings, they are the
ways of later kings."[15] According to this concept of time, history is
not a single line stretching through the ages, but a series of circles
which pass repeatedly through the same or similar points. This conception of the recurrence of history had a great effect upon Ssu-ma
Ch'ien. He was quick to recognize the unique in history. Speaking of
the phenomenal rise of Hsiang Yü (SC 7/76) he remarks: "From
ancient times to the present there has never before been such a thing."
But more often he was conscious of the constantly repeating patterns
of history, the rise and decay of states, the alternation of moral values
and of institutions and rites. He was also conscious of the recurrence
of types of personalities, as he showed by his grouping of men of the
same type into one chapter, or by using the same phrases to describe
figures of widely separated ages who belonged to the same category.[16]
These were all ideas which came to Ch'ien from his sources and his
predecessors. Neither the patterns nor the theories which attempted to
explain them were his own creation. It was his task, he felt, merely to
put his material into such order that the patterns would be clearest, the
lessons of history most apparent, and the ever recurring moral types
of mankind most readily identifiable.

With these old patterns and cycles of history Ssu-ma Ch'ien also inherited from his sources a crude theory of causation which attributed certain happenings to the action of fate (*ming*) or Heaven (*t'ien*). From fairly early times this Chinese concept of Heaven seems to have been quite vague and impersonal. There are no smiting angels, no gods who walk the earth, no divinities who intervene and turn the tide of battle, such as appear in early Western history. But there is a feeling that behind the continued good luck and success of a ruler or a kingdom is the aid and protection of some higher force. This idea is expressed, for example, in the *Tso Commentary* several times when it speaks of the success of the hero Ch'ung-erh who became Duke Wen of Chin: "Since Heaven has raised him up, what man can cast him out?" [17]

There has been much discussion as to whether, or to what extent, Ssu-ma Ch'ien accepted this belief in fate. The difficulty is that Ch'ien is seldom consistent in his avowal of any belief. He is extremely flexible in his opinions, changing his viewpoint and adapting his tone to fit the subject of each chapter. One may, for example, almost always predict what stand Pan Ku will take on a question, for his thinking follows the clearly defined orthodoxy of Latter Han Confucianism. But it is impossible to predict what Ssu-ma Ch'ien will say at any given point. It is equally impossible, as those who have tried will know, to deduce from all of Ssu-ma Ch'ien's scattered utterances a consistent system of thought. He seems rather to let himself be drawn along by his narrative, sighing in sympathy, moralizing, or chiding as the mood strikes him, and proclaiming quite the opposite when another mood is upon him.

Ssu-ma Ch'ien makes frequent reference to this vague aid of Heaven. Some of these opinions may not necessarily be his own, as they are quoted from earlier sources. Following the *Tso Commentary*, for example, he quotes the words concerning Ch'ung-erh: "Heaven is opening up the way for you" (SC 39/44), or concerning the ancestors of Wei: "Heaven will open up the way for them" (SC 44/2), or again of the rising power of Ch'u: "Heaven is now opening up the way for it and it cannot be opposed" (SC 39/75). But it was the brilliant and remarkable rise of Kao-tsu and his band of followers that most often inspired the attribution of Heaven's aid. Chang Liang had said of Kao-tsu, when the latter was still a minor official, that he was one of those to whom Heaven would give its aid (SC 55/7); and Kao-tsu on his deathbed asserted that his success had been due to the "Mandate of Heaven" (SC 8/84). Ssu-ma Ch'ien agreed that the miraculous success of Kao-tsu appeared to be due to help from Heaven, as he says in SC 16/4: "Was it not Heaven, was it not Heaven?" and again, speaking of the way Chang Liang always managed to help Kao-tsu out of difficulties, "Can we say that this was not Heaven?" (SC 55/30). He also says of the spectacular rise of Ch'in to power: "Was it not as though it had been aided by Heaven?" (SC 15/4).

This question of the role of Heaven in human history, and in particular of the so-called "Mandate of Heaven" (*t'ien-ming*), which conferred the right to rule upon a new dynasty, was the subject of considerable controversy in the early Han. In the time of Emperor Ching two scholars, Master Yüan Ku and Master Huang, were discussing the Mandate of Heaven in the emperor's presence. Master Huang, a Taoist, maintained that T'ang and Wu, who overthrew the rulers of the Hsia and Shang dynasties respectively and set up their own dynasties, had been guilty of regicide. This contradicted the traditional Confucian view that, acting under the Mandate of Heaven, these men had been absolved of their allegiance to their former sovereigns and were destined to found new dynasties. Master Yüan Ku then pointed out that, if his opponent's reasoning were true, the Han would also be guilty of regicide in overthrowing the Ch'in. At this crucial point the emperor put a stop to the discussion and, as Ssu-ma Ch'ien remarks, "After this scholars no longer dared openly to discuss questions of who had received the Mandate and who had committed regicide" (SC 121/17). At the beginning of the Latter Han, Pan Piao wrote a long essay, "A Discussion of the Mandate of Kings," *Wang-ming-lun* (HS 100A/8a), in which he asserted that only the heir of a family that had long been distinguished by its virtue and had received signs of divine election was qualified to accept the rule of the empire. This view had been expressed some years earlier by Ch'u Shao-sun. In a conversation between Ch'u and a friend which he has appended to SC 13/31, he writes:

The Mandate of Heaven is difficult to discuss; none but a sage can discern it. Shun, Yü, Hsieh, and Hou-chi [ancestors of the early dynasties] were all descendants of the Yellow Emperor. The Yellow Emperor divined the Mandate of Heaven and ruled the world, and his power and goodness penetrated deeply into later ages. Therefore his descendants were all later set up as emperors. This is the reward of Heaven for virtue. Men do not realize this and simply consider that these men all rose from the rank of commoners. But how could a fellow who is a commoner without any reason rise to become ruler of the world?

What Ch'u Shao-sun does not explain, however, is how the Liu family, if this reasoning is correct, could have risen to the position of rulers of the Han. Pan Piao, writing just after the downfall of Wang Mang when the newly restored Liu emperor was still contending with several pretenders to the throne, was careful to make clear that not only the rulers of the older dynasties but the Liu family as well were descended from a distinguished line of ancient times. For this purpose he made use of the assertion, accepted toward the end of the Former Han, that the Liu family were descendants of Emperor Yao, fourth of the ancient Five Emperors. According to this theory, the Liu family, as descendants of Yao, the Fire Emperor, ruled by virtue of the element fire. It was at this time that the Han accepted fire as its patron element, with its accompanying color red, in place of the element earth, which had been chosen in the reign of Emperor Wu. Thus Pan Piao could assert, as Ch'u Shao-sun had, that it was erroneous to suppose that a commoner who had no great ancestors could ever hope to become an emperor, and point to the Liu family to support his assertion. Pan Ku fully accepted this theory of the ancestry of the Lius. He recites their genealogy at the end of HS 1B/25a and repeatedly refers to the dynasty as the "Fire Han."

This genealogy, however, either did not exist in the time of Ssu-ma Ch'ien, or at least was ignored by him. In spite of his customary attention to genealogy, he can give no more than the vague appelations of

Kao-tsu's parents, the honorary title "Venerable Sire" (*T'ai-kung*), for his father, and "Dame Liu" (*Liu-ao*) for his mother.[18] And in *Shih chi* 16/3 he speaks of how Kao-tsu "rose from the lanes and alleys," i.e., from a very humble position, making no mention of any glorious descent from Emperor Yao. So this whole theory of the noble ancestry of the Liu family, with its broader implication that no family could receive the Mandate of Heaven to rule that did not possess a long and distinguished pedigree, was an invention of the time between Ssu-ma Ch'ien and Pan Ku.

The various references to this supernatural aid or Mandate of Heaven in the *Shih chi* might be dismissed by apologists as no more than a literary convention, a manner of speaking that Ch'ien carried over from an earlier and more superstitious age, were it not for one famous passage. At the end of his "Hereditary House of Wei" (SC 44/50), he writes:

The strategists all say that it was because Wei did not make use of the Lord of Hsin-ling that the state became so feeble and weak and was finally wiped out. But I consider that this is not correct. Heaven at this time had commanded Ch'in to pacify all within the seas, and its task was not yet completed. Although Wei might have had the services of an A-heng [wise minister of the Shang] of what use would it have been?

This statement of Ssu-ma Ch'ien has been the object of much criticism by commentators. One may argue that, to Ch'ien, viewing the massive and seemingly invincible expansion of the power of Ch'in, the fall of a small, weak state like Wei appeared indeed inevitable. We may not quarrel with the fact that Wei was destined to be destroyed, yet Ch'ien's way of expressing this inevitability as "the command of Heaven" seems unworthy of his customary realism. And the fact that he pessimistically denies that able ministers would have been of any help in the situation has won him the enmity of commentators who, themselves bureaucrats dedicated (like the strategists Ch'ien is refuting) to the thesis that good government depends upon the right men in public office, view it as an attack upon the very fundamentals of their trade. Yet it is typical of the human, fallible quality of Ch'ien's writing that even he, this once, should fall from the lofty plane of his usual clarity into what Croce has called "the pessimistic and sceptical view common to man when history, instead of seeming to have been enacted by him and to be proceeding by his own initiative, falls upon him like a heap of stones." [19] So appalling must have seemed the debacle that marked the downfall of the Chou to the early Chinese that only the invocation of a supernatural agent could explain and justify it.

But although his view of the fall of Wei is flatly fatalistic, Ch'ien completely reverses his position in the case of two other famous downfalls. At the end of his "Basic Annals of Hsiang Yü" (SC 7/76), after a description of the spectacular rise of this military leader, he says:

He boasted and made a show of his own achievements. He was obstinate in his opinions and did not abide by established ways. He thought to make himself a dictator, hoping to attack and rule the empire by force. Yet within five years he was dead and his kingdom lost. He met death at Tung-ch'eng, but even at this time he did not wake to or accept responsibility for his errors. "It is Heaven," he declared, "which has brought about my ruin, and no fault of mine in the use of arms!" Was he not indeed deluded?

Here we see Ch'ien expounding quite the opposite view, that men's failures are due primarily to their own faults and may not be wantonly attributed to Heaven or fate. In his biography of the Ch'in general Meng T'ien (SC 88/11) he takes the same position. Meng T'ien had worked to construct the Great Wall which protected Ch'in from the incursions of the barbarians but which was built at the cost of terrible suffering to the people. Meng T'ien was eventually forced to commit suicide by the eunuch Chao Kao and at his death, after protesting his innocence, he suddenly proclaimed that he was deserving of death after all because of his crime of "disturbing the arteries of the earth" when he constructed the walls and roads of the empire. Ssu-ma Ch'ien in his appraisal at the end of the chapter points out the terrible burden which these great works placed upon the people. He blames Meng T'ien and his brother for not trying to alleviate the ills of the common people but instead "toadying to the will of the emperor in beginning these constructions. Was it not right that for this he and his brother should meet with punishment? What is this 'crime of the arteries of the earth?' "

But perhaps the sharpest point of controversy in this question of fate was the downfall of Ch'in. To the end of his "Basic Annals of the First Emperor of Ch'in" (SC 6/87) Ch'ien has appended the famous essay "The Faults of Ch'in" (*Kuo-Ch'in-lun*), by Chia I.[20] In this essay on the phenomenal rise of Ch'in and the errors and crimes that led to its downfall Chia I states:

If Tzu-ying [nephew of the Second Emperor who was made ruler shortly before the dynasty fell] had had the talent of a mediocre ruler with even ordinary counselors, then although there was a rebellion east of the mountains he might have kept the territory of Ch'in intact and the ancestral sacrifices of the state need not have come to an end (SC 6/88).

Chia I is here emphasizing the point that success depends upon wise and benevolent rule and the use of good officials, and that the Ch'in had gone to pieces so quickly not because of any adverse fate but because of its own internal rottenness and the discontent of its people.[21]

But, as we have seen above in discussions of the Mandate of Heaven, if a scholar suggested that the Ch'in was not necessarily destined to fall, he called into doubt the right of the Han to overthrow and replace it and so moved into very dangerous ground. Pan Ku disagreed with Chia I's opinion that Tzu-ying might, by good government, have saved his state. When he remarked so to friends, he was summoned by Emperor Ming to expound his views, which he did in a short essay that has now been appended to the very end of SC 6/111, after Chia I's essay. His point, which seems an acceptable one, is that by the time of Tzu-ying the situation had degenerated beyond hope of repair. "When the river has burst its dikes it cannot again be dammed up; when a fish has rotted to pieces it cannot be put back together again" (SC 6/113). In other words, as did Ssu-ma Ch'ien in the case of the downfall of Wei, he felt that there is a point beyond which no amount of good government and wise counsel can save a perishing state. But the emperor scented treason in Ssu-ma Ch'ien's approval of Chia I's views and was in no mood to listen to disinterested discussions of historical causation. "Ssu-ma Ch'ien," he declared, "wrote his book as the work of one family, making a name for himself in later ages. But because he fell into error and suffered punishment, he turned around and used veiled words to criticize and slander, attacking his own times. He was no righteous scholar!" [22]

All of these stories, of course, do not prove that either Ssu-ma Ch'ien or Pan Ku held consistently to a belief in fate. What they do show, however, is the difficulty that the Chinese historian faced in trying to make objective statements about history and its causes. If he evoked a vague fatalism, then other scholars and bureaucrats at once attacked him for ignoring the all-important human causes in history. But if he were too frank about the human failings of rulers or the reasons for the change of dynasties, he was likely to become entangled in perilous discussions of imperial destiny. We may not agree with Emperor Ming that Ssu-ma Ch'ien was guilty of disloyalty to his age by endorsing the view that the Ch'in was not necessarily fated to fall. But the attitude of the emperor is enough to tell us why Ssu-ma Ch'ien and his fellow historians used, indeed were forced to use, "veiled words" in their writing. It is hardly surprising that, even had they wished to, they could not always be consistent in their views.[23]

Finally something must be said about Ssu-ma Ch'ien's economic thought.[24] As in other aspects of his thought, his scattered statements on this subject are not sufficiently detailed and clear to allow any systematic analysis. But it can be said that he favored a laissez-faire policy and was clearly opposed to the efforts of Emperor Wu to take over private trade monopolies for government profit. Although he agreed with most contemporary scholars that farming was the most honorable enterprise, the basis of national well-being, he was realistic enough to recognize that far greater profits were to be gained in industry and trade. Because he dared to express this view frankly, he was severely criticized by later Confucianists who felt that nothing favorable should ever be said about the merchant class lest farmers be tempted to give up their labors and enter trade. Both Pan Piao and Pan Ku complain that Ch'ien, in his biographies of wealthy merchants, "honors those who were skilled at making a profit and heaps shame on those in poverty and low station" (HS 62/25b). As in the case of many criticisms of the *Shih chi,* this is based upon a distorted view of Ch'ien's statement. What he says, qualifying himself very carefully, is: "If a man is not a gentleman of talent who has deliberately sought retirement, and if he grows old in poverty and lowliness, and still insists upon talking about 'benevolence and righteousness,' then he ought to be ashamed of himself." In other words, what Ch'ien is criticizing is not the fact that people grow old poor, but the fact that, having failed to make any money, they adopt a self-righteous attitude and insist it is wholly because they have been following lofty moral principles. Such hypocrisy he could not abide.[25]

One can make a profit, Ch'ien points out, by conducting his business astutely, by building up a trade in sauces and pickles, by cornering a salt monopoly. Profit indeed at times seems to rule all mankind.[26] But, as he is careful to add, profit is not a fit motivation for governments. Governments are made up of gentlemen who are concerned with higher and more altruistic motives. Therefore he is absolutely opposed to the government interfering with the economic life of the nation for the purpose of competing with the people for profit.

This is probably all that one may venture to say about the thought of Ssu-ma Ch'ien. As I have said, his statements are full of contradictions and ambiguities. He expounds his ideas subtly and often with deliberate vagueness, and his writing, no matter how one forces it, will produce no "system" of thought. Yet in a sense the *Shih chi* is the work of a philosophical school, the school of Ssu-ma T'an and Ssu-ma Ch'ien. As such, how can we define its characteristics, and where does it fit into the history of Chinese thought?

The *Shih chi* is not, of course, primarily the statement of a single school of thought, as are the other works that are roughly contemporary with it, the *Huai-nan Tzu,* the *Ch'un-ch'iu fan-lu* or the *Yen-t'ieh-lun.* Philosophically it represents no more than a general approach to life and history, an attitude of mind. The mind of Ssu-ma Ch'ien is, first of all, like all the best minds of the early Han, dedicated to rationalism. The element of the miraculous and the supernatural is remarkably small in the *Shih chi,* comparing favorably not only with Christian and Buddhist historiography but even with that of the classical West. It is confined for the most part to those sections derived from older works such as the *Tso Commentary,* or the speeches and assertions of the magicians of Han times which Ssu-ma Ch'ien, though he reported them, clearly condemned. At times he even took pains to attack the superstitious beliefs of his time, as in SC 86/39, where he denies the tale that at the command of Prince Tan the heavens rained grain and horses grew horns.

Another characteristic of Ch'ien's writing that he shares with many of the men of the early Han is his eclecticism. His father had studied the major philosophies of the day and written a brief survey of their teachings, and Ch'ien, too, was obviously familiar with the literature of these various schools. In his day the Confucian Classics had only just received official sanction as the basis of learning and it was still possible for a man to select his ideas from a variety of sources without appearing heretical. In his preface to the biographies of the wandering knights (SC 124), for example, Ch'ien quotes from such diverse authors as Han Fei Tzu, Chuang Tzu, Hsün Tzu, and Kuan Tzu. But as the Confucian school grew to a position of unchallenged dominance in the following centuries this eclecticism came to be frowned upon. When Pan Ku wrote a new preface to this chapter to replace that of his predecessor which he found offensive, he confined himself to quotations from the *Analects* and *Mencius.*

The third characteristic of the thinking of Ssu-ma Ch'ien is his realism. We have already noted the position of importance which he accorded to figures such as Hsiang Yü and Ch'en Shê, who, although they were never unanimously recognized in their rule and eventually fell from power, exercised great actual authority in their time. Equally significant is the way he relegated puppet rulers such as Emperor Hui to minor positions. This realistic treatment of history stands in contrast to the more careful consideration for the form and name of authority, rather than its reality, that marks the *Han shu* and later histories. But even more striking is the contrast in Ssu-ma Ch'ien's whole attitude toward the past. He rejected the Taoist concept of history as a steady devolution from the ancient days of primal simplicity and naturalness. Again, though he paid high tribute to the Confucian golden ages, the days of the sage emperors Yao and Shun, Yü, T'ang, and the founders of the Chou, he did not advocate any forced attempt to return to the ways of these times. On the contrary he felt that the men of his day had much to learn, not from these utopias of the far distant past, but from the troubled times of the late Chou and Ch'in that had just closed. As he writes in SC 18/5:

One who lives in the present age and considers the ways of the past has his own mirror wherein he may see that the two are not necessarily entirely alike. The emperors and kings each had different rites and different things which they considered important. And if a man hopes to win success and establish a lasting family, he cannot afford to confuse them!

Again, in discussing the way in which the Ch'in rose to power (SC 15/5), he insists that his age can learn much from the history of this period. "Why," he asks, "must one learn only from ancient times? . . . Take for your model the kings of later ages," he advises, "for they are near to us and the forms of their customs are like ours." Such a view of the past was probably rare in Ch'ien's own day. It was to become even rarer as the Confucian idealization of the ancient kings and their glorious ways gained universal acceptance among the intellectuals of the Han. The *Han shu* never tires of describing these wise kings of ancient times and contrasting them with the sad spectacle of the present.

The last and perhaps most important mark of Ssu-ma Ch'ien's writing is his humanity. He assembled the old records and chronicles of the past, copied out their entries, related their tales and recorded their dates, allowing himself only a few short personal remarks set aside from the body of his narrative at the beginning or end of his chapters. There are no massive collections of letters, poems, or intimate papers

of Ch'ien such as we possess for the great Sung historians. It is on
the basis of what he reveals of himself in his history alone that we
know him. And yet in these brief remarks he comes through as one
of the most warm and vivid personalities of Chinese historiography.
He wrote of history as though he had lived through it, as indeed he
must have done in his mind when he traveled about the country,
viewed the landmarks of the past, and talked with others about historical events. He possessed that deep love and sympathy for the past
that is the mark of all truly great historians. He did not merely stand
aside and record with cold detachment the lives of the men of the past,
but himself participated in their triumphs and sorrows, as he reveals
by his frequent outbursts of emotion, his sighs of pity and admiration
at the end of his chapters. No one was above his criticism, no one beneath his sympathy. It is this quality of warmth, intimacy, and humanity in his writing, more than anything else, perhaps, that has won for
his work the admiration of so many generations of readers and assured
it an imperishable position in the Chinese heritage.

SSU-MA CH'IEN'S THEORY OF LITERATURE

One aspect of Ssu-ma Ch'ien's thought, his theory of literature, demands special consideration because of its important bearing upon his
own work. Although there are scattered statements on the nature and
function of literature, mostly confined to poetry, in earlier works,
Ssu-ma Ch'ien's remarks represent perhaps the first exposition of a
general theory of literature. As such they occupy an important place
in the history of Chinese literary criticism.

Ssu-ma Ch'ien actually expounds two theories of the motivation and
function of literature. The first of these occurs in Ch'ien's conversation
with Hu Sui concerning his own writings, where he remarks:

I have heard my father say that Fu Hsi, purest and most virtuous of ancient
men, made the eight trigrams of the *Book of Changes;* the *Book of Documents* records the glorious age of Yao and Shun, and at that time the *Rites*
and *Music* were composed; the makers of the *Odes* celebrated the golden age
of T'ang and Wu in song. The *Spring and Autumn Annals* picks out the

good and condemns the evil, exalting the virtue of the Three Dynasties and praising the House of Chou. It does not confine itself solely to criticism and ridicule.

According to this theory, literature, in the main, is the product of peaceful, prosperous times and its primary purpose is to record these glorious times. This, according to the full passage, is the essential nature of the five Classics and of Ssu-ma Ch'ien's own work. It is important to note here that Ch'ien introduces the whole speech with the words, "I have heard my father say." In other words, this is actually Ssu-ma T'an's theory of literature, which his son is here repeating with apparent agreement. When we look back at the words of Ssu-ma T'an earlier in the chapter, we find confirmation of this point. T'an, in his words to his son just before his death, emphasizes the glory of the Han and of the reign of Emperor Wu, and his own duty, which he has failed to fulfill, to "set forth a record of all the enlightened rulers and wise lords, the faithful ministers and gentlemen who were ready to die for the right." Literature, according to this view, is the product of a great age and its purpose is praise.

But Ssu-ma Ch'ien relates this theory only once, attributing it to his father. Either from the first he did not believe in it, or he abandoned it in his later years. In his autobiography, after referring to his punishment, he writes:

I left the prison and pondered deeply to myself, saying: The writers of the *Odes* and the *Documents* were troubled and in distress and they tried to set forth the meaning of their desires and hopes. Of old when the Chief of the West was imprisoned at Yu Li, he spent his time expanding the *Book of Changes;* Confucius was in distress between Ch'en and Ts'ai and he made the *Spring and Autumn;* when Ch'ü Yüan was exiled, he composed his poem "Encountering Sorrow"; after Tso Ch'iu lost his sight he composed the *Narratives from the States;* when Sun Tzu had had his feet amputated he set forth the *Art of War;* Lü Pu-wei was banished to Shu but his *Lü-lan* has been handed down through the ages; while Han Fei Tzu was held prisoner in Ch'in he wrote the "Difficulties of Disputation" and "The Sorrow of Standing Alone"; most of the three hundred poems of the *Book of Odes* were written when the sages poured forth their anger and dissatisfaction. All these men had a rankling in their hearts, for they were not able to accomplish what they had hoped. Therefore they wrote about past affairs in order to pass on their thoughts to future ages.

Here we see Ch'ien expounding a very different theory according to which literature is not the product of peace and prosperity but of suffering and anger. It is motivated by frustration and disappointment in political life and its purpose is not that of bringing glory to the age through praise but the much more personal one of relaying the words of the author himself, of assuring him of an audience for his grievances in future ages and seeking his own immortal fame. In this second theory Ch'ien does not confine himself to the five Classics but includes other works of philosophy, history, and poetry of earlier ages. All literature, for him, springs from the same impulse and seeks the same aims and, as we have seen, Ch'ien's own history was only the latest in this series of writings.

This theory, the expression of Ch'ien's own, very personal beliefs, is repeated and referred to throughout his writings. In his letter to Jen An, he repeats the recital of great writers of the past and their motives for writing in the same words, adding himself to the list. In these parallel passages we see the two parts of the theory combined, the motivation of literature, suffering, and its objective, immortal fame. Elsewhere Ch'ien treats the two facets separately. In his biography of Ch'ü Yüan (SC 84/4) he dwells upon the anger and resentment which motivate literature. In a passage that rings with personal conviction he writes: "To be sincere and yet be doubted, to be loyal and yet suffer slander—can a man in such a situation be without anger? Did not Ch'ü Yüan's composition of the 'Encountering Sorrow' spring from this anger?" Ssu-ma Ch'ien, who was very much alive to the role of emotions and personal feelings in history, realized the importance of anger and resentment in men's behavior. At the end of his biography of Wu Tzu-hsü (SC 66/23), a man spectacularly motivated by hatred, he remarks: "How terrible indeed is the poison of anger in men!" Hardship and suffering, too, he saw as great forces molding the lives and character of men. At the end of his biography of Fan Chü and Ts'ai Tse (SC 79/49), he points out that luck and the right opportunities have a great deal to do with success. "But," he concludes, "if these two men had not known suffering and hardship, how could they have risen to such heights?" Great deeds, and in particular great literature, are the product, according to Ch'ien, of suffering and anguish, longing and anger. It is hardly a coincidence that these were the very feelings and experiences of Ch'ien himself.

The aim of literature, as we have seen, is the immortality of fame. In his biography of Confucius (SC 47/82) Ch'ien writes:

The Master said, "Alas! Alas! The superior man hates the thought of his name not being mentioned after his death. My way is not practiced. How shall I make myself known to later ages?" With this he used the historical records and made the *Spring and Autumn Annals.*

The first part of this passage is of course a quotation from the *Analects* (XV, 19). But the sentence "How shall I make myself known to later ages?" appears to be Ch'ien's own words which he puts into the mouth of the sage. Here, and in *Shih chi* 121/3, he is eager to make clear that Confucius wrote the *Spring and Autumn Annals* out of despair and frustration and that his object was to gain the recognition of later ages. In his biography of Yü Ch'ing, Ch'ien refers to this writer, author of a work entitled *Yü-shih ch'un-ch'iu,* in the following words: "He could not accomplish his aims, and so he wrote a book" (SC 76/21), and later adds, "If Yü Ch'ing had not known hardship and despair, then he would have been unable to write his book and make himself known to later ages" (SC 76/23).

For the Chinese the immortality of history was the great goal of life. Ch'ien emphasizes this search for fame in his general introduction to the *lieh-chuan,* the "Biography of Po I" (SC 61/15), quoting again the words of Confucius: "The superior man hates the thought of his name not being mentioned after his death." The superior man of ancient China could not join the common mob in its search for profit, nor could he strive for political power if he must use unjust means to acquire it. His only proper concern was his conduct and reputation, the kind of name he was going to leave behind in the world. Heaven, as Ch'ien points out in this chapter, does not invariably reward the good man nor does it always punish the wicked. We must look to mankind for our own reward, the reward of a good or bad name. The most terrible thing that could happen to a man was to blunder so badly, to go so morally awry, that he deserved not even pity or hatred, but only laughter. *T'ien-hsia-chih-hsiao,* the bitter, scornful laughter of the world is a phrase that rings through the *Shih chi,* marking the greatest fools of history, the men who left behind them an evil reputation.[27] And the greatest reward a man could receive was to make for himself a great name in history, "a name that," as Lu Chung-lien says in his letter (SC 83/17), "shall last until the decay of heaven and earth."

Hsün Tzu had optimistically declared of the superior man that "his body dies but his name grows ever more renowned." [28] But Ssu-ma Ch'ien has pointed out the one difficulty in this process. A man must have someone who will recognize his worth and transmit his name to future ages. An intermediary is needed if virtuous and deserving men, particularly those who did not succeed in achieving great power or eminence in their time, are not to be forgotten. "The hermit-scholars hiding in their caves may be ever so correct in their givings and takings, and yet the names of them and their kind vanish away like smoke without receiving a word of praise. Is this not pitiful?" writes Ch'ien in his biography of Po I (SC 61/17), and he repeats his lament in the biography of the wandering knights (SC 124/6) whose names have "vanished like smoke and are no longer known." It was Confucius, he points out, who insured the fame of Po I and Confucius' favorite disciple, Yen Hui, by praising them in his conversations, which were written down and transmitted to the ages. And it is Ssu-ma Ch'ien who is filling this same role by writing his own book, the history of all the great and deserving men of the past. His purpose, as he makes clear, is to insure immortal fame for himself and his father. But his generosity extends beyond himself to all men of worth, insuring to them likewise a fame of ever growing renown. Literature, then, was for him a vital part of human life, rising from deep emotional anguish and despair, and aiming at the highest of human goals, immortality. It is literature alone that will last "until heaven and earth decay!"

THE SHIH CHI *AS LITERATURE*

Professor Emery Neff, pointing out the vital role which the literary sense plays in the writing of history, remarks that "it has given historians their subtlest and profoundest insights into the human spirit." [29] It is undoubtedly partly because Ssu-ma Ch'ien possessed this literary sense in a degree seldom equaled by other historians of his country that his work has been so much read and so deeply reverenced in China, Korea, and Japan. Ch'ien's view of literature, which recognized the same motivation and objective for all types of writing, is enough to demonstrate that he was deeply concerned with the theory and practice of the art of letters. We find further proof of this interest in the fact that Ch'ien's heroes, the men toward whom he felt the warmest and most intimate sympathy, are so often men of literature—the poets Ch'ü Yüan and Chia I, and the father of all Chinese literature, Confucius.

Ch'ien believed that literature is a means of salvation, that a man's literary works are what will assure his fame and make him known to later ages. The poems of the poet, the discourses of the philosopher represent the very core and essence of their personalities. For this reason, when describing men of ancient times nothing is so appropriate as the quotation of their writings. In his biography of Ch'ü Yüan and Chia I, for example, Ch'ien does not devote great space to the facts of their lives, although in the case of Chia I he probably had access to many such facts and anecdotes. Instead he quotes in full those poems which he feels most clearly reveal their true personalities and aspirations. For, he felt, rather than in a list of dry data, the life of the poet exists in his own poems.

In other chapters Ch'ien copied songs, popular sayings, proverbs, letters, memorials, edicts, philosophical essays, funeral orations, stone inscriptions, any scrap of literature that he thought would bring to life his subject better than his own words could. Such miscellaneous writings had often been included in earlier works of a historical nature, such as the *Tso Commentary* or the *Intrigues of the Warring States*. But the fact that Ch'ien continued the practice in his own work and made it a recognized part of standard historical method was a fortunate event for Chinese historiography. Later historians might fall far short of Ch'ien's integrity and art, but no matter how inferior their own talent, so long as they continued to copy into their narrative the texts of such literary works, their histories could never become completely void of value and interest. From all the pages of Herodotus and Thucydides we can gather hardly more than a handful of oracular ditties or scraps of Homer quoted by the historians. But Chinese histories such as the *Shih chi* and *Han shu* often include so many poems and works of literature that they reach the proportions of literary anthologies of the period whose value is independent of the excellence or mediocrity of the historians themselves.

In the time of Ssu-ma Ch'ien there was as yet no concept of the poet as a particular type of individual or of poetry as a profession. Like other kinds of literature, poetry might be written by any man of intelligence and sensitivity with no further qualification than the desire to express an emotion. And like other types of literature, poetry was strongly political in tone, for politics, statecraft in the broadest sense of the word, was the one great concern of men of intelligence and moral sensitivity. The poems of the *Book of Odes* were composed anonymously by the common people or by court officials and aristocrats, not by particular men identified as "poets," and this tradition continued into the Han. The small amount of poetry that is attributed to the late Chou and early Han is the work of rulers, generals, and statesmen. The figure of Ch'ü Yüan, melancholy and emaciated, wandering in exile, bears a superficial resemblance to the romantic Western concept of "the poet." But it must be remembered that both Ch'ü Yüan and Chia I were primarily statesmen. They turned to poetry only after their careers as officials were frustrated, and their poetry was only a substitute outlet for the ideas and passions they longed to expend in the duties of office. In like manner the great representative of the early Han poetic spirit, Ssu-ma Hsiang-ju, was a government official whose writings are wholly concerned with the life of the court and affairs of state. Literature and politics in the Han were inseparable; there was no such thing as writing that was without political significance, as in later ages there was to be scarcely a major political figure who was not also a poet and litterateur.

Ssu-ma Ch'ien undoubtedly had a great fondness for poetry, as he did for music. Like most of the famous literary men of his time he wrote works in the *fu* or rimeprose form, though no completely reliable texts of these exist today. In addition he included in his history remarks on poetic interpretation [30] as well as a great many poems and songs attributed to the great men of the past. The poems of the *Book of Odes,* being for the most part anonymous, could not easily be worked into his narrative, though he used them as sources for facts and legends. But from the *Book of Documents* he copied the songs of Emperor Yü and his minister Kao Yao which he found so moving,[31] and from other earlier works songs attributed to Po I, Confucius, Ching K'o, Hsiang Yü, Kao-tsu, and many others. Ch'ien utilized these songs in his narrative with striking skill. Each comes at a crucial point in the chapter, at a moment of pause before or after the climax, summing up the essence of a life, the heart of the narrative. The contrasting portraits of Hsiang Yü and his opponent Kao-tsu are beautifully balanced by the songs of the two men. That of Hsiang Yü, a bitter lament for lost power, appears just before his final defeat, summing up the whole passionate and tragic pattern of his life (SC 7/69). The song of Kao-tsu, the victor, comes in a moment of peace, when the great battles are over and the emperor, with typical farsighted reflection, ponders the problem of who will carry on his work (SC 8/80).[32] The song of Ching K'o, expressing the fierce determination that governed his fate, comes in a scene of quiet parting as he sets out upon his fateful journey (SC 86/33); the song of Confucius in his old age foretells his approaching death and hints at his true stature, unrecognized by the men of his time (SC 47/85). Ch'ien was very emotional, as his frequent admissions of deep feeling show. But instead of pouring out his own feelings in the midst of his narrative, he entrusted them to these songs whose emotional power he knew must move his readers more deeply and poignantly than could any words of his own. In the "Treatise on The

River and Canals" (SC 29/14) he describes the great break in the dikes of the Yellow River at Hu-tzu which Emperor Wu and his attendants personally helped to repair. Overseeing the work in anxious solicitude, the emperor composed a song describing the scene. Ch'ien himself was a member of the party and, as he says at the end of the chapter, was much moved by the song of the emperor. But he relates the entire incident without a trace of personal feeling, leaving the song itself to convey all the terror, savagery, and sorrow of the scene.

Ch'ien was well aware of the dangers involved in using such poems and songs in a work of history. His chapter on Po I (SC 61) discusses the discrepancy between the account of Po I and his brother given by Confucius and the picture of their personalities conveyed by the song attributed to them, implying that the poem is unreliable. But where no such doubt or discrepancy stood in the way, he seems to have utilized poems whenever possible. This practice not only adds greatly to the power and effectiveness of his narrative, but gives his history, and later histories which followed his practice, a special value in the study of Chinese literature.

Ch'ien displays this same sense of the dramatic in his use of other types of literature. Chavannes has pointed out the historical importance of the stone inscriptions of the First Emperor of the Ch'in which Ch'ien has copied into his "Annals of the First Emperor" (SC 7).[33] Undoubtedly the inscriptions give valuable data on the ideals of the Ch'in, though, since they all say much the same thing, one would have been sufficient to convey this information. But this interest was not, it seems to me, the sole, or perhaps even the primary reason why Ch'ien included the inscriptions in his narrative. Year after year, as the people of the empire groaned in ever deepening oppression, as weird happenings and stirrings of revolt troubled the nation, the stone inscriptions continued without change to proclaim in resounding hyperboles the virtue and glory of the emperor and the peace and order of his reign. This striking contrast between pretension and reality, between what the First Emperor claimed to be and what he was, brings home to the reader more clearly than could any mere statement of the fact the megalomania and essential falseness of the Ch'in.

Something must be said about Ssu-ma Ch'ien's use of another literary device which figures prominently in Greek and Roman historical writing, the speech. I have already mentioned the intimate connection which existed in Chinese literature between rhetoric and history. In the discussions and expositions of the late Chou philosophers, it is most often not the compelling logic which wins an argument but the apt reference to the past, the evocation of historical fact. Thus, while history became an aid to effective argumentation, these speeches and debates themselves often in later ages became sources for a knowledge of the past. Many of Ch'ien's sources, such as the commentaries on the *Spring and Autumn Annals* or the *Intrigues of the Warring States,* were basically philosophical works which used historical ancedotes for didactic ends, and their favorite method of instruction was the debate or oration. It was inevitable, therefore, that Ch'ien's narrative, if it was not to be unbearably lean and dry, should be filled out with these records of speeches. Large sections of his history of the feudal states or whole biographies had to be constructed out of lengthy diplomatic debates set within the barest factual framework.

But this abundance of direct discourse constituted no fault in Chinese eyes. We have noted the tradition of the two ancient historians who recorded respectively the words and actions of the ruler, and the two Classics, the *Book of Documents* and the *Spring and Autumn Annals,* which were supposed to have derived from these records. Words (*yen*) were fully as important to the Chinese as deeds (*shih*). The reason for this, I believe, is the emphasis which Chinese thought places upon men's wills or intentions (*chih*). At the end of his biographies of famous assassin-retainers (SC 86/40) Ch'ien writes:

Of these five men from Ts'ao Mo to Ching K'o, some succeeded in carrying out their duty and some did not. But it is perfectly clear that they had determined upon the deed. They were not false to their intentions. Is it not right that their names should be handed down to later ages?

A modern historian writing of the rise of the Ch'in would probably do little more than refer to the plot of Ching K'o to assassinate the man who later became the First Emperor of the Ch'in. Since Ching K'o failed in his plot, it may well be argued that he had no influence upon the course of events and so does not deserve a place in a history of the period. But Ch'ien's work is not so much a record of the facts of history as a record of the hopes, ambitions, and wills of men. Whether a man succeeded or failed, whether he actually changed the course of history or not, is secondary to the question of what he wished and tried to do. It is for this reason that speeches, conversations, the declarations of intent, are often more important in the *Shih chi* narrative than the recital of actual deeds.

It should also be kept in mind that almost all literature at this time was the product of one class, the scholar-officials, and was designed primarily to be read by men of this class. Its principal concern was politics, the ordering of the state, and it was particularly interested in the question, so important to these men, of how a minister can most effectively counsel and influence his lord or superior. Chapter after chapter of the *Shih chi* is concerned with the problem of the success or failure of ministers in advising rulers. Ch'ien even devotes a special chapter to men who were famous for using the humorous anecdote or witty retort to advise and reprimand an erring ruler (SC 126). The modern reader may weary at times of the endless highflown speeches and memorials that fill the chapters of Chinese history and seem about to crowd the facts quite off the page. But we must remember that it was often precisely this rhetoric, and its success or failure, that interested the Chinese student of history. Works of history were for him the handbooks of political theory and practice.

Ssu-ma Ch'ien displays great skill in his presentation of these dramatic scenes of debate and persuasion. In his biography of Li Ssu (SC 87) he relates in full the long, overpowering speeches of the eunuch Chao Kao which eventually forced Li Ssu and Hu Hai to consent to his plan to change the heir to the throne. In the biography of Han Hsin (SC 92) we are given again and again the long list of felicitous argu-

ments by which, over his repeated refusals, K'uai T'ung at last persuaded Han Hsin to revolt.[34] In the biography of Liu An (SC 118) we
have the opposite situation, in which the loyal minister Wu Pei employs all the devices of rhetoric in a vain attempt to dissuade the prince
from his plan to start a rebellion. The modern historian would probably be content to note that Wu Pei tried unsuccessfully to dissuade
the prince or that K'uai T'ung talked Han Hsin into starting a revolt.
But the Chinese reader, himself a minister or candidate for an official
career, would want to know exactly how these men argued their cases.
He was less interested in the final effect of the rhetoric than in the
rhetoric itself, for what it might teach him for his own use, and for
what it revealed of the character of the counselors and the counselled.

This use of conversations and speeches to reveal and criticize the
personalities of his subjects is a favorite device of Ssu-ma Ch'ien. There
was an old story that Confucius and Lao Tzu once met and talked together in the Chou capital. Ch'ien splits the story in two. In his biography of Confucius (SC 47/14) he recounts Lao Tzu's remarks in which
the Taoist warns Confucius of his fatal tendency to be too honest in
appraising and criticizing the faults of others; in the biography of Lao
Tzu (SC 63/5) he puts Confucius' tribute to the mystical worth of the
Taoist sage. Thus he makes use of the comments of a third party to
build up his picture of the personality and stature of each man. In his
biography of the Legalist philosopher Lord Shang (SC 68/16) he in-
serts the long critique of Shang's character by Chao Liang which serves
effectively to point out all the faults and evils of the man. In this way
the historian, without ever resorting to direct comment of his own, can
convey through the conversations and criticisms of his characters a
clear picture of their true personalities. Ku Yen-wu has pointed out in
particular the way Ch'ien frequently ends his biographies with the remarks of a third person upon the subject of the chapter.[35] These remarks, underlined by their position at the very end of the narrative,
serve to sum up the historian's own opinion. The most wry and biting
of Ch'ien's indirect criticims is perhaps that which ends his chapter on
economics (SC 30/44). After a long and impersonal description of the

economic policies advocated by the Legalist Sang Hung-yang and put into practice by Emperor Wu, Ch'ien notes that at this time there was a drought and the emperor asked his officials how they might obtain rain. "The prefectural officials," answers P'u Shih, a violent opponent of Sang Hung-yang and his policies, "are supposed to look out for food taxes and clothing levies, and that is all. Now Hung-yang has the officials sitting in the market and lined up in the stalls selling goods in search of profit. If Your Majesty were to boil Hung-Yang alive, then I believe Heaven would send us rain." With this suggestion Ch'ien ends his narrative.

It is probably as useless to question the reliability of Ch'ien's conversations and speeches as to ask the same question concerning the speeches of Herodotus and Thucydides. Those for the earlier periods we know Ch'ien copied almost verbatim from his sources, for in most cases we have the sources with which to check. In the case of Ch'in and Han times he may have had documents, reports, memorials, or court records to draw upon that we cannot know about now. Some chapters, such as the biographies of the five sons of Emperor Ching (SC 59) involve court investigations, trials, testimony of witnesses, etc., and may very well be based upon reports which were sent to the central government and preserved there where Ch'ien could use them. But these explanations cover only a limited number of cases. How much did Ssu-ma Ch'ien and Pan Ku, or Herodotus and Plutarch, for that matter, know about what kings said to their concubines and eunuchs in the seclusion of palace chambers? In many cases we may suppose almost nothing. Their reports of these conversations are probably based on no more than rumor, intuition, and art. But there is one interesting point to notice in the speeches of the *Shih chi*. Very often the Han orators, such as Shu-sun T'ung (SC 99) or Yüan Ang (SC 101), in their speeches refer to historical events of the Ch'in and early Han—events related earlier in the *Shih chi* but of so secret a nature as to make us wonder how even Ch'ien knew of them. In the face of this fact, we must assume one of two things: either Ch'ien not only invented his stories of the scandals of the inner court but also took the

trouble to insert references to these secret affairs in speeches attributed
to men of a later time; or else these seemingly secret affairs were public
knowledge in the Han. When we read that Empress Lü mutilated the
late emperor's favorite concubine, Lady Ch'i, and called her the "human swine," we may suspect Ch'ien of reporting mere gossip. But
when we read that Yüan Ang warned Emperor Wen of the danger of
paying greater honor to his concubine than he did to his empress with
the words, "Has Your Majesty alone not seen the 'human swine?'"
(SC 101/8), we must conclude that such gossip was commonly known
and accepted as fact not only by Ch'ien himself but by the rulers and
officials of the time.

Toynbee has written of the Greek historians:

The semi-fictitious speech . . . is clearly a dangerous instrument in a historian's hands, and yet we have discovered nothing equivalent to take its
place. . . . The Hellenic method of portrayal may be excessively "idealized"
or "subjective," but we have no right to criticize Solomon's architecture so
long as we refuse, in our own case, to venture beyond the limits of David.[36]

We may well doubt the reliability of the *Shih chi*'s elaborate speeches
and secret counsels, its intimate conversations and whispered remarks,
insisting that Ch'ien could not have had any record of such utterances.
But we must admit that without the use of these Ch'ien could never,
in the space at his command, have built up the series of vivid and life-
like portraits that have caught the fancy of generations and lived in the
memory of his readers. And this, we must not forget, was his primary
aim—that the men of his history should be remembered. With less art
he might never have been able to achieve it.

These characteristic traits of Ch'ien's writing and thought are perhaps nowhere better illustrated than in his "Hereditary House of Confucius" (SC 47). This chapter has been the subject of much controversy.
Admirers of the *Shih chi* have termed it a key section in the history
and a literary masterpiece, while critics such as Professor Creel have
condemned it as "a slipshod performance" "full of anachronisms, in-
coherence and absurdities." [37] Much of the biography, there can be no
doubt, is historically suspect. By Han times the body of lore surround-

ing the life of Confucius had already swelled to considerable proportions and was still growing. Ch'ien in his biography was presenting,
rather uncritically, to be sure, no more than the picture of Confucius
held by most men of his age, avoiding, as always, the obviously absurd
and apocryphal. It is not, needless to say, the picture of Confucius held
by later ages of Chinese scholars, nor by historians today, which is one
reason it has attracted criticism. In addition the charge made by Pan
Ku that Ch'ien favored Taoism over Confucianism has led scholars to
be especially suspicious of the biography. Professor Creel, himself a
biographer of Confucius, even goes so far as to assert that the whole
chapter is a satire, intended to damn Confucius while it appears to
praise him.[38]

Since this charge of Taoist sympathies appears so often in discussions
of the *Shih chi,* it may be well at this point to go over briefly some of
the evidence for and against it. The statement of Taoist sympathies, as
I have noted in Chapter Two, was first made by Yang Hsiung when,
referring to the discussion of the Six Schools by Ssu-ma T'an, he attributes T'an's opinions to Ch'ien.[39] But though Ch'ien copied T'an's
eulogy of Taoism into the biography of his father, as any good biographer might do, he gives no indication in any other part of the *Shih
chi* that he shares his father's Taoist leanings. So it must be assumed
that the charge of Taoist sympathies is based solely on Ssu-ma T'an's
opinions in SC 130.

There are, as a matter of fact, a number of indications that Ch'ien
did not share his father's preference for Taoism over Confucianism or,
at least, for the father of the Taoist school, Lao Tzu, over Confucius.
First is the fact that he placed the biography of Confucius in the "Hereditary House" section of his history, among the great feudal leaders
of the past, while that of Lao Tzu appears in the last or "Memoirs"
section. Furthermore, Lao Tzu is not given a whole chapter, but is
lumped together with Chuang Tzu and the Legalist philosophers Shen
Pu-hai and Han Fei Tzu. In view of the low opinion of Legalism held
by Ch'ien and his contemporaries, it is hardly exalted company. The
biography of Lao Tzu itself is no more than a collection of doubtful

legends and attempts to identify the figure of the Taoist recluse, ending with Ch'ien's declaration that "nowadays no one knows which story is correct" (SC 63/8). In other words, as Arthur Waley puts it, "Ssu-ma Ch'ien's 'biography' of Lao Tzu consists simply of a confession that for the writing of such a biography no material existed at all." [40] A true admirer of Taoism, one feels, would have attempted to do better.

Finally we may compare the descriptions which Ch'ien gives in his Table of Contents of the "Hereditary House of Confucius" (SC 130/43) and the chapter containing the biography of Lao Tzu (130/47):

Confucius:

The house of Chou had already declined and the feudal princes acted according to their own selfish desires. Confucius grieved that rites and music had fallen into decay and disuse. He sought out and arranged the Classics, making clear the way of the king, in order to correct the discordant age and turn it back to the right. He set forth his writings so as to constitute the institutions, usages, and laws for the whole world, handed down to posterity in the comprehensive records of the Six Classics. So I made the "Hereditary House of Confucius."

Lao Tzu:

Li Erh—"non-action and self-transformation. That which is pure and still of itself becomes upright."

This description of Li Erh (Lao Tzu) is copied from the end of his biography. The remainder of the passage deals with Han Fei Tzu.

We might continue this list with further passages evidencing Ch'ien's very positive admiration for Confucius (though by no means for all Confucianists) and his coolness toward the Taoist philosophers, but this is sufficient, I believe, to demonstrate that, unless one is prepared to discover incredible subtleties of meaning in Ch'ien's writing, the old charge of Taoist sympathies may well be dismissed.

With that ghost at least for the moment laid, let us return to the "Hereditary House of Confucius." This seems to have been the first attempt to write a full-length biography of the sage. Before Ch'ien's time there existed only scattered references to Confucius in the commentaries on the *Spring and Autumn Annals,* the anecdotes and say-

ings recorded in the *Analects,* and a number of stories concerning him
in the ritual texts and the writings of Mencius, Hsün Tzu, and other
philosophers. Ch'ien, by selecting what he wished from these various
materials, was therefore able with considerable freedom to build up the
picture of Confucius which accorded best with his ideas and those of his
age. It is for this reason that the chapter is of such importance in a study
of the thought and literary technique of the *Shih chi.*

As a biographer Ch'ien seems to have been more interested in the
failures of history, the tragic heroes of the past, than in the successes.
Men such as Hsiao Ho, Ts'ao Ts'an, Wei Ch'ing, or Kung-sun Hung,
who passed relatively uneventful lives and died in their beds, respected
and full of years, provided little to stir the emotions or draw the interest
of the historian, and their biographies are accordingly rather flat and
colorless. It was the tragic tales of men like Wu Tzu-hsü, Hsiang Yü,
Ch'ü Yüan, or Chia I that aroused his sympathy and called forth his
best writing. It is not surprising, therefore, that he should make of Confucius a tragic hero in the same pattern as these others. The principal
themes of his biography of Confucius, as of those of his other tragic
heroes, are despair, frustration, and the animosity of an evil age. Understandably, later critics have mistaken this picture of Confucius, the mis-
fit and the failure, as proof of a basic hostility on the part of Ch'ien
toward his subject. But such a view, I believe, represents a complete
misunderstanding of what Ch'ien was trying to do in this chapter.

Like so much of the *Shih chi,* the biography of Confucius is essentially a dramatic piece of writing which falls naturally into a definite
series of scenes and acts. It begins with a recital of the ancestry of Confucius, his birth, childhood, and early years up to the age of fifty. In
this first section are introduced all the principal themes which dominate
the chapter, the disappointment which Confucius meets in his efforts to
enter an active political career, the moral chaos and degeneration of his
time, and the hostility of his contemporaries toward him and his ideas.
Of particular importance is the scene of the meeting between Confucius
and Lao Tzu in the Chou capital. Lao Tzu, seeing Confucius off on his
journey home, advises him not to be so outspoken in his criticisms of

others, warning him of the danger that awaits one who is too frank in exposing the faults of men. Later scholars, who prefer to imagine Confucius as a sage without flaws, have been offended at the implication that Confucius should have any such failings, and find it darkly significant that the criticism should come from a Taoist patriarch. Yet the entire remainder of Ch'ien's biography of Confucius is a revelation of the consequences of this flaw, the unfortunate proclivity for criticizing others too openly. No matter how much he admired his subjects, Ch'ien never failed to point out the flaws of character that so often hastened their downfall. Mencius failed because of the untimeliness of his ideas —"His ways were unsuited to the times" (SC 74/4); Ch'ü Yüan was defeated by his own boastful arrogance—"No one but myself could do this!" (SC 84/3). In the same way Ch'ien reveals the flaw that was to contribute so much to Confucius' failure: "He who exposes the faults of others endangers himself" (SC 47/14). Without this key to the personality of Confucius, which Ch'ien gives the reader through the words of Lao Tzu, we might be at a loss to understand why he met with such opposition and failure in his lifetime.

The second act of Confucius' biography shows us the sage in his period of power when for a time he achieved high office in the government of Lu. But the effects of his good government alarm the neighboring states, and they plot his overthrow. The ruler of Ch'i sends a troop of entertainers and dancing girls to distract the duke of Lu from affairs of state, achieving such success by this device that Confucius resigns his post in disgust and leaves the state. His brief moment of triumph ends with a sigh and a song as he warns of the power of women and departs upon his years of wandering.

The third section covers the ten or so years during which Confucius and his band of disciples journey from state to state seeking an opportunity to put their doctrines into practice. The time is one of repeated frustration, hardship, and danger. Again and again Confucius is ignored by the feudal lords or actually repulsed, and we are given long speeches by his opponents on the faults and inadequacies of his doctrines. As one critic points out, Ch'ien uses the two words *pu-yung,* "he was not used," as a kind of refrain running through the whole biography.[41] Over and over we see Confucius trying earnestly to find some way to put his doctrines into practice. Over and over he is turned away, slandered, or physically attacked, and the description of his efforts ends with these two words *pu-yung,* "he was not used." Not only is Confucius attacked by the politicians of his day. He and his disciples are also bitterly criticized by another class of men, the recluses, who warn them of the futility of attempting to gain power in a decadent age and advise them to flee from the world. And when Confucius, in his almost pathetic desire to find an outlet for his talents, considers taking employment with some military upstart of dubious character, even his own disciples turn upon him with criticism. Alone in his consuming desire to save the world, he is surrounded by hostility from all sides. In the song of Chieh-yü, the madman of Ch'u, copied from *Analects* XVIII, 5, Ch'ien catches up the atmosphere of isolation, futility, and deepening tragedy which marks this period of Confucius' life: "O phoenix, phoenix, how has your virtue declined!"

It is in this section also that we find Confucius described by the men of Cheng as "a homeless dog" (47/42). The incident is not original with Ch'ien, for we find it in the *Han-shih wai-chuan* (9/10a). Ch'ien merely adopted it from this or some other earlier work. But the fact that he chose this epithet shows that he wished to emphasize the humiliation and lack of recognition suffered by the sage in his lifetime. For the more strongly he emphasizes the outward and material failure of Confucius' life, the greater will appear the moral and spiritual triumph achieved by the sage's teachings in the centuries after his death.

Confucius returns at last from his long and fruitless wanderings to his home in Lu, and his biography enters upon an interlude of comparative calm and optimism. For the first time, in a number of sayings and anecdotes drawn from the *Analects,* we have an intimate picture of the personality and daily life of the teacher and his disciples. We see him, resigned at last to political failure, engaged in the labors that are to insure his immortality, teaching his followers, and arranging and editing the Classics. But this is no more than a brief, sunny interlude, and with the ominous capture of the unicorn, we enter upon the fourth and last act of the sage's life. Confucius, distressed that his ideas have failed so completely to gain acceptance, writes the *Spring and Autumn Annals* to insure the recognition of posterity. With a song prophetic of his true moral grandeur ("Mount T'ai crumbles, the great beam breaks"), the sage signals his approaching death. At his death, Duke Ai of Lu, who ignored Confucius while he lived, sends to the funeral an extravagant eulogy which Ch'ien has copied in full. To the picture of the meanness and hostility which confronted Confucius all his life the biographer adds this last, bitter variation—hypocrisy.

So ends the life of Confucius, a life of almost unrelieved hardship, disappointment, and failure. It is only in the very closing pages of his biography that Ch'ien suddenly reverses the whole picture and shows us Confucius at last triumphant. His tomb becomes the center of a community of disciples. Sacrifices, lectures, festivals, and archery contests are held there, and his personal belongings preserved for later generations to see. The founder of the Han worships there, along with feudal princes and high ministers. In his remarks at the end of the chapter, Ch'ien quotes one last song, this time from the *Book of Odes:* " 'The great mountain, I look up to it; the great road, I travel it.' [42] Although I cannot reach it," he adds, "my heart goes out toward it. When I read the works of Confucius, *I try to imagine what sort of person he was."* This last is a phrase Ch'ien uses only twice, here and at the end of his chapter on Ch'ü Yüan (SC 84/36). Of all the great men of the past, it was perhaps these two that he would most have liked to have known. He then relates how he himself visited the mortuary temple of Confucius, viewing the carriage, the clothes, and other belongings of the sage, and "wandering about, unable to tear myself away." He concludes:

There have been many kings, emperors, and great men in history who enjoyed fame and honor while they lived and came to nothing at their death, while Confucius, who was but a common scholar clad in a plain gown, became the acknowledged Master of scholars for over ten generations. All people in China who discuss the six arts, from the emperors, kings, and princes down, regard the Master as the final authority. He may be called the Supreme Sage.[43]

As we have seen in the discussion of Ch'ien's theory of literature and elsewhere, he viewed Confucius as the father of Chinese letters, a man driven by frustration and despair to seek in literature a rectification of the woes of life, and the recognition of later ages. And by his adoption of the symbol of the unicorn and the closing words of the *Kung-yang Commentary,* Ch'ien has made it clear that he considered himself to be motivated in his own writing by the same aims and ideals. It is not surprising, therefore, that he should emphasize the apparent failure and lack of recognition suffered by Confucius in his lifetime, and contrast it with the glory achieved by the sage through his writings in after ages. The themes of frustration and despair, the ominous decadence of the age, the gloomy songs and constant repetition of the words *pu-yung,* the long speeches and harangues against Confucius, the attacks upon his life, the sickening hypocrisy of the funeral oration— all these are deft instruments used by Ch'ien to create his image of the sage, an image which strongly reflects the despair and failure of Ch'ien's own life. It is a very human, moving, and often pathetic portrait, and one which, understandably, has often disturbed scholars of later generations who would prefer a sunnier version of the sage's life. Yet in the end the failure of Confucius is reclaimed by the judgment of history, defeat in the very last moment turns to triumph, and the man who could find no employment in his lifetime becomes after his death the teacher of kings. The story was one that affected Ch'ien deeply, for it was, he no doubt hoped, in some small measure the story of his own life.[44]

THE STYLE OF THE SHIH CHI

In his narrative Ch'ien drew freely upon all the literature of the past, both the Confucian Classics and the works of the philosophers, using any facts or anecdotes that he considered reliable and important. Pan Piao had made the criticism, repeated by his son, that Ch'ien, in utilizing the Classics and other early works "was often careless and sketchy and differed from his sources." [45] We need not at this point go into a detailed discussion of exactly how Ch'ien utilized his sources; a few examples will suffice to show what Pan Piao and Pan Ku were probably criticizing.

First is the fact that, when quoting from sources that used obscure or archaic words, or were unusually terse and difficult, Ch'ien frequently substituted more common words or paraphrased, rather than quoting verbatim, the harder passages. This practice seems to be very old in Chinese historiography. There is reason to believe that the editor or editors of the *Book of Documents* worked to put the wording of their miscellaneous sources into a uniform style and grammar, and the same is true of the compiler of the *Tso Commentary*. Ch'ien was therefore only continuing a custom already in use and one which by no means ended with him. When Pan Ku adapted material from Ch'ien, for example, he revised Ch'ien's wording to conform to his own ideas of style and clarity, and Ssu-ma Kuang did the same when he quoted from either historian.[46] Ch'ien not only paraphrased in the language of his time the extremely difficult and archaic style of very ancient works such as the *Book of Documents,* but also freely amended more recent works, such as the *Tso Commentary,* when its peculiar style and language made it difficult to follow.[47] His aim was obviously to make his own work as easy to read as possible without doing violence to the meaning of the original. But that he should have used the canonical books at all as sources inevitably drew criticism, especially in later ages when the Classics acquired an aura of sanctity not unlike that which has surrounded the Bible in the West. Thus Su Hsün reprimands Ch'ien for breaking up and scattering through his narrative passages from the *Documents,* the *Tso,* and the *Analects,* which, he says, violates the original beauty of their form as cutting up brocade to make garments violates the beauty of the original cloth.[48]

Occasionally Ch'ien added to his narrative events and accounts that do not appear in his sources as we have them today. The most striking example of this is the many fantastic and dubious tales which fill the "Hereditary House of Chao." As he indicates at the end of this chapter

(SC 43/96), Ch'ien was acquainted with an official of his time named Feng Wang-sun who was a descendant of a ministerial family of Chao, and these tales, which do not appear in older accounts of the state, may have come from this man, though it is hardly to his credit that Ch'ien included them in his history. At other times he added merely a phrase, a single sentence or fact, from what source we do not know. We have already noted how, in his biography of Confucius, in order to explain Confucius' reasons for writing the *Spring and Autumn Annals,* he has the sage exclaim: "How shall I be known to later ages?" This remark is to be found in none of the extant sources which Ch'ien used in this chapter, and it has been assumed that he added it out of his own imagination, a sacrilege for which he has been severely chastised.[49] Again, in his biography of Chang I (SC 70/17) he writes: "When Chang I went to Ch'in, he pretended that he lost hold of the cord [used to steady oneself when climbing in and out of a carriage] and fell out of the carriage, and for three months he did not attend court." But Ch'ien's only known source for this chapter, the *Intrigues of the Warring States* (Ch'in 2, 3/16a), merely says: "When Chang I arrived, he said he was ill and did not attend court." Where Ch'ien got his more detailed account, whether from some written source now lost or from popular story, we do not know.[50]

Another point to be noticed in Ch'ien's writing is his frequent carelessness about names and birthplaces. Pan Piao comments on this defect, noting that Ch'ien occasionally failed to give the full birthplace even of men who were his contemporaries, or forgot to record their full names at the beginning of their biographies.[51] This carelessness, though hardly a major fault, makes his work hard to read, as in the "Hereditary House of Wu" (SC 31) where, after referring to Wu Tzu-hsü, he suddenly mentions a Wu Yüan without explaining that the two are the same person. Pan Piao generously attributes this defect to Ch'ien's lack of time, and indeed, considering the clumsiness of writing materials in Ch'ien's day and the official duties that must have constantly pressed him, we may not wonder at such oversights. Fortunately the historians of the Pan family were allowed to work under more leisurely and favorable circumstances, and they established the practice, followed in later historical works, of carefully recording at the beginning of each biography the full name and birthplace of the subject.

This impression of rapidity, if not actual haste, in Ch'ien's work is borne out by the whole style of the *Shih chi*. His writing is surprisingly direct. As Pan Ku remarks, "He discourses without sounding wordy; he is simple without being rustic." Ch'ien was very sparing in his use of such literary devices as parallelism, metaphor, and symbol. Compared to the polished, high-sounding phrases of his predecessor Chia I or his contemporary Ssu-ma Hsiang-ju, his prose seems almost plain. In Han times the writing of essays and poetic descriptions such as the *fu* was extremely popular. These writings, like the philosophical works of pre-Han times, employed historical allusions, extended metaphorical or allegorical passages, or sometimes simply long lists of things such as trees, animals, buildings, etc., to achieve their rhetorical effect. Their purpose was not to tell a story but to persuade, instruct, or merely dazzle. Ch'ien himself was capable of writing this type of prose, as is shown by his beautiful and carefully composed letter to Jen An with its balanced sentences, literary flourishes, and lists of examples from history. But he seems to have realized that this style, with its extreme attention to literary effect, sometimes at the expense of clarity and good sense, was not suited to the kind of narrative and discussion that he wished for his history. Instead he developed, as Professor Naitô has pointed out, a style quite different from anything his age had known, or could even recognize for the new creation that it was.[52]

I hesitate to comment further on a subject as delicate and abstruse as Chinese prose style. But one thing may be easily noted about Ch'ien's sentences. This is their free, conversational tone. One is tempted to believe that he often wrote almost exactly as he spoke. When Pan Ku adopted passages from the *Shih chi,* for example, he was able to cut out a great many particles and helping words and yet retain for all practical purposes the full meaning of the original. Occasionally Pan Ku also reworked a sentence which in the *Shih chi* seems involved and clumsy, as though jotted down just as it came into the author's mind. Ch'ien's thoughts, particularly in passages where he is arguing back and forth on a question, as in his prefaces to the "Chronological Tables" or to the biographies of the wandering knights, seem to move about too fast for his powers of ordered presentation. He makes a point and suddenly turns to something quite different, or appears to go back and contradict what he has just said. For this reason he is frequently obscure and hard to follow. This is almost never true of Pan Ku. When he worked over the *Shih chi* material, he filled in the gaps in thought where the meaning was unclear or, if he disagreed with Ch'ien, discarded the whole passage and wrote one of his own in his clear, orderly style.

In rare instances Ch'ien used rhetorical devices in the style of the essays and *fu* of the period. In his introduction to the "Wandering Knights" or his autobiography, he employs a series of historical examples to emphasize his point. At other times he uses a metaphor or symbol, such as the ivory chopsticks, symbol of decadence (SC 14/4); the homeless dog, epithet of Confucius the unknown sage; or the wild peach, symbol of rustic modesty and virtue (SC 109/21). But unlike contemporary works such as the *Huai-nan Tzu* where these devices are employed in wearisome profusion, he is very sparing in their use, and thereby gains greater power and effectiveness.

Ch'ien had a novelist's feeling for a good story. His sources provided him with many, some of them amounting to rather lengthy historical romances. Such for example is the tale of Ch'ung-erh, later Duke Wen of Chin, in the *Tso Commentary,* which Ch'ien relates in *Shih chi* 39, or the tragic account of King Ling of Ch'u retold in *Shih chi* 40. These, not the dry facts of the past but the vivid, moving stories of great men, were what really interested him, and he repeats them with obvious gusto. He gives special attention to the role of women in history (a lesson which Thucydides might better have learned). Three times he relates the tale of the princess of Ts'ai, engaged to Duke Huan of Ch'i, who playfully rocked the boat when she and the Duke were out rowing one day, and so unnerved him that he immediately sent her back home and precipitated a war between the two states (SC 14,

32 and 35). With equal interest he tells of the ladies of the palace of Ch'i who laughed at the crippled general Hsi K'o and occasioned his resentment (SC 32/36); the colorful queen dowager of Chao who threatened to spit in the face of the next person who suggested she change her choice for the heir apparent (SC 43/81); and the sad and terrible tales of the imperial consorts of the Han rulers (SC 9 and 49). In fact, it was probably this fondness for a good story that at times led him to recount events of dubious reliability. Yang Hsiung remarks on this aspect of the *Shih chi:* "Tzu-ch'ang [Ch'ien] had great love; it was a love for the strange." "Great love that could not endure, that was Tzu-ch'ang." [53] There are two interpretations of the phrase *pu-jen,* "could not endure." One theory is that it means that Ch'ien's many tales and stories are "not worthy" of being handed down to later ages as models. But just before this Yang Hsiung has said: "The sayings of the *Huai-nan Tzu* are not so useful as those of The Grand Historian. A sage will find things to adopt from The Grand Historian." The second interpretation, which seems much more natural and likely, is that Ch'ien "could not endure" to leave anything out of his history. In his biography of Chang Liang (SC 55/22) Ch'ien tells the story of the four aged recluses [the *ssu-hao* famous in Chinese poetry and art] who came to the court of Kao-tsu at the invitation of the heir apparent. According to Ch'ien, Kao-tsu had long attempted to persuade these worthy old men to visit his court, but they had consistently refused. When he discovered that the heir apparent had succeeded in attracting them, he was forced to recognize the young man's superior virtue and abandon his plans to change his choice of an heir. Pan Ku repeats the story in *Han shu* 40/9a, but Ssu-ma Kuang in his *Tzu-chih t'ung-chien* rejects it on the grounds that it is inconsistent with common sense. This and similar episodes of a dubious nature, he remarks, are examples of Ssu-ma Ch'ien's "fondness for the strange and great love." [54]

One more aspect of Ch'ien's style remains to be noted, and that is the unusually personal and emotional quality of much of his writing. Chavannes has characterized the narrative style of the *Shih chi* as just the opposite—cold and impersonal.[55] It is quite true that in the body of his narrative Ch'ien seldom interjects his own feelings or reactions. These he has reserved for special sections at the beginning or end of his chapters. Chavannes, however, concludes from this contrast between what he characterizes as the traditional narrative style of the Han—simple, concise, cold, and impassive—and the emotional and personal quality of Ch'ien's own expressions of opinion, that the narrative sections must not have been original with Ch'ien but were copied directly from earlier sources. This conclusion seems to me hardly justifiable. The treatises on the "Feng and Shan Sacrifices" (SC 28), or "The River and Canals" (SC 29), or the biographies of Li Kuang (SC 109), Ssu-ma Hsiang-ju (SC 117), or Kuo Hsieh (SC 124), for example, are all in this simple, impassive style. Yet it is hard to conceive that complete treatises and biographies on these subjects could possibly have existed for Ch'ien to copy from. Any modern historian is allowed to have two styles: one when he gives a simple, direct account of historical facts, another when he ventures upon his own reactions and opinions. I see no reason to believe that Ch'ien was not equally capable of composing in two styles. The fact that he kept the two strictly apart, to a degree unknown in Western historical writing, was due to the dictates of Chinese custom, which demanded such a separation.

Often, as I have pointed out, Ch'ien utilized the words of one of his characters, or a poem or song, when he wished to convey emotion in the body of his narrative. Occasionally just at the close of his narrative he indulges in a few sentences of personal comment to sum up his feelings on the subject. At the end of his description of the endless humbug which surrounded the great sacrifices of Feng and Shan and the pathetic efforts of Emperor Wu to achieve immortality, for example, he concludes: "The Son of Heaven grew increasingly weary and disgusted with the queer and inane tales of the magicians. And yet he was bound and tied by them and could not free himself, for always he hoped to find the truth" (SC 28/88). This brief description of the deluded ruler, prey of every clever charlatan (which Pan Ku in his treatise on the same subject, HS 25, significantly omits) gains its emotional power precisely because it comes at the end of a completely impersonal recital of the facts.

Most of Ch'ien's remarks are confined to the special sections set off by the words, "The Grand Historian says." These passages are personal and emotional in the extreme. Over and over he says "I have seen," "I have heard," "When I visited," "When I read," etc. Repeatedly he speaks of himself as "imagining," "weeping," "sighing," or uses the word *pei,* "I am moved," or "It is pitiful." Indeed, Ch'ien is so emotional and personal in these sections that he is quite untypical of Chinese historians. A brief glance at the corresponding sections of the *Han shu* will reveal the contrast between Ch'ien and Pan Ku on this point. Pan Ku occasionally quotes the opinions and experiences of Ch'ien or his own father, Pan Piao. But he never once uses the pronoun "I" in his writing, even when he is clearly speaking in the first person; never does he give any indication that he has been to the places he mentions or met any of the descendants or associates of the men he describes. Scarcely ever does he intimate that history is for him anything more than a collection of written materials.[56] Sometimes he allows himself an expression of sympathy, usually, in good Confucian style, for the plight of the common people. Yet compared to Ssu-ma Ch'ien he seems almost glacial in his restraint. This truly impersonal style of Pan Ku was followed by later historians, perhaps because the passionate concern of Ch'ien for his subject was inimitable. It is more reassuring to the reader, undoubtedly, to believe that his author is going about the task of relating the facts of history objectively and free of personal emotional involvement. But the loss of interest and literary effectiveness, as we can see when we compare the pages of the *Shih chi* and the *Han shu,* is great indeed.

Judgments upon the style and emotional impact of writing, especially when the writing is in a foreign language, are highly personal and hardly subject to scientific proof. Chavannes can scarcely be denied his right to remark that the narrative of the *Shih chi* strikes him for the most part as cold and impersonal. I should only like to note in conclusion that other readers may hold, and often have held, quite different opinions. I quote for example a comment on the *Shih chi* by another foreigner, the Japanese historian Rai Sanyô (1780–1832):

I delight in reading the *Shih chi* and always have a few volumes of it on my desk. I read it and sigh, I break into song, I weep or I laugh. Ah, the men of his day looked upon Tzu-ch'ang's work as so much trash. How little they realized that, a hundred generations later, there would be men who, reading it, would sigh or sing, weep and laugh! [57]

APPENDIX A

SELECTED TRANSLATIONS

FROM THE *SHIH CHI*

[The following passages contain some of the more important remarks and discussions of Ssu-ma Ch'ien. They have been selected to represent his concept of history and the past, the ideals and methods that guided him in his work, and the personal quality of his writing. Most of these key passages have already been discussed or referred to in the chapters above. This selection does not pretend to encompass all the important passages of the *Shih chi* but only those that seem to me to relate most directly to the life, methods, and opinions of the historian.]

SC 1/65–67: *Basic Annals of the Five Emperors*

The Grand Historian remarks: Scholars frequently speak of the Five Emperors of antiquity. Yet the *Book of Documents* records only Emperor Yao and his successors, while when the various schools of philosophers tell of the Yellow Emperor, their words are not authoritative and reasonable so that learned men find it difficult to accept them. Thus the questions of Tsai Yü on the "Virtues of the Five Emperors" and the "Successions and Clans of the Emperors," which Confucius has transmitted to us, are not taught by some Confucian scholars. I myself have travelled west as far as K'ung-t'ung, north past Cho-lu, east to the sea, and in the south I have sailed the Yellow and Huai Rivers. The elders and old men of these various lands frequently pointed out to me the places where the Yellow Emperor, Yao, and Shun had lived, and in these places the manners and customs seemed quite different.[1] In general those of their accounts which do not differ from the ancient texts seem to be near to the truth. I have examined the *Spring and Autumn* and the *Narratives from the States,* and these show clearly that the "Virtues of the Five Emperors" and the "Successions and Clans of the Emperors" are genuine. However, many scholars fail to study the matter deeply enough and cannot see that what appears in these texts is not false. The ancient books [2] are often incomplete and have gaps, but what has been lost from them can sometimes be found in other records. It is indeed difficult to explain such things to men of shallow views and scant knowledge who are not fond of study or deep reflection and whose minds cannot recognize the true significance of things! I have brought together these records and put them in order, selecting those parts which seemed most reasonable and reliable, composing this Basic Annals as the beginning of my book.

SC 13/3–4: *Preface to the Chronological Table of the Three Dynasties*

The Grand Historian remarks: The chronicles of the Five Emperors and the Three Dynasties extend back to high antiquity. For the Yin dynasty and before, we cannot compile any genealogical records of the feudal lords, though from the Chou on down they can usually be constructed. When Confucius arranged the *Spring and Autumn* from the old historical texts, he noted the first year of a reign, the time when the year began, and the day and month for each entry; such was his exactitude. However, when he wrote his prefaces to the *Book of Documents,* he made only general references and did not mention year and month. Perhaps he had some material, but in many cases there were gaps and it was impossible to record exactly. Therefore, when there was a question of doubt, he recorded it as doubtful; such was his circumspection. I have read the genealogical records, which have complete dates entered from the Yellow Emperor on down. I have examined these chronologies and genealogies, as well as the "Record of the Cycle of the Five Elements." But these ancient texts disagree and contradict each other throughout. I can hardly consider as meaningless the example of the Master in not attempting to assign the exact year and month to events. Thus, basing my work on the "Virtues of the Five Emperors," the "Successions and Clans of the Emperors," and the *Book of Documents,* I have made this chronological table of the generations from the Yellow Emperor down to the era *kung-ho* (841 B. C.).

SC 15/2–6: *Preface to the Chronological Table of the Six States*

[This table, arranged by year, lists in parallel columns one below the other the histories of the states of Chou, Ch'in, Wei, Han, Chao, Ch'u, Yen, and Ch'i for the years from 475 to 206 B. C. Chou, representing the central court, is not counted among the Six States, nor is Ch'in, the state which eventually conquered and swallowed up the six; hence the title Table of the Six States.]

Reading the Chronicle of Ch'in, I come to the time when the Ch'uan-jung barbarians defeated King Yu and Chou moved east to the city of Lo. At this time Duke Hsiang of Ch'in was first enfeoffed among the feudal lords [3] and constructed the altar of the west, using it to serve the Lord on High.[4] Here is the first sign of usurpation. The *Ritual* says: "The Son of Heaven shall sacrifice to Heaven and Earth; the feudal lords shall sacrifice to the famous mountains and great rivers within their domains." [5] At this time Ch'in followed many of the customs of the barbarians, putting violence first and disregarding benevolence and righteousness. It held the position of an enfeoffed subject, and yet it imitated the suburban sacrifice of the Son of Heaven. Such behavior is enough to fill a gentleman with fear!

Then I come to Duke Wen who advanced out of Lung and drove back the I and Ti barbarians. He worshipped the Treasures of Ch'en [6] and made his camp between Ch'i and Yung. Then Duke Mu applied himself to the task of governing and extended the state east to the Yellow River, standing as an equal with Duke Huan of Ch'i and Duke Wen of Chin among the peers of the Middle Kingdom.

After this the ministers of the feudal lords took over the management of their respective governments, the high officials handed their offices down from generation to generation, and the six lords of Chin seized power in their state,[7] conducting military campaigns and forming alliances until their authority outweighed that of the feudal lords. Eventually when T'ien Ch'ang assassinated Duke Hsien and became prime minister of the state of Ch'i, the feudal lords simply sat back and made no move to punish him, so busy was everyone within the four seas in struggling for his own military success. In the end the three states divided up Chin among themselves and T'ien Ho [8] overthrew and took possession of Ch'i. This was the beginning of the great period of the Six States. All worked to strengthen their arms and encompass their enemies. Plots and deceptions were employed and the strategies of the Vertical and Horizontal, the Short and Long alliances appeared. The land swarmed with false titles and oaths and agreements could not be trusted. Although men exchanged hostages and split tallies,[9] they still could not enforce promises.

Ch'in was originally only a small state in a distant and out-of-the-way place, rejected by the feudal lords of the Middle Kingdom and regarded the same as the barbarians. But after the time of Duke Hsien it was always one of the leaders of the feudal lords. The best Ch'in had in the way of virtue and honor could not compare even with the worst in violence and cruelty of Lu or Wei; in arms it could not weigh up to the strength of the three states of Chin. And yet in the end it conquered the world! This was not necessarily because of the advantages of steep and secure terrain or the result of fortunate circumstances. Rather it was as though Heaven had aided it.

Some say that things begin life in the east and come to maturity in the west. Thus one must begin his dynastic undertaking in the southeast, and he will always reap his success in the northwest. Therefore we find that Emperor Yü arose among the Western Ch'iang; T'ang began in Yü-po; the Chou attained kingship by attacking the Yin from Feng-kao; Ch'in became emperor by rising in Yung-chou; and the ascendancy of the Han was from the lands of Shu and Han.

When Ch'in had already accomplished its aims, it burned all copies of the *Odes* and *Documents,* and in particular the historical records of the feudal lords, because they contained criticisms and slander of the Ch'in. The reason the *Odes* and *Documents* reappeared is because a number of copies were stored with private families. But the historical records were preserved only in the archives of Chou and so they were lost. What a pity! What a pity! We have only the Annals of Ch'in and it does not even record days and months; its text is brief and incomplete.

Yet there is much that can be learned from the methods and stratagems for gaining power used by the Warring States. Why must one learn only from ancient times? There was much violence in Ch'in's seizure of the world. But because it was able to change with each different age, its success was great. There is a book which says: "Take for your model the kings of later ages." [10] Why is this? Because they are near to us and their ways and customs are like ours; their counsels are easy and simple to practice. Scholars are misled by tradition and see only that the time the Ch'in held the position of emperor was very short, without examining the end and beginning of the affair. Therefore they all mock the Ch'in and do not deign to speak of it. This is no different from trying to eat with your ears and a form of nonsense I find very regrettable! Thus I have followed the Annals of Ch'in and made a continuation from the end of the Spring and Autumn period, beginning with King Yüan of Chou and recording the dates and events of the Six States down to the Second Emperor of the Ch'in, in all a period of two hundred and seventy years. I have recorded all that I have heard of the beginning of ascendancy and decay. In later years there may be gentlemen who will read what I have done.

SC 44/50: *The Hereditary House of Wei*

The Grand Historian remarks: I have visited the ruins of the old city of Ta-liang.[11] The people around the place told me that when Ch'in overthrew Liang, it dug canals from the Yellow River and flooded Ta-liang. In three months the city walls collapsed and the king begged to surrender. Thus Wei was eventually destroyed. The strategists all say that it was because Wei did not make use of the Lord of Hsin-ling [12] that the state became so feeble and was finally wiped out. But I consider that this is not correct. Heaven at this time had commanded Ch'in to pacify all within the seas, and its task was not yet completed. Although Wei might have had the services of an A-heng,[13] of what use would it have been? [14]

SC 61: *The Biography of Po I and Shu Ch'i*

Although in the world of learning there exist a large number and variety of books and records, their reliability must always be examined in the light of the Six Classics. In spite of deficiencies in the Classics of the *Odes* and *Documents,* we can nevertheless know something about the culture and institutions of the times of Yü (Emperor Shun) and the Hsia dynasty. When, for instance, Emperor Yao wished to retire from his position, he yielded the throne to Shun of Yü. When Shun in turn yielded to Yü, the various court officials made their recommendations in favor of Yü and he was given the throne for a period of trial. After he had discharged the duties of the imperial office for some twenty years and his merits and ability were already manifest, only then was the rule finally ceded to him. This proves that the empire is a precious vessel,[15] the heritage of the ruler, and that its transmission is a matter of extreme gravity. Yet there are some theorists who say that Yao tried to yield the empire to Hsü Yu and that Hsü Yu was ashamed and would not accept it but fled into retirement.[16] Again, in the time of the Hsia dynasty we have similar stories of men called Pien Sui and Wu Kuang.[17] Where do people get stories like this?

The Grand Historian remarks: When I ascended Mount Ch'i [18] I found at the top what is said to be the grave of Hsü Yu. Confucius, we know, eulogizes the ancient sages and men of wisdom and virtue, and quite specifically mentions such figures as T'ai-po of Wu [19] and Po I. Now I am told that Hsü Yu and Wu Kuang were men of the highest virtue, and yet in the Classics there appears not the slightest reference to them. Why would this be?

Confucius said, "Po I and Shu Ch'i never bore old ills in mind and had not the faintest feelings of rancor." [20] "They sought to act virtuously and they did so; what was there for them to repine about?" [21]

I am greatly moved by the determination of Po I. But when I examine the song that has been attributed to him,[22] I find it very strange.

The tales of these men [23] state that Po I and Shu Ch'i were two sons of the ruler of Ku-chu. Their father wished to set up Shu Ch'i as his heir, but when he died, Shu Ch'i yielded in favor of Po I. Po I replied that it had been their father's wish that Shu Ch'i should inherit the throne and so he departed from the kingdom. Shu Ch'i likewise, being unwilling to accept the rule, went away and the people of the kingdom set up his second son as ruler. At this time Po I and Shu Ch'i heard that Ch'ang, the Chief of the West, knew well how to look after the old, and they said, "Why should we not go and follow him?" [24] But when they had gone they found that the Chief of the West was dead and his son, King Wu, had taken up the tablets of rule from his father, whom he honored with the title of King Wen, and was marching east to attack Emperor Chou of the Yin. Po I and Shu Ch'i clutched the reins of King Wu's horse and reprimanded him, saying, "The mourning for your father is not yet completed and yet you take up shield and spear. Can this conduct be called filial? As a subject you seek to assassinate your lord. Is this what is called righteousness?" The king's attendants wished to strike them down, but the king's counselor, T'ai-kung, interposed, saying, "These are just men," and he sent them away unharmed.

After this, King Wu conquered and pacified the people of the Yin and the world honored the house of Chou as its ruler. But Po I and Shu Ch'i were filled with shame and outrage and considered it unrighteous to eat the grain of Chou. They fled and hid on Shou-yang Mountain,[25] where they tried to live by gathering ferns to eat. When they were on the point of starvation, they composed a song:

> "We ascend this western hill
> And pluck its ferns.
> He replaces violence with violence,
> And sees not his own fault.
> Shen Nung, Yü, and Hsia,
> How long ago these great men vanished!
> Whom now should we follow?
> Alas, let us depart,
> For our fate has run out!" [26]

They died of starvation on Shou-yang Mountain. When we examine this song, do we find any rancor or not?

Some people say: "It is Heaven's way, without distinction of persons, to keep the good perpetually supplied." [27] Can we say then that Po I and Shu Ch'i were good men or not? They clung to righteousness and were pure in their deeds, as we have seen, and yet they starved to death.

Of his seventy disciples, Confucius singled out Yen Hui for praise because of his diligence in learning, yet Yen Hui was often in want. He ate without regret the poorest food, and yet suffered an untimely death.[28] Is this the way Heaven rewards the good man?

Robber Chih day after day killed innocent men, making mincemeat of their flesh. Cruel and willful, he gathered a band of several thousand followers who went about terrorizing the world. But in the end he lived to a great old age.[29] For what virtue did he deserve this?

The import of these examples is perfectly apparent. Even in more recent times we see that men whose deeds are immoral and who constantly violate the laws and prohibitions end their lives in luxury and wealth and their blessings pass down to their heirs without end. And there are others who carefully choose the spot where they shall place each footstep, who "speak out only when it is time to speak," [30] who "walk on no by-paths and expend no anger on what is not upright and just," [31] and yet, in numbers too great to be reckoned, they meet with misfortune and disaster. I find myself in much perplexity. Is this so-called "Way of Heaven" right or wrong?

Confucius said, "Those whose ways are different cannot lay plans for one another." [32] Each will follow his own will. Therefore he said, "If the search for riches and honor were sure to be successful, though I should become a groom with whip in hand to get them, I would do so. But as the search might not be successful, I will follow after that which I love." [33] "When the year becomes cold, then we know how the pine and the cypress are the last to lose their leaves." [34] When the whole world is in foul and muddy confusion, then is the man of true purity seen. Then must one judge what he will consider important and what unimportant.[35]

"The superior man hates the thought of his name not being mentioned after his death." [36] As Chia I has said:

> "The covetous run after riches,
> The impassioned pursue a fair name.
> The proud die struggling for power
> And the people long only to live." [37]

"Things of the same light illumine each other; things of the same class seek each other out. Clouds pursue the dragon; the wind follows the tiger. The sage arises and all creation becomes clear." [38]

Po I and Shu Ch'i, although they were men of great virtue, became, through Confucius, even more illustrious in fame. Though Yen Hui was diligent in learning, like a fly riding on the tail of a swift horse, his attachment to Confucius made his deeds renowned.[39] The hermit-scholars hiding away in their caves may be ever so correct in their givings and takings, and yet the names of them and their kind vanish like smoke without receiving a word of praise. Is this not pitiful? The gentlemen living in retirement in their country cottages strive to make perfect their actions and establish a name for virtue, but if they do not somehow ally themselves with a man of worth and importance,[40] how can they hope that their fame will be handed down to posterity?

SC 66/23: *The Biography of Wu Tzu-hsü*

[Wu Tzu-hsü's father, an official of Ch'u, fell victim to the slander of court rivals and was seized and held as a hostage. Word was sent to his two sons, Tzu-hsü and Shang, that if they would come and surrender themselves, they might save their father. Shang, for the sake of filial piety, went, although he knew he would be put to death. But Tzu-hsü fled to the state of Wu, where he eventually won favor, led an army against Ch'u, and avenged the death of his father and brother.]

The Grand Historian remarks: How serious a thing is the poison of hatred in men! If a ruler must not arouse hatred among his ministers and subjects, how much more important that he do not do so among his equals![41] If Wu Tzu-hsü had followed his father, Shê, and died with him, he would have been of no more significance than a mere ant. But he set aside a small righteousness in order to wipe out a great shame, and his name has been handed down to the ages after. How moving! At that time Tzu-hsü suffered affliction at the River,[42] and begged for his food by the roadside, but not for a moment in his determination did he forget Ying.[43] He bore all secretly and silently, and in the end achieved merit and fame. Who but a man of burning intention could have accomplished such a deed?

SC 67/53: *Biographies of the Disciples of Confucius*

The Grand Historian remarks: Scholars have often spoken about the "seventy disciples" of Confucius.[44] Those who wished to praise them have sometimes exaggerated the facts, while those interested in disparaging them have done injury to the truth; both groups alike discuss the matter without ever having known the men they are talking about. There is a register of the disciples preserved by the K'ung family and written in archaic characters which I believe to be generally accurate. I have used this list of names and surnames of the disciples, combining with it the questions and answers of these men found in the *Analects,* and arranged the material in this chapter. Material that seemed doubtful I have omitted.

SC 69/62: *Biography of Su Ch'in*

[Su Ch'in was a famous strategist and diplomat of the Warring States period and the proponent of the Vertical Alliance, a sort of security pact among six feudal states designed to block the expansion of the state of Ch'in. He was eventually assassinated because of his secret and devious plotting among the various states. After his death his brothers carried on his campaign for the Vertical Alliance.]

The Grand Historian remarks: Su Ch'in and his two brothers all achieved fame among the feudal lords as itinerant strategists. Their policies laid great stress upon stratagems and shifts of power. But because Su Ch'in died a traitor's death, the world has united in scoffing at him and has been loath to study his policies.[45] There are a great many varying stories told about Su Ch'in. Indeed, even affairs that occurred in a different age, if they are of the same type, are all attributed to the figure of Su Ch'in. Su Ch'in arose from the humblest beginnings to lead the Six States in the Vertical Alliance, and this is evidence that he possessed an intelligence surpassing the ordinary person. For this reason I have set forth this account of his deeds, arranging them in proper chronological order, so that he may not forever suffer from an evil reputation and be known for nothing else.

SC 86/39–40: *Biographies of the Assassin-Retainers*

[This chapter relates the lives of five retainers who undertook to assassinate the enemies of their lords. The most famous of them is Ching K'o who, for Crown Prince Tan of Yen, attempted to stab to death King Cheng of Ch'in, who later became the First Emperor of the Ch'in dynasty.]

The Grand Historian remarks: When people these days tell the story of Ching K'o, they assert that at the command of Crown Prince Tan the heavens rained grain and horses grew horns. This is of course a gross error. They likewise say that Ching K'o actually wounded the King of Ch'in, which is equally untrue. At one time Kung-sun Chi-kung and Master Tung[46] were friends of Hsia Wu-chü[47] and they learned exactly what happened. I have therefore reported everything just as they told it to me. Of these five men from Ts'ao Mo to Ching K'o, some succeeded in carrying out their duty and some did not. But it is perfectly clear that they had all determined upon the deed. They were not false to their intentions. Is it not right, then, that their names should be handed down to later ages?

SC 88/11: *Biography of Meng T'ien*

[Meng T'ien and his brother, Meng I, were powerful military leaders at the court of the First Emperor of the Ch'in, but were later forced to commit suicide by the eunuch Chao Kao. Both protested their innocence of any wrongdoing, but Meng T'ien, when he found it was of no avail, consoled himself by saying that he deserved death for the crime of "disturbing the arteries of the earth" when he constructed the walls and roads for the northern part of the empire.]

The Grand Historian remarks: I have travelled to the northern border and returned by the Direct Road.[48] As I went along I saw the towers of the Great Wall which Meng T'ien constructed for the Ch'in. He cut through the mountains and filled up the valleys, opening up a direct road. Truly he made free with the strength of the common people! Ch'in had only recently destroyed the feudal states; the hearts of the people of the world were not yet at rest and the wounded were not yet healed. T'ien was a renowned general, yet he did not take this opportunity to urge that the ills of the common people be attended to, that the old be cared for or the orphan preserved; he did not strive to bring about the well-being of the mass of people. Instead he toadied to the will of the Emperor in undertaking these constructions. Was it not right that for this he and his brother met with punishment? What is this "crime of the arteries of the earth?"

SC 100/11–12: *Biographies of Chi Pu and Lüan Pu*

[Chi Pu, who fought with Hsiang Yü against the Han, was forced into hiding when Hsiang Yü was defeated and a price put on his head. In order to escape capture, he allowed himself to be chained and sold as a field slave. He was later pardoned by Kao-tsu and became an official. Lüan Pu had been a friend of the King of Liang, P'eng Yüeh, in his poorer days. When P'eng Yüeh was accused of treason and executed by Kao-tsu, Lüan Pu dared to defy the Emperor's orders by weeping and praying before the severed head of P'eng Yüeh that hung exposed in the marketplace of Lo-yang. He was seized and condemned to die by boiling, but was pardoned at the last minute for his faithfulness and bravery, and later rose to high position.]

The Grand Historian remarks: With a spirit like that of Hsiang Yü, Chi Pu made a name for bravery in Ch'u. From time to time he commanded armies and several times he seized the enemy pennants. He may truly be called a brave and fine man. Yet he suffered punishment and disgrace and became a slave, and did not commit suicide. Why did he stoop to this? Because he chose to rely upon his abilities. Therefore he suffered disgrace without shame, for there were things he hoped to accomplish and he was not yet satisfied. Thus in the end he became a renowned general of the Han. Truly the wise man regards death as a grave thing. When slaves and scullion maids and lowly people in their despair commit suicide, it is not because they are brave; it is because they know that their plans and hopes will never again have a chance of coming true. Lüan Pu wept for P'eng Yüeh and faced the boiling water as though it were his true destination. This is indeed what it means to know the right place to die, not counting death as important in itself. The most brave and determined men of ancient times could do no better than these two!

SC 123/43–46: *Memoirs on Ta-yüan*

[In 138 B. C., an envoy, Chang Ch'ien, was sent on a diplomatic mission as far as western Turkestan. The information he brought back with him from his travels changed the whole Chinese conception of the geography of the lands to the west of them. Ssu-ma Ch'ien used this account as the basis for this chapter on Ferghana, called by the Chinese Ta-yüan, and the other countries of central Asia.]

The Grand Historian remarks: The *Basic Annals of Emperor Yü* [49] records that the source of the Yellow River is in the K'un-lun Mountains, mountains some 2,500 *li* high, the place where the sun and moon in turn go to hide when they are not shining. It is said that on their heights are to be found the Fountain of Sweet Water and the Pool of Jade. Now Chang Ch'ien has been sent beyond the land of Ta-hsia (Bactria), tracing the Yellow River to its source, and he found no such K'un-lun Mountains as the *Basic Annals* records. Therefore, what the *Book of Documents* states about the mountains and rivers of the nine provinces of China is nearer the truth, while when it comes to the wonders mentioned in the *Basic Annals of Emperor Yü* or the *Classic of Hills and Seas,* I cannot accept them.

APPENDIX B

ON THE DATING OF
SSU-MA CH'IEN'S LETTER
TO JEN AN

There are at present two theories on the dating of Ssu-ma Ch'ien's famous letter written to his friend Jen An, *tzu* Shao-ch'ing, the text of which is found in *Han shu* 62 and *Wen hsüan* 41. I should like here to examine in some detail these theories and the evidence upon which they are based.

In the beginning of his letter, Ssu-ma Ch'ien thanks Jen An for a letter which he received from his friend some time before, explaining why he has been so long in answering it. He then says: "Now, Shao-ch'ing, you are accused of this terrible crime. The days and months have gone by and it is drawing close to the end of winter" (literally, "the third month of winter," the twelfth month of the Han year). In a note on this (*Liu-ch'en-chu Wen-hsüan* ch. 41/11b), the T'ang commentator Lü Hsiang says: "An was a prisoner in jail because of the affair of the Crown Prince Li." Although Lü Hsiang does not elaborate upon this statement, his note indicates that he believes that the crime Jen An was accused of was that of aiding the crown prince in his attempted rebellion in *Cheng-ho* 2, 91 B. C., so that the letter must have been written near the end of that year.

This is the theory adopted by Chou Shou-ch'ang in his *Han-shu chu-chiao-pu* ch. 41/7b. He gives as further proof the fact that Ssu-ma Ch'ien states immediately afterwards: "I am forced to go in attendance upon the Emperor to Yung." In the first month of *Cheng-ho* 3, 90 B. C., according to HS 6/37a, the emperor did in fact go to Yung, and this is the trip, according to Chou Shou-ch'ang, to which Ssu-ma Ch'ien is referring.

At first glance this theory seems to fit the facts very well. But let us examine in detail exactly what happened in 91 B. C.

The biography of Jen An and his friend, T'ien Jen, was written by Ch'u Shao-sun [1] and appended to the end of SC 104. According to this account, both Jen An and T'ien Jen were retainers of the famous general Wei Ch'ing and later were promoted by the emperor to official positions. Jen An was made protector of the Northern Garrison, one of the two garrisons which guarded the city of Ch'ang-an,[2] and some time after was transferred to the position of regional inspector (*tz'u-shih*) of I Province in Szechwan. Later he seems to have been transferred back to his original post, for in 91 B. C. he was acting as superintendent of the Northern Garrison.

In the summer of 91 B. C., the emperor went to his palace at Kan-ch'uan, some 200 *li* northwest of the capital, to escape the heat. At this time the crown prince Li and his mother, Empress Wei, became involved in the famous "black magic" affair and were accused of trying to kill the emperor by means of secret arts.[3]

In the early part of the seventh month, the palace of the crown prince was searched for evidence of the crime, and at this time the emperor returned from Kan-ch'uan to the Chien-chang Palace in Ch'ang-an. On the day *jen-wu* of this month, September 1 by the Western calendar, the prince announced that Chiang Ch'ung, the official who was in charge of the investigation into his conduct, had revolted, using this as an excuse to send out troops to massacre Chiang Ch'ung and his party. He forged credentials, opened the prisons, and attempted to take over the capital by force. One of his acts was to march to the south gate of the Northern Garrison, summon Jen An, who was in command, give him the false credentials, and demand that Jen An dispatch troops to aid him. Jen An accepted the credentials, but shut the gate of the garrison and would not send out any troops, upon which the prince withdrew. In the meantime the lieutenant chancellor Liu Ch'ü-li, with a force of loyal troops, attacked the prince and after five days of bloody battle defeated him. On the day *keng-yen* of the seventh month, September 9, the prince managed to escape from the city and flee.

Jen An's friend, T'ien Jen, director of Justice, was held responsible for allowing the prince to slip through the city gates. The imperial secretary Pao Sheng-chih interceded for T'ien Jen, asking that he be given a hearing, but the emperor was in a rage and would not think of ordinary legal procedure. Pao Sheng-chih committed suicide in fear and T'ien Jen was cut in two at the waist.[4] Things moved very rapidly at this time.

What had happened to Jen An in the meantime? According to Ch'u Shao-sun's account in SC 104, the emperor at first believed in the loyalty of Jen An. But a subordinate who had been beaten and humiliated by Jen An sent a memorial to the emperor declaring that Jen An had agreed to help the prince. The emperor thereupon said: "This man is an old official. When he saw the rebellion break out, he wanted to sit by and see which side would win and then go along with the winner. He is double-hearted. An has committed a great many crimes worthy of death, but I have always let him live. Now he has acted fraudulently and is not loyal in his heart." The emperor then had Jen An sent to jail and executed.

The question arises of just when this execution took place. We have no way of telling for certain. In HS 6/37a, Pan Ku records the execution of T'ien Jen between the time of the rebellion and the suicide of the crown prince on the day *hsin-hai* of the eighth month, September 30, but he does not mention the execution of Jen An. In HS 66/4a, however, he says that Jen An was accused of being disloyal because he accepted the credentials of the prince, and that both he and T'ien Jen were cut in two. He relates this before he mentions the suicide of the crown prince, so it would appear that he believed Jen An was executed about the same time as T'ien Jen, i.e., between September 1 and September 30.

This of course is not positive proof of the death date of Jen An. The fact that, according to Ch'u Shao-sun, the emperor became suspicious of Jen An only after receiving a report from An's subordinate would suggest a delay in time. But in view of the general hysteria of the times and the emperor's rage, it seems hard to believe that the affair was still unsettled and that Jen An could have been in jail and alive by the eleventh or twelfth month of the year, when Ssu-ma Ch'ien is supposed to have written him.

There is one more fact that makes Chou Shou-ch'ang's theory seem improbable. When Ssu-ma Ch'ien apologizes for not answering Jen An's letter sooner, he says: "At that time I had to accompany the Emperor on a trip to the east." But the emperor did not go to the east either in 91 B. C. nor in the previous year, 92 B. C.; he was around Ch'ang-an the whole time. The last time the emperor had been to the east was in 93 B. C. Ssu-ma Ch'ien would hardly use this trip as an excuse for not writing if he had been back in Ch'ang-an for two years before answering Jen An's letter at the end of 91 B. C.

Chavannes accepts the theory that Ssu-ma Ch'ien's letter was written when Jen An was in prison on charges of having aided the crown prince in 91 B. C., but adds a new interpretation of his own. In the Introduction to his *Mémoires historiques,* p. xliii, he says that Jen An wrote to Ssu-ma Ch'ien asking for Ch'ien's help in getting him set free. But this would mean that Jen An must have written to Ssu-ma Ch'ien sometime *after* the rebellion in the seventh month of 91 B. C. In such a case Ssu-ma Ch'ien could not possibly say that he had been busy attending the emperor on a trip to the east. Nor does the tone of Ch'ien's letter suggest that it could have been written when things were as upset as they were in late 91 B. C. Finally,

Ch'ien's reply suggests that the letter from Jen An was not a plea for personal intercession on his behalf but a general suggestion that Ch'ien should use his influence at court in helping the advancement of deserving men. Ch'ien refers to Jen An's advice only at the beginning and end of his letter, devoting all the rest of his space to his own troubles.

It is worth noting that neither Yen Shih-ku, in his notes on the *Han shu* text of the letter, nor any of the other commentators on the *Wen hsüan,* suggest that the crime of Jen An mentioned in Ch'ien's letter refers to the affair of the crown prince. Pan Ku, in his biography of Ssu-ma Ch'ien, says: "Jen An, an old friend who was regional inspector of I Province, sent Ch'ien a letter." But as we have seen, in 91 B. C. Jen An was not the regional inspector of I Province but the superintendent or *shih-che* of the Northern Garrison. So it seems that Pan Ku believed the letter had been written at an earlier time when Jen An was still regional inspector.

The second theory on the dating of Ch'ien's letter is that of Wang Kuo-wei, advanced in his study of the life of Ssu-ma Ch'ien (*op. cit.,* under the date *T'ai-shih* 4). He places the letter in the eleventh month of *T'ai-shih* 4, 93 B. C. This year, he notes, fits perfectly with Ch'ien's description of his activities in his letter. In the third month the emperor went to Mt. T'ai; in the fourth month he visited Pu-ch'i. Both places are in the eastern provinces. In the fifth month he returned to the capital and declared a general amnesty. In the twelfth month, the emperor went to Yung (HS 6/36a). According to this theory, if Ch'ien wrote in the eleventh month he would be quite correct in saying that he had been busy attending the emperor on a visit to the east and that, as the last month of the year drew near, he would again be forced to go with the emperor, this time to Yung. But how are we to account for the fact that Jen An was accused of a crime at this time?

Wang Kuo-wei refers to the words of Emperor Wu recorded by Ch'u Shao-sun: "An has been guilty of a great many crimes worthy of death but I have always let him live." In other words, Jen An had been in serious trouble at least once before his final tragic end, and this must be why Ch'ien says: "You are now accused of this terrible crime."

It should be remembered that during the Han, and particularly in the late years of Emperor Wu's reign, officials were thrown into prison on the slightest charges; there is hardly a famous man of the age who was not at some time at least reprimanded and removed from his post. So it is not surprising that Jen An should have been accused of some crime in 93 B. C. We recall that he was for a time regional inspector of I Province, but later we find him back at his old job as superintendent of the Northern Garrison. It is quite possible that he was removed from his post in I Province because of some misdemeanor, and at that time he was put in prison, but was later pardoned and restored to official position.

If this supposition is true, we may reconstruct the situation as follows. In late 94 or early 93 B. C., Jen An, who was then regional inspector of I Province in Szechwan, wrote to Ssu-ma Ch'ien suggesting that he use his influence to promote worthy men at court. Hence when Pan Ku mentions the letter from Jen An he is quite correct in calling him "regional inspector of I Province." But shortly after he received the letter, Ssu-ma Ch'ien was forced to go with the emperor on a tour of the east, returning to the capital in the fifth month, after which, as he says, he was kept busy with official duties. In the seventh month, a general amnesty was declared, so it is unlikely that Jen An was in prison at this time. But some time between the seventh and eleventh months, Jen An was accused of some crime and put in prison. In the eleventh month, Ch'ien wrote to him explaining why he had not answered Jen An's letter and telling of his own misfortune. Some time later, Jen An was pardoned and made superintendent of the Northern Garrison. This theory also helps to explain how the letter of Ch'ien came to be preserved. If Ch'ien had written to Jen An when he was in prison on charges of having aided the crown prince in his revolt, and Jen An was shortly after executed, it is hard to see how Ch'ien's letter, unless he circulated copies himself, would have or could have gotten into the hands of anyone who would preserve it. Thus, although we may not agree with Wang Kuo-wei that there can be "no doubt" that the letter was written in 93 B. C., we must admit that this theory is more convincing. If it offers no positive proof, it at least avoids the obvious difficulties and contradictions of the older theory shared by Lü Hsiang, Chou Shou-ch'ang, and Chavannes.

NOTES

I. THE WORLD OF SSU-MA CH'IEN

1. All page references to the *Shih chi* are to the Japanese edition entitled *Shiki kaichû kôshô,* edited and with a commentary in Chinese by Takikawa Kametarô (see Bibliography under *Shih chi*). The title *Shih chi* is usually translated "Historical Records," following Chavannes' rendition, "Mémoires historiques." As pointed out by many scholars, the title *Shih chi* was not given to his work by Ssu-ma Ch'ien himself. In the first few centuries after his death his book was referred to as *T'ai-shih-kung shu* or *T'ai-shih-kung chi,* "The Book" or "The Records of The Grand Historian." The oldest use of the term *Shih chi* in reference to Ssu-ma Ch'ien's history seems to be that which appears in the biography of Wang Su (d. 256 A. D.), in the *San-kuo-chih, Wei-chih* 13. (For a translation of this biography, see R. P. Kramers, *K'ung Tzu Chia Yü,* pp. 54–72.) It would appear, then, that this title came into use sometime during late Han or Wei times, probably as an abbreviation of the old title *T'ai-shih-kung chi.* Logically speaking, therefore, the correct translation should be "Records of the Historian." See Cheng Hao-sheng, *Ssu-ma Ch'ien nien-p'u,* pp. 70–72. In a note on page 68, however, Kramers (*op. cit.*) cites the opinion of Dr. William Hung of Harvard that the word *Shih chi* is used by Wang Su as a generic term for a work of history. The term is so used, of course, in Han times and even in the *Shih chi* itself to refer to the records of the historians of the feudal period, such as Confucius used in compiling the *Spring and Autumn Annals.* The word *shih* in this term, however, always refers to the official historians of the Chou state and its feudatories so that, even interpreted as a generic term, it would still be translated as "records of the historian(s)."

In addition to the *Shih chi* there are a few minor works extant which have been attributed to Ssu-ma Ch'ien. The *Han shu* Treatise on Literature (HS 30/53b), lists eight *p'ien* of *fu* by Ch'ien. Of these only one, the *Pei Shih-pu-yü Fu* or "Lament for Unemployed Gentlemen," survives, though there is considerable doubt as to the authenticity of the present text. It has been translated by Prof. James R. Hightower in his study, "The *Fu* of T'ao Ch'ien," HJAS 17, 197–200. There are also fragments of a treatise on economics, the *Su-wang miao-lun* or "Subtle Discussion of [?] the Uncrowned King," apparently patterned on *Shih chi* 129. Wang Kuo-wei believes it to be a work of the third or fourth centuries A. D. Finally the *Kao-shih-chuan* 2/9a of Huang-fu Mi (215–282) describes the friendship of Ch'ien and a recluse named Chih Chün and records an exchange of brief letters between the two. But there is no earlier evidence to corroborate this story or the authenticity of the letters. These works and anecdotes appear to be too fragmentary and suspect to merit consideration in this study. For a discussion of the works, see Cheng, *op. cit.,* p. 63 and pp. 122–24. The texts of the works are reprinted in *ibid.,* pp. 145–46.

2. *Fu-hsing* or *chung-hsing*. As Prof. Lien-sheng Yang has pointed out, *chung* in this case does not mean "in the middle" but "again," i.e., "re"-storation; hence the two terms are synonymous. See his article "Toward a Study of Dynastic Configurations in Chinese History," HJAS 17 (1954), 332.

3. The exceptions are the conventional phrase "translating and retranslating their languages," used by Ch'ien himself in SC 130/26 or "retranslating their languages ninefold," used by Chang Ch'ien (SC 123/17), which indicate at least an awareness of the variety of languages that existed in Central Asia, and the brief remark in SC 123/31: "Although the countries from Ta-yüan [Fergana] west to An-hsi [Parthia] all speak different languages, their customs are generally similar and their languages mutually intelligible."

4. Note a similar passage in *Li chi* Sec. 32, 54/17b–19a: "The men of Yin honored the gods and led their people in the serving of the gods. They placed the gods first and rites after. . . . The faults of their people were restlessness and lack of quietude, contentiousness and lack of shame. The men of Chou honored rites and the administration of human affairs. They served the spirits and reverenced the gods but kept at a distance from them. They drew near to man and kept faith with him. . . . The faults of their people were an excessive concern with profit and cleverness, elegance without modesty, insubordination and delusion." Since it is impossible to determine the exact dating of this chapter of the *Li chi,* it is not possible to say which version of the idea, this or Ssu-ma Ch'ien's, is older.

5. Gilbert Murray, *Five Stages of Greek Religion,* pp. 59–60.

6. *Ch'un-ch'iu fan-lu* 13/57.

7. Quoted in the section *Tu-shih tsung-p'ing* at the beginning of the *Shih-chi p'ing-lin.* I can find no biographical information on this man, Li T'u, *tzu* Hsing-hsüeh.

8. See Naitô Torajirô, *Shina jôkoshi*, 11.

9. The self-styled "King" Yen, last ruler of the state of Sung, SC 38/42. He conforms in all details to the traditional pattern of the cruel and decadent terminator of a dynasty. The state of Sung was ruled by the descendants of the kings of the Shang dynasty. It is interesting to note that, though the Chou dynasty began with the typically wise and virtuous founding fathers—King Wen, King Wu, the Duke of Chou—it did not end with an evil ruler as the earlier dynasties had ended. This is undoubtedly because all the opprobrium was transferred to the first and second emperors of the Ch'in who followed, and who were the great villains of the Han people. The Han did not overthrow and replace the Chou, but the Ch'in. Therefore Han writers bent all their efforts to drawing as black a picture as possible of the wickedness of the Ch'in, while they pictured the last Chou rulers as simply weak and ineffective.

10. Ch. 4/7a. Chuang Tzu, who urged men to set their eyes upon more lofty ideals, naturally had only scorn for this concern for fame.

11. "The *Fu* on the Owl," SC 84/28 and *Wen hsüan* 13.

12. *Li chi* 26/18a.

13. *Hsün Tzu* 5/16.

14. *Ch'un-ch'iu fan-lu* 15/70.

15. See the speech by the official Wu-ch'iu Shou-wang to Emperor Wu when the so-called cauldrons of Chou were discovered: "From the time of Kao-tsu the Han has continued the Chou" (HS 64A/16b).

16. How far the problem remains unsolved even today is interestingly illustrated in a recent interpretation of Ssu-ma Ch'ien by a writer of the new communist regime. The writer first praises Ch'ien for championing the rights of the people against the oppression and tyranny of Emperor Wu's administration, then censures him for seeing only the negative aspects of Emperor Wu's policies and failing to perceive that his foreign wars and expansion brought power and glory to the nation. See Chi Chen-huai, *Ssu-ma Ch'ien,* 90–94 and 111.

17. "Criticism of the Elders of Shu" (SC 117/69–74; *Wen hsüan* 44). Ssu-ma Hsiang-ju's proclamation is a magnificent example of Han rhetoric expounding the ideal of imperial glory extending out beyond the borders of the nation. It ends with a poetic description of the emperor, the extraordinary man, pictured as a swan soaring above the heads of the uncomprehending masses: "The watcher has not yet glimpsed his meaning, the listener does not comprehend his voice. The bright swan has soared to the dome of heaven, but the spreaders of nets still search for him, alas, in the marshy wastes!"

18. The best account of the economic policies of Emperor Wu and his immediate successor, and the objections to them posed by the Confucianists, is found in the *Yen-t'ieh-lun* or "Discourses on Salt and Iron," trans. by Esson Gale. Although the debate upon which these discourses are based did not take place until 81 B. C. and was probably not written up by Huan K'uan until several decades later, a comparison with the later chapters of the *Shih chi* shows that they represent essentially the arguments of the economic advisers of Emperor Wu and their Confucian opponents.

II. THE BIOGRAPHY OF SSU-MA CH'IEN

1. See bibliography.

2. *Han shu* (hereafter abbreviated as HS) 62 writes *"Huo-cheng";* there is much discussion by commentators, but the general opinion is that the HS reading is correct.

3. According to the *Tso chuan* Duke Shao 29, Chung was the son of Shao-kao, the emperor who preceded Chuan Hsü, while Li was the son of Chuan Hsü himself. But this passage of the *Tso* also contains the dubious genealogy of the Liu family which some scholars believe was inserted in the *Tso* by Liu Hsin (d. 23 A. D.). This may account for the fact that Ssu-ma Ch'ien does not refer to these genealogies of Chung and Li. Clearly, however, they were regarded as two distinct families and the question arises why Ch'ien seems to derive his ancestry from both. Ssu-ma Chen, author of the *So-yin* commentary to the *Shih chi,* states that Hsiu Fu was a descendant of the Li family but believes that Ch'ien wished as much as possible to give the impression that he was also related to the Chung family which was in charge of astronomical affairs. On the other hand he may have had too little information to say exactly how he was related to these ancient and probably purely legendary personages.

4. All of the above comes, with some condensation, from the *Narratives of the States* 18/2b–3a (Ch'u 2).

5. The source of this statement is unknown.

6. Both kings encountered rebellions led by their sons. Chin, at this time under the rule of Duke Wen, the famous Ch'ung-erh, was very powerful, and aided King Hsiang in his struggles. So it is not surprising that the family should move to Chin (SC 4/69–74).

7. Sui Hui, also called Shih Hui, fled to Ch'in in 620 (*Tso* Duke Wen 7). At this time he was not yet general of the Central Army. Shao-liang was the old kingdom of Liang. It was conquered by Ch'in and the name changed to Shao-liang. But at this time it was part of Chin.

8. His name was Ssu-ma Hsi; he was three times the prime minister of the state of Chung-shan. *Intrigues of the Warring States* 33 (Chung-shan).

9. Some commentators would read *po* for the *chuan* of the present text, i.e., "masters of the arts of swordsmanship and boxing."

10. The Wei dynasty commentator on the HS, Ju Shun, says that this is the K'uai-wai who appears in the "Memoirs of Assassin Retainers," SC 86. But in the present text of this chapter there is no such name. It has been suggested that K'uai-wai is the same as Kai Nieh, a famous master of swordsmanship of Yü-tz'u, a district of Chao, who discussed his art with Ching K'o. The assumption is that in the old text which Ju Shun saw, the names were still the same but later came to be written differently. *Huai-nan Tzu* 9/16b mentions a Ssu-ma K'uai-wai who was a swordsman and the Latter Han commentator on the *Huai-nan Tzu*, Kao Yu, identifies him as a descendant of the earl of Ch'eng, Hsiu Fu.

11. According to the Latter Han scholar, Ying Shao, quoted by Yen Shih-ku in his commentary on the HS, King Hui of Ch'in wished to make an attack upon Shu. Ssu-ma Ts'o supported this plan, but Chang I argued that it would be to greater advantage to attack Han. The king decided in favor of Ts'o's suggestion.

12. In 316 B. C., according to SC 15/81.

13. The HS writes his name as Ch'i.

14. According to SC 5/57 the name was changed in 327 B. C. Commentators dispute this date, but it is certain that the change took place many years before the time of Lord Wu-an. Perhaps the sentence belongs earlier in the narrative.

15. In 260 B. C. Lord Wu-an, Po Ch'i, was a famous general of Ch'in. This was the notorious battle in which Po Ch'i, after defeating the Chao forces, massacred some 450,000 Chao soldiers who had surrendered to him (SC 73/8).

16. Po Ch'i had become very powerful and had many enemies at court. Although Ch'in had been victorious against Chao, the battle was very costly and Po Ch'i opposed King Chao's plans for any further military expeditions. Angered and suspicious of his loyalty, the king in 257 B. C. sent Po Ch'i a messenger bearing a sword with orders to commit suicide. Presumably Ssu-ma Chin was ordered to die at the same time. Tu-yu was some 10 *li* west of the Ch'in capital of Hsien-yang (SC 73/12).

17. Most commentators identify Lord Wu-hsin as Wu Ch'en, a man of Ch'en, who took part in the revolt against Ch'in led by Ch'en Shê and set himself up as King of Chao in 209 B. C. (SC 48/11). But Hsiang Liang,

uncle of Hsiang Yü, who died in 208, also called himself Lord Wu-hsin and he may be the person meant.

18. In 206 B. C., SC 7/38 records: "The general of Chao, Ssu-ma Ang, several times distinguished himself in battle. Therefore Hsiang Yü set up Ang as king of Yin, ruling over Ho-nei with his capital at Ch'ao-ko."

19. The following year, 205, when Kao-tsu marched east again from Han. SC 8/46 says that Kao-tsu "took the King of Yin prisoner." *Chin shu* 1/1a, in the Annals of Emperor Hsüan, traces the ancestry of Ssu-ma I (later given the posthumous title of Emperor Hsüan), the grandfather of Ssu-ma Yen, founder of the Chin dynasty, back to this Ssu-ma Ang.

20. The HS writes the name with slightly different characters.

21. HS 19A/21a under the title *nei-shih,* notes that there were four markets in Ch'ang-an with masters in charge of them.

22. Wu-ta-fu. See HS 19A/25a.

23. In Han-ch'eng hsien of present day Shensi. This was the area of the old Shao-liang, later Hsia-yang, where the Ssu-ma family had lived for generations.

24. *T'ai-shih-kung.* There is much dispute among commentators about the origin, rank, and salary of this position. The only completely reliable report is that of Ch'ien himself, who says in his letter to Jen An: "My father . . . dealt with affairs of astronomy and the calendar, which are close to divination and the worship of the spirits. He was kept for the sport and amusement of the Emperor, treated the same as the musicians and jesters, and made light of by the vulgar men of his day." At this time, then, the official duties of the position were concerned only with astronomy and did not include the writing of history, which Ssu-ma T'an and his son undertook privately. For this and other reasons which he mentions in his Introduction, pp. ix–xi, Chavannes translates the title as *"duc grand astrologue."* But as I have pointed out in Chapter III, affairs of astronomy and the keeping of historical records were from early times closely associated in Chinese history and we know from notices in the *Shih chi* itself that men with the title of *T'ai-shih* in the Chou period had something to do with the keeping of historical records. So although their actual duties did not call for it, it is obvious that both Ssu-ma T'an and his son believed that both they and their ancestors should rightly deal not only with astronomical affairs but also with the keeping of historical records. Keeping in mind then that at this particular time they were not officially historians, I see no great objection to translating the title as "Grand Historian." If we were to follow Chavannes' translation, we should have to render the title of the

Shih chi, mistakenly translated by him as "Mémoires historiques," as "Records of the Astrologer," which would be simply misleading.

Later on in this text and elsewhere we find the title given as *T'ai-shih-ling,* and this is probably the correct form which Ssu-ma Ch'ien has usually abbreviated as *T'ai-shih.* I cannot agree with Chavannes' rendering of the word *kung* as *"duc."* There is no indication that Ssu-ma T'an ever received any honorary title of nobility which would justify this translation. On the other hand, as Wang Kuo-wei has pointed out (*op. cit.,* p. 6a–7b) the word *kung* was used frequently in the Han as an honorary suffix about equivalent to our "Mr." or "Master." It thus had no more of the technical sense of a noble title than does the word *tzu* (technically "viscount") in the names Lao Tzu, Chuang Tzu, etc. An examination of the SC text here and elsewhere will show that quite regularly Ch'ien uses *T'ai-shih* when referring to the office, and *T'ai-shih-kung* when referring to the particular person, his father or himself, who held the office. I have therefore translated the former as "Grand Historian" and the latter as "The Grand Historian" much as we distinguish by the use of the article in English between the office of "mayor" and "the Mayor," meaning the man who holds the office. As to why Ssu-ma Ch'ien uses the phrase "The Grand Historian" to refer to both himself and his father, see Chapter IV, pp. 131–32 and note 38. In the following section it is fairly easy to distinguish whether he means his father or himself, though in the closing paragraph where he calls his history "The book of The Grand Historian" it is possible that the title should be in the plural to include Ssu-ma T'an also.

25. Mentioned in SC 27/93 as an authority on astronomy.

26. A man of Tzu-ch'uan; his *tzu* is Shu-yüan (SC 121/25).

27. Master Huang (*Huang Tzu*), mentioned as Scholar Huang (*Huang Sheng*) in SC 121/16. See Chapter V, p. 145. This is an example of the Han usage of the words *tzu* and *sheng* as titles of respect.

28. *Book of Changes, Hsi tz'u* B/3b.

29. The Confucianists at this time, as indeed later, paid a great deal of attention to details of ritual, dress, etc.; hence this criticism.

30. The text here has the word *chien* (man radical) which T'an has used above to describe the parsimony of the Mohists. Commentators suggest it should be corrected to the homophone *chien* (tree radical), with the meaning I have given.

31. Following the HS reading, which seems preferable to the SC. The second part of the sentence is a reference to *Lao Tzu* 7.

32. This criticism may be found in two works of earlier date, the *Yen-*

tzu ch'un-ch'iu Sec. 1, 8/29a, and *Mo Tzu* Sec. 39, 9/21a. Ssu-ma T'an's criticism here was noted by Yang Hsiung in his *Fa yen* Sec. 7, 5/2a, where he wrongly attributes it to Ssu-ma Ch'ien. Yang Hsiung's reply is that in ancient times men could, while pursuing an agricultural life, find time in three years to complete the study of one Classic. But the scholars of his own day, he complains, have become too engrossed in petty details and furbelows and hence take much longer in their study. Pan Ku (HS 30/27a) repeats and elaborates on Yang Hsiung's point, declaring that the ancient scholars, by concentrating only upon the general meaning of a book, could complete their study of the Five Classics by the time they were thirty. For a translation of the HS passage, see Tjan Tjoe Som, *Po-Hu T'ung,* 143.

33. "Also" probably means "The Mohists as well as the Confucianists." The passage is based on *Han Fei Tzu* Sec. 49, 19/1b and Sec. 50, 19/7b. In the latter chapter Han Fei remarks that both the Mohists and Confucianists declare they are following the ways of Yao and Shun, though they do not agree at all in their practices.

34. Literally "so that the threes and fives shall not be lost." This phrase "threes and fives" is found in a number of late Chou and Han works, though the exact meaning is obscure. An examination of its various usages suggests it indicates something like "the proper order," "the real situation." It seems to derive from the terminology of the *Book of Changes.*

35. *Lao Tzu* 37.

36. The present SC text reads: "The Sage does not perish," a phrase suggesting some idea of immortality. Ssu-ma Chen says the phrase comes from the *Kuei-ku Tzu,* but it is not found in our present text of that work. The HS writes "The Sage is without skill"; this accords with the thought of Lao Tzu and seems preferable.

37. This section resembles the thought and wording of the *Huai-nan Tzu* 7/6b. The *Huai-nan Tzu,* written sometime before the death of the prince of Huai-nan, Liu An, in 122 B. C., was contemporary in composition with this essay. Both works most likely drew upon earlier Taoist writings.

38. The SC text writes only "spirit," but the HS has the double phrase "spirit and substance," which seems preferable.

39. Neither the SC nor HS texts mentions Ssu-ma Ch'ien's *tzu,* Tzu-ch'ang. See Chapter V, note 51.

40. In Han-ch'eng hsien. See Note 23 above. Another theory would put it in Hsia-yang hsien, but this seems unlikely. See Cheng Hao-sheng, *op. cit.,* pp. 10–12. There are several theories as to the date of Ch'ien's birth. The date indicated by Chang Shou-chieh and followed by Wang Kuo-wei, Cheng Hao-sheng, and Ch'ien Mu, 145 B. C., is most generally accepted.

41. That is, north of the Yellow River on the southern side of the hills. At this time T'an was not yet employed at court and the family presumably made a living farming and raising animals.

42. According to Ssu-ma Chen, the *Po-wu-chih* calls Ch'ien a man of Hsien-wu Village in Mou-ling. Mou-ling was a suburb of the capital and it is probable that T'an and his family moved there when he took office as Grand Historian around 140. This statement is not found in the present text of the *Po-wu-chih,* which is of doubtful authenticity, but Wang Kuo-wei believes it is based upon a Han dynasty document of registration and is completely reliable. Ch'ien had probably already had some instruction in a village school and then continued his schooling at Mou-ling. There are three theories on the meaning of "old writings" (*ku-wen*). One is that Ch'ien studied with the authority on the *Book of Documents* Fu Sheng. But this is absurd, since Fu Sheng would by this time have been over 140 years old. The second is that "old writings" simply refers to old books such as the *Tso chuan,* etc. The third is that he studied the so-called "old texts" with K'ung An-kuo at this time. HS 88/14b states that Ch'ien inquired about the "old text" version of the *Book of Documents* from K'ung An-kuo and used sections of it in his own work. But Wang Kuo-wei believes that this took place some ten years later, when Ch'ien was about twenty. See Wang Kuo-wei, pp. 3a–4a.

43. Emperor Yü was supposed to have died at Hui-chi and on top of the mountain was a cave called The Cave of Yü.

44. *Chiu-i* in Honan, the burial place of Emperor Shun.

45. Lu and Ch'i, the states of Confucius and Mencius, were noted as the seat of Confucian learning. Note that Ch'ien makes a point of saying that he studied Confucianism, but never mentions any study of Taoism.

46. Near Ch'ü-fu, the home of Confucius.

47. Chavannes, Introd., p. xxxi, suggests that Ch'ien deliberately uses this phrase in imitation of Confucius, "who encountered difficulties between Ch'en and Ts'ai." Although there may be some truth in this, there seems to be no reason to doubt that Ch'ien actually did get into some kind of difficulties at these places. In his concluding remarks to SC 75 he writes: "I once visited Hsüeh. Its customs are rustic and countrified, and there are a great many ruffians and tough young men. It is very different from Tsou and Lu. I asked someone the reason for this and he replied, 'Lord Meng-ch'ang invited all the wandering knights and criminals from around to come to Hsüeh and set up some sixty thousand families here.'"

48. The exact date of this is uncertain. The *lang-chung* were palace attendants and, as we see later on, often accompanied the emperor on his

travels. According to the system suggested by Kung-sun Hung and adopted in 124, promising students of eighteen or older were selected for a year's instruction and those who passed examinations at the top of the class were qualified to become *lang-shih,* i.e., *lang-chung.* See SC 121/11 and HS 6, *Yüan-shuo* fifth year. Ch'ien started on his travels in 125 B. C. and must have been away from the capital for several years, so it is possible that on his return he underwent this instruction and attained his position because of his good grades. Or it may be, as he modestly says in his letter, that he was appointed simply because of his father's influence at court.

49. In 111 a military expedition was sent to the southwest, which created five new commanderies out of territory brought under Han rule. See SC 116, the chapter which Ch'ien wrote about the tribes of the southwest largely on the basis of his experiences at this time. This by no means ends the recital of Ch'ien's travels. Judging from the remarks he made in other chapters, he must have made a number of other trips in attendance on the emperor. He was one of the most widely traveled men of his age, a fact which helps to account for the wealth of material and broad outlook of his history. For a full list of places he is known to have visited, see Cheng Hao-sheng, pp. 32–40.

50. The great Feng Sacrifice at Mount T'ai, symbol of the divine election of the ruling house.

51. The area around Lo-yang.

52. Emperor Wu consulted the Confucianists and other court officials on the proper procedure for the sacrifice, but when they could not agree upon the type of ceremony he wanted, he discarded their suggestions and did not employ them, making up his own ritual instead (SC 28/73). This may be why Ssu-ma T'an was unable to take part in the ceremony, though it is more likely that he was simply too old and feeble. At any rate it was a great blow to him that he could not be present at this most solemn and auspicious of all ancient Chinese rites.

53. The emperor had already traveled to the east early in the year, leaving Ssu-ma T'an at Lo-yang. Ch'ien, after making his report at Ch'ang-an, journeyed east to join the imperial party, stopping to see his father on the way. The Feng Sacrifice took place in the summer and Ch'ien traveled with the emperor back to the capital by a northern route without seeing his father again, so T'an must have died during the summer or fall while Ch'ien was away. See Wang Kuo-wei, p. 5a.

54. These sentiments, in reversed order, are expressed in the *Classic of Filial Piety, Hsiao-ching.*

55. This refers to the *Book of Odes,* particularly to the hymns of the

section *Ta-ya* in praise of the Chou ancestors, which were supposed to have been written by the Duke of Chou. T'ai-wang, Wang Chi, Kung Liu, and Hou Chi are all ancestors of the Chou kings, Hou Chi being the founder of the family in the time of Emperor Yao.

56. 481 B. C., the end of the "Spring and Autumn" period. Actually it was 372 years earlier.

57. In 108. As in the so-called "three-year mourning period," this does not mean three full years but only to the beginning of the third year. Here the title *T'ai-shih-kung* is written *T'ai-shih-ling*.

58. Ie., books kept in the imperial libraries. It is probable that T'an had already collected a good deal of material which Ch'ien at this time began to work over.

59. In the spring of 110, when Emperor Wu first performed the great Feng and Shan sacrifices at Mount T'ai, he stopped to rest at a spot on the northeast side of the mountain where there existed what were said to be the remains of an ancient Illustrious Hall or *Ming t'ang*. At this time he expressed a desire to rebuild the hall, but upon consultation with court scholars could ascertain no detailed information on the shape or dimensions of the famous structure traditionally supposed to have existed in early Chou times. In this critical moment a man of Ch'i-nan named Kung-yü Tai appeared bearing a plan of what he claimed was the Illustrious Hall of the Yellow Emperor. Emperor Wu accordingly ordered a structure built to this design on the spot and four years later, in 106, when he again visited Mount T'ai, he performed sacrifices in the Hall, which he repeated, as indicated by our text, in 105 (SC 28/76, 84). As this account makes clear, the scholars of this time had no accurate information concerning the great audience hall of the Chou called *Ming t'ang* mentioned in the fourteenth section of the *Li chi*. For a treatment of the confused and voluminous lore on the subject of the *Ming t'ang*, see Alexander Coburn Soper, "The 'Dome of Heaven' in Asia," The Art Bulletin XXIX (1947), 238–241, and William Edward Soothill, *The Hall of Light*.

60. Ssu-ma Ch'ien, Hu Sui and a group of other court officials at this time worked to draw up a new calendar to replace the faulty one which the Han had inherited from previous ages. Although there was much discussion and a number of proposals, Wang Kuo-wei believes that the initiative for the reform and most of the actual work were due to Ch'ien alone. Detailed accounts of the discussions and the new calendar are found in SC 26 and HS 21. In the eleventh month the emperor sacrificed to *Shang-ti* in the Illustrious Hall and, because of the auspicious position of various stars and planets at this time, changed the era name to *T'ai-ch'u*. But ac-

cording to HS 6/31b the new calendar was not actually promulgated until the fifth month. (For an explanation of how the fifth month can come after the eleventh month, see below.) At this time it was announced that the Han year would begin with the first month and that the Han would honor yellow, color of the element earth. There had been many proposals before this that the Han change the beginning of its year and select an element to honor in order to show that it was a new dynasty entirely independent of the preceding Ch'in. But it was not until this year that the great step was finally taken. According to Han belief, the Hsia dynasty had begun its new year on the first month, *cheng-yüeh*, with the cyclical sign *yin*. The Shang dynasty had begun with the twelfth month, cyclical sign *ch'ou*, and the Chou dynasty with the eleventh month, sign *tzu*. It was thought that succeeding dynasties should follow this order, rotating among the eleventh, twelfth, and first months as their beginning. In *Analects* XV, 10, Confucius is reported to have told Yen Yüan that one should "follow the seasons of Hsia," i.e., begin the year with the first month. The Ch'in dynasty, however, instead of moving forward to the first month, had gone back one month, beginning its year with the tenth month, cyclical sign *hai*, and the Han had until this time continued the Ch'in practice, beginning its year with the tenth month. The Han calendar reform returned to the reputed practice of the Hsia, in accordance with the advice of Confucius, beginning its year with the first month, the first month of spring, some time in our own February. The correction of the calendar was an achievement of great and far-reaching significance. After this, with the exception of one attempt by Emperor Ming of the Wei (reign 227–239 A. D.), no dynasty ever tried to return to the old system of rotating the beginning of the year. Hence in China, Japan, and Korea today, wherever the old-system calendar is used, it is this so-called calendar of the Hsia, set up by Ssu-ma Ch'ien and his associates, that is followed.

61. For a discussion of the significance of this section of the translation see Chapter III, p. 87 *passim*.

62. The HS writes "There must be someone who can carry on and make them clear." The last four characters parallel a phrase from SC 27/83 describing how the Five Emperors and Three Dynasties "carried on and investigated" the ancient affairs of astronomy.

63. Cf. Mencius' theory that a true king will appear once every five hundred years (*Mencius* 2B/13 and 7B/36). See also Chapter III, p. 87.

64. A man of Liang who rose to position of *chan-shih*, a high post connected with the household of the empress and heir apparent. See HS

19/19a. He and Ch'ien worked together revising the calendar, and Ch'ien had the highest regard and feeling for him (SC 108/15).

65. Tung Chung-shu. The following exposition of the *Spring and Autumn Annals* is almost entirely a paraphrase of sections of Tung's *Ch'un-ch'iu fan-lu,* hereafter referred to as CCFL.

66. Note that the HS omits this phrase. This is one of the many indications that Pan Ku either chose to or had to be more cautious in his references to imperial institutions than his predecessor.

67. It is a great temptation to render this sentence in some such manner as: "I had thought of setting forth my ideas in abstract sayings (*k'ung-yen*), but I have decided that it would be more cogent and explicit to manifest them through actual events." (See Nivisen, "The Problem of 'Knowledge' and 'Action' in Chinese Thought Since Wang Yang-ming," *Studies in Chinese Thought,* p. 114.) This is probably the way many later Chinese scholars have understood it. But the text later on makes it clear that both Ssu-ma Ch'ien and Hu Sui believed that the *Spring and Autumn Annals* actually *does* embody *k'ung-yen,* theoretical principles or judgments, so that this translation is impossible. See the discussion of this term in Chapter III, pp. 87–89.

68. This parallels a passage in the CCFL Sec. 2, 1/9a, which reads: "The *Odes* describes the will, and therefore is preeminent for its unspoiled naturalness. The *Rites* regulates distinctions, and therefore is preeminent for order and refinement. Music intones virtue, and therefore is preeminent in its influencing power. The *Documents* records achievements, and therefore is outstanding concerning events. The *Changes* explores heaven and earth, and therefore is best for calculating probabilities. The *Spring and Autumn* rectifies right and wrong, and therefore stands preeminent in ruling men." As will be seen, Ch'ien's description in wording and meaning agrees with Tung Chung-shu's in all cases except music. His discussion of music follows the teaching of Hsün Tzu, beginning with the pun on *yüeh* "music" and *lo* "joy," and emphasizing that music is the bringer of harmony and order to all human life. As Hsün Tzu writes, "Music is the supreme governor of mankind" (*Hsün Tzu* 14/2b). In his essay on music, SC 24, Ch'ien expands this teaching of Hsün Tzu's, adding various examples of how the power of music has brought peace and order to the nations and even influenced supernatural beings.

69. See CCFL Sec. 7, 5/1a.

70. This quotation is not found in the *Changes* itself but in a work on it, the *I-wei t'ung-kua-yen,* A/5b.

71. A quotation from the *Wen-yen* commentary on the *Changes* under the hexagram *k'un*.

72. This section is based on CCFL Sec. 17, 6/3b.

73. This is apparently an old saying. It is found also in a memorial by Chia I, HS 48/26b, and in the *Ta-Tai Li-chi* 2/1b.

74. The theory of the Kung-yang school, widely accepted in the Han, that Confucius wrote the *Annals* to serve as the model for the rulers of a new dynasty.

75. A stock phrase in Han rhetoric. The traditional interpretation is that barbarian peoples will come to China in submission from such distant places that they have no knowledge of the Chinese language but must translate their own languages into an intermediary language, from which they will then be retranslated into Chinese. See Note 3, Chapter I.

76. Causing injury or allowing it to come to one's body was, according to Chinese thought, a grave offense against one's parents.

77. For the interpretation of this phrase *yin-yüeh* I have followed the note by Yen Shih-ku in the HS. The more common interpretation is "subtle and terse," i.e., the writers of the *Odes* and *Documents* were subtle and terse when they tried to set forth, etc. But this seems out of place when Ch'ien's entire theory is that literature is motivated by suffering and dissatisfaction.

78. Two sections of the present *Han Fei Tzu* 4. In this case and the *Lü-lan* above, more commonly known as *Lü-shih ch'un-ch'iu,* Ch'ien has substituted these ways of designating the books for their more common titles in order to make his clauses conform to a four-character pattern.

79. Why this four-character phrase is tacked on here I cannot say. Perhaps Ch'ien added it as an afterthought to show that he did not mean literally that he began his history with Emperor Yao. More likely, however, it belongs to the following section, the Table of Contents, which begins with a mention of the Yellow Emperor.

80. Most of the rulers of the previous dynasties and feudal states claimed descent from one or another of the Five Emperors.

81. Hsia, Shang and Chou. The HS writes *chüeh* instead of *t'ung,* i.e., "the great task" instead of "the task of unification."

82. A former petty clerk in the Ch'in administration who aided Kao-tsu in his conquest of the empire and rose to the highest position in the Han court. He was famous as the compiler of the Han legal code. See SC 53.

83. A general of Kao-tsu famous for his brilliant and clever military strategy. See SC 92.

84. Another former Ch'in official who handled affairs of weights and

measures and the calendar for the Han court. See SC 96. HS 30/39b lists a work of his in 16 sections under the school of *Yin-yang;* the book is now lost.

85. The famous literatus of the Ch'in who compiled the code of rites and etiquette for Kao-tsu's court. See SC 99.

86. A high official of the early Han. When he served as minister to the fief of Ch'i, he became acquainted with a Taoist named Master Kai, who expounded to him Taoist ideas on government. Ts'ao Ts'an was much impressed and put them into practice with great success in Ch'i and later when he became Prime Minister of the central court (SC 54).

87. The poet and statesman Chia I, author of the *Hsin shu,* which is still extant. He is generally regarded as a Confucianist, and Pan Ku in HS 30/31b lists his book under the Confucian school. It is not clear why Ch'ien identifies him here as a Legalist, though it may be because he advocated the policy of weakening the feudal lords and strengthening the central government which was usually associated with Legalist thinkers. See his biography in HS 48. His biography in SC 84 does not deal extensively with his political ideas.

88. A student of the doctrines of Shen Pu-hai, Lord Shang, and the school of Legalism, who became a high official under Emperor Ching. He was the most outspoken advocate of the policy of stripping power from the feudal lords (SC 101). HS 30/41b under the Legalist school lists a work by him in 31 sections, now lost.

89. The famous Confucian official under Emperor Wu (SC 112). HS 30/32a under the Confucian school lists a work by him in 10 sections, which is now lost. At this point something may be said about these lost works of the early Han statesmen. An examination of the one work that is still extant, the *Hsin shu* of Chia I, will show that it is made up largely of short essays and memorials on specific subjects of government policy. The most famous of these, the essay on "The Faults of Ch'in," is included in the *Shih chi* (end of SC 6), while Pan Ku has copied in others which were submitted to the throne as memorials in his biography of Chia I (HS 48) and his "Treatise on Food and Money" (HS 24). In other words, the most important and representative sections of Chia I's book are preserved in the histories of the period. We may perhaps surmise from this that the other works listed under the names of Ch'ao Ts'o, Kung-sun Hung, etc., were mainly or perhaps entirely collections of memorials which they presented to the throne and represented no more than duplicate copies of the memorials which Ssu-ma Ch'ien and Pan Ku copied into their histories under the names of these men. If such was the nature of these books, it

will help to explain how Ssu-ma Ch'ien and Pan Ku happened to have access to the texts of these memorials which they used in their works, and may also suggest why the books were allowed to fall into oblivion. One is often appalled when looking over ancient Chinese bibliographies at the number of seemingly important works that have been lost. But although there were undoubtedly a number of regrettable losses, I would suggest that most of these works were allowed to disappear either because they were not worth the labor of copying and preserving, or because the bulk of their contents had already been copied into some other larger work, such as one of the major histories, that was in no danger of becoming lost.

90. The present text lacks any indication of who says this. I have taken it as the words of Ssu-ma Ch'ien and for convenience's sake continued the narration in the first person down to the end of the chapter, although there are no pronouns in the latter part.

91. The phrase refers to the last of the eight treatises, that on economic practices, SC 30.

92. Or, punctuating differently, "This is the book and postface of the Grand Historian."

93. Ssu-ma Chen states that *Ming-shan,* "Famous Mountain," was a term for the Imperial Archives, but Yen Shih-ku takes it in its literal meaning of a famous mountain, i.e., some secluded place where Ssu-ma Ch'ien deposited a copy of his work to escape damage in case war or some natural catastrophe should destroy the capital.

94. I.e., this is the seventieth and last of the *lieh-chuan* chapters. In his Table of Contents above, Ch'ien does not list this chapter itself.

95. This last sentence is not found in the HS text. I am inclined to agree with commentators who consider it a later interpolation.

96. There has been much discussion among commentators concerning the ten missing chapters of the *Shih chi.* Some deny that they were ever written, while others claim that some, such as the annals of emperors Ching and Wu, were suppressed. The evidence seems to be insufficient to permit any conclusive decision. See *Shiki kaichû kôshô,* X, 102–105, and Yü Chia-hsi, "On the Missing Chapters of Ssu-ma Ch'ien's Work Shih Chi," *Fu Jen Sinological Journal,* XV (1947), 1–91.

97. Shao-ch'ing is the *tzu* of Jen An. On the date and circumstances of this letter, see Appendix. A second text of the letter, containing slight variations, is found in *Wen hsüan* 41. Chavannes has translated the letter in Appendix I to his Introduction, pp. ccxxvi–ccxxxviii.

98. The *Li chi* Sec. 41, 59/10a says: "A Confucian . . . shall recommend worthy men and work to advance them."

99. A paraphrase of Ch'ü Yüan's words, "Alone in my sadness and despair, to whom shall I speak?" (*Li sao, Ch'u-tz'u* 1/49a).

100. I.e., for whose benefit would I be working if no one understands or appreciates me, and who indeed would even listen to my suggestions?

101. A reference to the famous story of the *ch'in* player Po Ya, who had only one true friend, Chung Tzu-ch'i, who understood his playing. When his friend died, he smashed the instrument and never again played.

102. An old saying, also found in *Intrigues of the Warring States* 6/7a (Chao 1), where a man is said to be willing to *die* for one who appreciates him.

103. The pearl of Marquis Sui and the jade of Lord Ho, two precious objects of ancient times, used as metaphors for extraordinary talent and worth. Hsü Yu and Po I were two legendary figures renowned for purity of conduct (SC 61).

104. On the question of why Jen An was in prison, see Appendix.

105. *Chi-tung,* the last month of winter. According to *yin-yang* theories, winter is the time for administering punishments, so that if cases involving capital punishment were still pending, they were apt to be settled in haste at the end of winter. Note for instance that the marquis of Wei-ch'i and Kuan Fu were executed on "the last day of the twelfth month" because their rivals feared that the beginning of spring might bring a pardon for them (SC 107/27). See also Hulsewé, *Remnants of Han Law,* I, 104.

106. The area north-west of Ch'ang-an where sacrifices were performed.

107. While Confucius was visiting in the state of Wei, Duke Ling of Wei drove with his wife and favorite eunuch Yung Ch'ü in a carriage about the city, instructing Confucius to follow in another carriage behind. Confucius considered such conduct disgraceful and left the state. In his "Hereditary House of Confucius" (SC 47/41), Ssu-ma Ch'ien says that Confucius went to Ts'ao, but the text here indicates as his destination Ch'en, the state Confucius had visited earlier.

108. The philosopher Shang Yang once asked Chao Liang who was the greater, himself or Po-li Hsi. Chao Liang replied scornfully that Po-li Hsi had gained the recognition of the king of Ch'in by his wisdom, but that Shang Yang had depended upon the introduction of the eunuch Ching Chien to secure an interview with the king (SC 68/17).

109. The eunuch Chao T'an was riding once with Emperor Wen of the Han, when Yüan Ssu (Yüan Ang) remonstrated with the emperor, saying that only heroes and great men should share the imperial carriage, not "remnants of the knife and saw," as eunuchs were called (SC 101/6). Because Chao T'an's personal name is the same as that of Ch'ien's father, he

avoids writing the name here by referring to him as "a man of the same name."

110. The sentence is largely a paraphrase of Yüan Ssu's remonstrance to Emperor Wen (SC 101/6).

111. "To await punishment" is a conventional phrase of humility used when referring to official service. It means that one is unworthy and actually deserving of punishment; it has nothing to do with Ch'ien's later punishment.

112. Ch'ien is here referring to the five "merits" which he says characterized the great men of ancient times. In SC 18/2 he writes: "In ancient times there were five grades of merit among government servants. The first was that of men who, by their virtue, set up great families and maintained their fiefs and their merit was called 'loyalty.' Next were those who served by their words and their merit was called 'labor.' Next were those who served by strength, called 'achievement.' Next were those who brought glory to their position, called 'eminence.' Finally there were those who held office for a long time, and their merit was called 'longevity.'" It is the modest lament of Ch'ien that he has not been able to achieve any of these distinctions.

113. This may mean the traditional function of the Ssu-ma family, the writing of history. Or it may simply refer to family affairs of wealth and property; i.e., Ch'ien had done nothing to increase the family fortune.

114. I.e., being busy with official duties, he could not think of doing great things for himself or his family and friends.

115. Li Ling was appointed as a *shih-chung,* an attendant at court (HS 54/9b).

116. The title of the Hsiung-nu ruler.

117. According to Hsiung-nu custom those who recovered the bodies of the dead from the battlefield could claim the dead men's property. See SC 110/25.

118. The "Wise Kings of the Left and Right" were the two highest ranking military leaders under the *Shan-yü,* hereditary commanders of the eastern and western sections of the Hsiung-nu nation respectively (SC 110/21).

119. This expedition of Li Ling against the Hsiung-nu, one of the most famous and brilliant of Han military exploits, was the first time the Chinese had opposed infantry against the Hsiung-nu cavalry in barbarian territory. Initially Li Ling won a smashing success, the news of which, when it reached the court, caused great rejoicing. But without reinforcements, which the Emperor failed to send, he could not follow up his victory. The Chinese

were forced to retreat, fighting as they went, until they reached a valley only some 100 *li* from the frontier. When a Chinese captain turned traitor and informed the barbarians that no reinforcements were on the way, the Hsiung-nu surrounded Li Ling's forces and attacked in overwhelming numbers. Most of the Chinese died fighting, only some 400 of the original force of almost 5,000 reaching the border in safety. Li Ling, realizing the hopelessness of the situation, buried the army's treasures, dismissed his men, and surrendered to the Hsiung-nu. Emperor Wu, famous for the severity with which he treated his unsuccessful generals, expected Li Ling to die with his men. When the news of the surrender reached the court, he was sick with rage. The court united in condemning the unfortunate general, only Ssu-ma Ch'ien daring to speak out on his behalf. A year later, the emperor realized that he had been to blame for not dispatching reinforcements and sent word for Li Ling to return to China, but met with a refusal. Later, when it was reported that Li Ling was instructing the Hsiung-nu in military science, the emperor ordered the death of all members of Li Ling's immediate family. Embittered by this act of imperial vengeance, Li Ling refused all invitations to return to China, and remained among the Hsiung-nu until his death in 74 B. C. See HS 54 and Dubs, *History of the Former Han,* II, 13–16.

120. This was also said of Li Ling's grandfather, the famous general Li Kuang (SC 109/10), and of the ancient general Jang Chü (SC 64/5).

121. The Erh-shih General Li Kuang-li (not to be confused with Li Kuang above), was so called because he had formerly led a successful expedition against the city of Erh-shih (Sutrishna), the capital of Ta-yüan, or Fergana (SC 123/34). He was the leader of the present expedition, commanding 30,000 cavalry troops. But he failed to make contact with the enemy and returned with no great deeds, while all the glory went to his subordinate, Li Ling. Li Kuang-li was a brother of Emperor Wu's favorite at this time, the Lady Li, and so it was especially impolitic of Ssu-ma Ch'ien to appear to criticize him.

122. The crime of "defaming the emperor" (*wu-shang*), was of the utmost gravity and generally punished by execution. See Hulsewé, *op. cit.,* p. 169 *ff.* Hence Ch'ien at this time no doubt expected death. But there were occasional cases in which castration was substituted for the death penalty, as happened with Ssu-ma Ch'ien. See Hulsewé, p. 385–6. It may well be that the emperor felt that Ch'ien was too valuable a man to lose, and ordered the death sentence commuted to castration so he could continue to make use of Ch'ien's services. Ch'ien Mu in his article "An Examination and Interpretation of the Title Tai Sze Kung" [*sic*], *Academic Review* I

(1953), 57, suggests that Ch'ien himself *requested* the punishment in order to be able to finish writing his history. There is no conclusive evidence of this; certainly Ch'ien himself could hardly be expected to give us any. But it is an interesting suggestion and worth bearing in mind as we read Ch'ien's repeated expressions of his deep sense of shame and his explanation of why he did not choose the customary course of suicide.

123. One of the much criticized measures of Emperor Wu's fiscal policy was this system of commutation of punishments on payment of large sums of money, because it placed the poor at a complete disadvantage and led the government officials to trump up charges against wealthy men whenever the treasury needed money.

124. Tallies and documents bestowed by the emperor when he awarded territories or privileges to distinguished subjects.

125. Cf. Ch'ien's remarks at the end of SC 81: "It takes bravery to resign yourself to death. Death itself is not difficult; it is choosing the right place to die that is hard."

126. Persons condemned for minor crimes were made to wear special clothing or marks, like the scarlet letters of early America.

127. *Li chi*, Sec. 1, 3/7a. The same statement is also found in a memorial by Chia I, HS 48/30a. The meaning is not that officials of the government are outside the law but that any man who has the moral qualifications to hold high office also has the conscience to commit suicide if he is guilty of a crime without being forced to undergo legal procedure to prove his guilt. It is because of this custom among officials of committing suicide rather than undergo imprisonment and trial that Ch'ien goes to such lengths to excuse his own departure from the accepted practice. See Hulsewé, *op. cit.*, p. 296.

128. King Wen, chief or earl of the West, was imprisoned by Emperor Chou of the Shang because he was too powerful. It is very daring of Ssu-ma Ch'ien to include a great sage like King Wen among his list of condemned men. It was probably this sort of unorthodox boldness that shocked later Confucianists like Pan Ku. This is only one of many indications that the letter is a genuine work of Ch'ien.

129. Famous minister of the First Emperor of the Ch'in. After the emperor's death, he was defeated by a rival at court and executed (SC 87). The traditional five punishments of the old Chou law were tattooing, cutting off the nose, cutting off the feet, castration, and execution. But the Ch'in had its own customs and other lists are given for the five punishments inflicted upon Li Ssu.

130. The marquis of Huai-yin, Han Hsin, suspected by Emperor Kao-tsu

of treason, was tricked into coming to visit the emperor at Ch'en, and there seized and fettered (SC 92).

131. P'eng Yüeh was set up by Kao-tsu as king of Liang, but later dethroned and thrown into prison (SC 90). Chang Ao succeeded his father, Chang Erh, as king of Chao, but was later implicated in a plot to revolt against Kao-tsu and was seized and forced to commit suicide (SC 89).

132. The marquis of Chiang, Chou Po, led a coup d'état which seized power from the relatives of Empress Lü and restored it to the Liu family, but he was later accused of plotting rebellion and put into prison (SC 57).

133. The marquis of Wei-ch'i, Tou Ying, distinguished himself as a general in the Rebellion of the Seven States, but later became involved in a court squabble and was executed (SC 107).

134. Chi Pu, who had fought with Hsiang Yü against the Han, fled into hiding to avoid being punished after the Han was victorious, and served incognito as a slave to Chu Chia (SC 100).

135. Kuan Fu, a retainer of Tou Ying (See note 133 above) was involved in the same brawl with his master and condemned to death (SC 107).

136. A quotation from the *Ping fa* (*Art of War*), by Sun Wu, 5/16b & 17b.

137. Ssu-ma Ch'ien is implying that it was not concern for his own family that kept him from suicide. We know nothing about his wife, but he seems to have had only one child, a daughter. In spite of the affection he might have felt for them, the little family would hardly have detained a Chinese gentleman who sincerely felt it his duty to commit suicide.

138. Note that Ch'ien uses this same phrase "masterful and sure" to describe the subjects of his "Memoirs," p. 57 above.

139. The *Wen hsüan* text differs somewhat here, reading: "I have gathered up and brought together the old traditions of the world that were scattered and lost; I have examined these affairs, arranging their beginnings and ends, considering the principles behind their success and failure, their rise and decay, reaching back into antiquity to Hsien Yüan [the Yellow Emperor] and down to the present, comprising 10 Tables, 12 Annals, 8 Treatises, 30 Hereditary Houses, and 70 Memoirs, in all 130 chapters."

140. As the famous recluses of antiquity, to preserve their purity from the contamination of the world, were wont to do.

141. By this Ch'ien almost surely means the judgment of posterity concerning the worth of his history and whether it justifies his decision to suffer humiliation for the sake of its completion. Needless to say, Ch'ien has been amply vindicated by the glowing praise of two thousand years. Although the common people of the Han appear to have believed that the

souls of the dead dwelt on Mt. T'ai (see Edouard Chavannes, *Le T'ai Chan,* p. 13 and p. 399), there is little indication that Ch'ien or others of his class seriously entertained any such conception of a life after death. His remark earlier in the letter that should Jen An be executed "then in the long journey hereafter your spirit would forever bear me personal resentment" I take to be no more than a conventional manner of speaking used primarily for literary effect. See Wang Ch'ung's specific denials of a conscious life after death, *Lun hêng* 15, translated by Alfred Forke, Pt. I, pp. 191–201, and the twelfth of the "Nineteen Old Poems of the Han" translated by Arthur Waley, *170 Chinese Poems,* pp. 65–66.

142. Cf. *Book of Changes,* 7/11b, *Hsi-tz'u* A: "Writing does not fully convey one's words, and words do not fully convey one's thoughts."

143. The *Wen hsüan* text adds at the end the conventional phrase, "With respect I salute you again." It is worth noting that in his letter Ch'ien uses the word *ju* (shame) a total of nineteen times, employing it as a kind of doleful refrain. It is powerful writing like this that has won him the admiration of generations of his countrymen.

144. His biography is found in HS 66.

145. All of these works except the *Genealogical Origins* (*Shih pen*) and the *Spring and Autumn of Ch'u and Han* (*Ch'u-Han ch'un-ch'iu*) are still extant.

146. "Hsiang-po," *Odes, Hsiao-ya* section, a poem of anger written by a eunuch who had suffered slander.

147. "Cheng-min," *Odes, Ta-ya* section. Most of Pan Ku's appraisal is taken from an essay by his father Pan Piao on the merits and faults of the *Shih chi* quoted in Piao's biography, *Hou-Han-shu, lieh-chuan* 30A/4a–5a. The criticism that Ch'ien's judgments differ from those of Confucius and the Classics dates back to Yang Hsiung. See the end of Yang Hsiung's biography, HS 87B/19a.

III. THE BEGINNINGS OF CHINESE HISTORIOGRAPHY

1. *Shuo-wen chieh-tzu* 3B/4b, by Hsü Shen, preface dated 100 A. D. He defines *shih* as "one who records affairs" and explains the character as a hand holding "middle" (*chung*), defining "middle" as "correct" (*cheng*).

2. See Wang Kuo-wei's essay "Explaining the word *Shih*," in *Kuan-t'ang chi-lin* 6 and Naitô, *Shina shigakushi,* p. 5.

3. Naitô, *Shigakushi,* pp. 80–81.

4. H. G. Creel, *Studies in Early Chinese Culture,* p. 57 and *passim.*

5. *Mémoires historiques,* Intro. p. clv.

6. This parallel which Chavannes draws between Greek and Chinese historical writing, though basically apt, presents certain difficulties. Nothing in the brief, disconnected pronouncements of the *Book of Documents* or the similarly brief poetic recitals of legend in the *Odes* can compare in scope and popular appeal to Homer. Although the *Odes* and *Documents* may have been far richer and more interesting to the men of the late Chou and early Han than the bare text of the *Spring and Autumn,* they were by no means as easy to read and understand. And when the *Tso Commentary* on the *Spring and Autumn* began to be better known and read at the end of the Former Han, the situation was actually reversed. The *Tso Commentary* is so rich, so dramatic, and so full of strange and supernatural doings, that it has often rather scandalized later scholars. As Fan Ning (339–401) says in his preface to the *Ku-liang Commentary:* "The *Tso-shih Commentary* is beautiful and rich, but it errs by dealing with the supernatural." In other words, read with the *Tso Commentary,* the *Spring and Autumn* became far more fascinating and appealing as literature than the archaic and obscure *Book of Documents.*

7. *Li chi,* Sec. 13, 29/5b.

8. "Treatise on Literature," HS 30/18b.

9. *Ta-Tai Li-chi,* Sec. 48, 3/3a.

10. SC 4/54 & 62. It is important to note that the whole eerie story of the ancestry and birth of Pao Ssu is in the form of a quotation from this ancient historian. Nowhere does Ch'ien indicate that he himself believed this or other similar fantastic tales that he relates at second hand. Like Herodotus, he felt it his business to record what people said, but not necessarily to believe it.

11. SC 5/47. "The Chronicle of Ch'in," the only other local chronicle besides the *Spring and Autumn Annals* that existed in the early Han, has been appended to the end of SC 6. It begins with the ruler who preceeded Wen, Duke Hsiang, 777–766, but is only a bare outline of successions and deaths of rulers.

12. That the *Spring and Autumn Annals* in late Chou and early Han times meant the *Annals* with the *Kung-yang* text appended may account for the fact that Ssu-ma Ch'ien in his review of the composition and transmission of the *Annals* makes no reference to the *Kung-yang* at all. See SC 14/7, introduction. In SC 121/28, he does, however, call Tung Chung-shu a follower of the *Kung-yang* school, clearly because by Tung's time the rival *Ku-liang* school was beginning to come to prominence, necessitating a distinction between followers of the two commentaries.

13. See Naitô, *Shigakushi*, pp. 81–82, and Karlgren's important study, *On the Nature and Authenticity of the Tso Chuan.*

14. It has often been pointed out by Western scholars that the attempts of the commentaries to discover these subtle moral judgments, particularly in the exact wording of the chronicle, generally end in confusion, contradiction, and sheer absurdity. It may be noted, however, that the Chinese themselves, or at least the best minds among them, have long been aware of these absurdities. The Sung scholar and historian Ou-yang Hsiu disagreed with a number of the interpretations found in the three commentaries and denied the theory that the exact time-span of the *Annals* had any mystical significance. See *Ou-yang Wen-chung-kung chi* 18, his essays, "A Discussion of the *Ch'un-ch'iu*," and "Some Questions on the *Ch'un-ch'iu*." No less an authority than Chu Hsi stated flatly that attempts to read a hidden meaning into each word of the chronicle were absurd (*Chu-tzu yü-lei* 83/1b), while the Sung historian Cheng Ch'iao vigorously attacked this word-by-word theory of interpretation, calling it "a freakish and absurd theory invented by early Confucianists to delude posterity" (preface to his treatise on "Disasters and Portents," *T'ung chih,* 74). For a recent constructive attempt to explain the wording of the *Annals,* see the excellent article by George A. Kennedy, "Interpretation of the *Ch'un-ch'iu*," JAOS 62 (1942), 40–48.

15. E.g., the statement in one of the Han apochryphal works on the *Annals:* "Confucius said, 'I, Ch'iu, have perused the historical records, drawn upon the ancient plans and diagrams, and examined and brought together evidence of the evolutions of the past to form the laws for the imperial system of the Han." *Ch'un-ch'iu-wei Han-han-tzu,* in *Ku-wei-shu* 12/1b, *Shou-shan-ko ts'ung-shu.*

16. CCFL Sec. 33, 9/5b. The *Ch'un-ch'iu fan-lu* of Tung Chung-shu is important not only because of its influence upon Ssu-ma Ch'ien but also because it represents a step between the *Kung-yang Commentary* itself and the standard commentary on the *Kung-yang* by Ho Hsiu of the Latter Han. Prof. Shigezawa Toshio of Kyoto University has performed a noble service by arranging the many scattered remarks of Tung Chung-shu in his CCFL into the form of a year-by-year commentary on the *Annals* so that we may now use it conveniently and easily along with the other commentaries on the *Annals.* It is found in his *Studies in Chou and Han Thought (Shû-Kan shisô-kenkyû).*

17. CCFL Sec. 4, 3/5b.

18. E.g., Duke Chuang fourth year, sixth month.

19. This is the theory of the three ages, enunciated in the *Kung-yang*

under Duke Yin, first year, and again at the very end of the *Kung-yang*. This idea is also found in *Mo Tzu* 10/10a in a slightly different form. Tung Chung-shu makes much of this theory in his interpretation of the *Annals*.

20. *Kung-yang*, Duke Ting, first year.

21. For the benefit of readers unfamiliar with the Chinese unicorn, the "small deer with a horn," I may say that to the best of my knowledge the origin of this legend in China is as obscure as that of the similar legend in Europe.

22. *Fa yen* 10/7b.

23. *Lun heng* 29/10b.

24. *Lü-shih ch'un-ch'iu* 17/2b.

25. SC 81/5, i.e., with lies or meaningless promises.

26. SC 8/63.

27. SC 129/7.

28. CCFL Sec. 17, 6/3b.

29. *Analects* VII, 1.

30. *Li chi* Sec. 19, 37/16b.

31. Ch'ien was not the only Han writer to ignore or violate Confucian modesty by using the word *tso*. Yang Hsiung, when asked why he presumed to say that he had "made" his *Classic of the Great Mystery* (*T'ai-hsüan-ching*) replied, "The affairs I have discussed are 'transmitted' but the actual writing was an act of 'making'" (*Fa yen* 5/3b). But Pan Ku, with his usual strict orthodoxy, went to pains to avoid using the word *tso*. He says that Ssu-ma Ch'ien "made the 'Basic Annals'" (HS 100B/1a), but describes his father, Pan Piao, as "a transmitter and not a maker" (100A/11b) and himself as "one who takes writing and transmitting as his task" (100A/19b). Furthermore, in his own table of contents to the HS (100B), though he followed the general form of the table of contents of the *Shih chi*, he substituted *shu* in all the places where Ch'ien had written *tso*. Wang Ch'ung repeats the theory that a sage "makes" and a worthy "transmits," but says that neither term is applicable to his own works, which are "discussions" (*lun*), the next grade after *shu*. He classifies the *Shih chi* as a work of "transmitting" (*shu*), *Lun heng* 29/8b. According to the T'ang commentator on the *Han shu*, Yen Shih-ku, the fact that Ssu-ma Ch'ien used the word *tso* in his table of contents was because he was imitating the "prefaces" to the sections of the *Book of Documents* traditionally believed to have been composed by Confucius. These, after relating briefly the circumstances which occasioned the particular speech or document, end with the words "The . . . was made." See Yen Shih-ku,

K'uang-miu cheng-su 5/41. If this is so, it is another instance of how Ssu-ma Ch'ien directly imitated the work, or what he took to be the work, of Confucius.

32. The exception is the modern scholar Ts'ui Shih, author of the *Shih-chi t'an-yüan,* who insists that any material dealing with events later than 123 in the *Shih chi* is an interpolation. See *Shiki kaichū kōshō* X, 73–4. "Such men," Takikawa remarks, "search for oddities, strive for novelty, and make it their duty to think up strange theories solely to startle men's ears and eyes."

33. This is the meaning which Ssu-ma Chen gives the sentence in his "Supplementary Preface to the *Shih chi.*" For some reason this preface is not in the Takikawa *Shih chi,* but will be found in most other editions such as that of the *Po-na-pen.*

34. This usage of the phrase in Han times is attested by Pan Ku's description of the *Discourses on Salt and Iron* by Huan K'uan: "He hoped by examining into good and bad government *to set up the model for one school of thought*" (HS 66/16b).

35. Cheng Ch'iao, "General Preface to the *T'ung chih.*"

36. Even Ssu-ma Ch'ien's statement is an example of "veiled" writing. He says nothing of himself, but simply makes a few apparently irrelevant remarks about Confucius and the *Annals* before commenting on the subject of the chapter, the Hsiung-nu.

37. E.g., in the biography of Chang Liang, SC 55/10 & 17, the use of the phrase "a discussion is found in the affairs of Hsiang Yü" or "a discussion is found in the affairs of Huai-yin." Ssu-ma Ch'ien unfortunately did not use this system of cross-references very often, but Pan Ku employed it more freely, particularly when he shifted the material he took from the *Shih chi* here and there in his own work.

38. Chi Chen-huai, *op. cit.,* 113–114.

39. Su Hsün, *"Shih-lun"* B, *Chia-yu-chi* 8/2a–b.

40. Ssu-ma Ch'ien's account of the struggle between Hsiang Yü and Kao-tsu, according to Pan Ku, is based on the *Ch'u-Han ch'un-ch'iu,* a work listed in the Treatise on Literature, HS 30/17b, as in 9 *p'ien* by Lu Chia. Although neither the *Shih chi* biography of Lu Chia (SC 97) nor that in the *Han shu* (HS 43) mention this work by Lu Chia, it has generally been accepted as genuine. The work was lost in the Southern Sung. Fragments which are quoted in other works have been collected in the *Hou Chih-pu-tsu chai ts'ung-shu* 7 and elsewhere. Just what the form of the original work was it is impossible to tell from these fragments. Liu Chih-chi remarks that, like the *Yen-tzu ch'un-chiu* and *Lü-shih ch'un-ch'iu,* it was not arranged by year and month, but beyond this we know nothing

(*Shih t'ung* 1/4a). It may be inferred from Liu Chih-chi's statement, however, that to get his material into the form of Basic Annals for each year for Kao-tsu and Hsiang Yü, Ssu-ma Ch'ien must have had to do considerable rearranging. Thus I think we may, lacking further information, discuss at least the form, if not the content, of these chapters as though it were the work of Ch'ien himself.

41. See *Fa yen* 13/2b: "The sage makes virtue his business and considers strange happenings as secondary."

42. SC 50/7. Compare the parallel passage in *Chung yung* 24: "When a nation is about to rise there will always be omens of fortune and good luck; when a state is about to perish there will always be omens of evil and bad luck."

43. The reporting of various natural catastrophes and odd occurrences which the Han people considered portentous was also an effective device used by the bureaucratic class to express indirect criticism of the government, since human misrule was believed to be the cause of such prodigies. See the study by Hans Bielenstein, "An Interpretation of the Portents in the Ts'ien-han-shu," BMFEA 22 (1950), 127–143.

IV. THE FORM OF THE SHIH CHI

1. See *Shiki kaichû kôshô* X, 75–91. In his article on the origins of the forms of the *Shih chi*, YCHP 37 (1949), 95–120, Ch'eng Chin-tsao discusses and refutes the theory that the form of the *Shih chi* is imitated from that of the *Lü-shih ch'un-ch'iu*. He also takes up the theory that Ssu–ma Ch'ien modeled his work after the now lost work *Shih pen*. As Prof. Ch'eng points out, this theory is not mentioned by any of the Six Dynasties or T'ang writers on the *Shih chi*, but is first suggested by Sung critics. The *Shih pen*, however, was lost in the early Sung, so that none of the scholars who advance this idea could have actually seen the *Shih pen* in its original form. Ch'eng's own theory, which I have followed, is that, although Ch'ien had hints and precedents of various types on which to base his work, the essential form of the *Shih chi*, with its five divisions, is his own creation.

2. In Han times Taoism was often referred to as Huang-Lao, the teachings of the Yellow Emperor and Lao Tzu.

3. *Mémoires historiques*, Intro., li.

4. SC 28/85. In SC 1/13, Ch'ien says that the Yellow Emperor was so called because he received signs of the virtue of the element earth. But he does not assign elements to the other four emperors.

5. In SC 130/26, for example, he mentions the former, while in SC 1/5

he refers to the "family of Shen Nung" who had been rulers before the Yellow Emperor.

6. Not so the T'ang commentator Ssu-ma Chen, who wrote a supplementary chapter, the "Basic Annals of the Three Luminous Ones," covering a miscellany of confused legends concerning these early mythical figures and appended it to the *Shih chi.*

7. E.g., Pan Ku's remarks at the end of his biography of Ch'ien, HS 62: "Although there are literary remains from the ages before T'ang and Yü [Yao and Shun], their words are not canonical. Therefore it is impossible to speak clearly about the affairs of the Yellow Emperor and Chüan Hsü."

8. See SC 1/65–67.

9. Ch'u Shao-sun was an Erudit (*po-shih*) around 55 B. C. and served at the courts of emperors Hsüan and Ch'eng. He is mentioned briefly in HS 88/17a and *passim* in the biography of his teacher, the Confucian scholar Wang Shih, but beyond this little is known of his life. Ch'u took upon himself the thankless task of making additions and continuations to the *Shih chi.* Whether, as he declares at the end of SC 126/13, he was motivated by a sincere desire to transmit the facts of history to later generations, or merely hoped to share in Ssu-ma Ch'ien's glory by associating his name with the *Shih chi,* we cannot say. Whatever his intention, his temerity in appending his remarks to the end of Ch'ien's chapters has won him nothing but condemnation from all later commentators on the *Shih chi.* Indeed one is sometimes perplexed by the severity with which they attack him for his "stupidity" and "vulgarity." Had he had the wisdom to publish his remarks separately, he would probably not have met with such scorn; but so long as his sentences stand side by side with those of Ssu-ma Ch'ien he is bound to suffer. His material is often without organization or direction, consisting mostly of anecdotes or conversations on some point of ritual or institutional history. Such questions obviously interested him, and he shows the typical Han love of systems based on tidy numerical categories. He is often trivial and verbose, and much of his material seems not to have been reliable, for Pan Ku seldom makes use of it in the *Han shu.* Nevertheless his remarks are occasionally informative and interesting, and if they do not represent a worthy continuation to the *Shih chi,* they at least show a commendable desire to carry on the writing of history where Ssu-ma Ch'ien left off. His most effective single piece of writing is probably the biography of Tung-fang So which he appended to SC 126/15. Fortunately for us Ch'u Shao-sun had the thoughtfulness (or audacity, if one takes the traditional attitude) to affix his name plainly to all his additions so that they are readily distinguishable from the original text. Other meddlers have

been less honest and there is clear evidence that at some time sentences or sections have been tacked on to Ssu-ma Ch'ien's text in a number of places. Some of these are comments copied back from the *Han shu* and so identifiable; others reveal their spuriousness by internal evidence and have been clearly noted by commentators. A complete list of these later additions is found in *Shiki kaichū kōshō* X, 105–111.

10. It is customary to laugh at the crude and superstitious ideas of the early Han thinkers, but in this case Ssu-ma Ch'ien and Ch'u Shao-sun have the laugh. The Latter Han Confucian scholar Cheng Hsüan apparently accepted these stories as literal truth and the Sung Confucianists went to lengths to explain how such miracles were possible. See Cheng Hsüan's commentary, *Chien,* and that of Chu Hsi, *Chi-chuan,* to *Odes, Ta-ya,* "Sheng-min" and *Shang-sung,* "Hsüan-niao."

11. E.g., Chavannes' opinion, *Mémoires historiques,* Intro., p. clxxvii.

12. There is another reason which may help to explain why Ch'ien chose to place the story of Hsiang Yü in his "Basic Annals" rather than elsewhere. This is the fact that, even if he had chosen to recognize the reign of the puppet emperor I who was set up in 206 by Hsiang Yü after the murder of the last ruler of the Ch'in, he would still have a gap in the chronology of his annals between the murder of Emperor I by Hsiang Yü's henchmen in late 206 and the formal assumption of the title of emperor by Kao-tsu in 202. The Han covered up this gap by setting the beginning of its reign back five years so that it began in 206. But in actual fact, as Ch'ien recognized, there was a period of three years, from the end of 206 to the beginning of 202, when there was not even a nominal emperor ruling, so that Ch'ien wisely chose to treat the whole period in "Annals" in terms of the man who came closest to being the actual ruler during this period, Hsiang Yü.

13. The oldest extant example of the use of such chronological tables in western historiography is probably the "Chronological Canons," the second part of the *Chronicle* of the great historian of the Christian Church, Eusebius (*ca.* 260–*ca.* 340 A. D.). These were tables with the dates of Chaldean, Greek, Roman, and other chronologies listed in columns down the center of the page, with notes on important events in both margins. Eusebius says that he was largely indebted for this plan to the Greek historian Castor of Rhodes, who, drawing upon earlier attempts by the Greeks to compile comparative lists of events in world chronicles, drew up a synchronistic table or "canon" of Oriental, Greek, and Roman history ending with the year 61 B. C. See James T. Shotwell, *The History of History,* I, 247 and 353. Professor Shotwell also quotes the Preface to Eusebius' *Chronicle* in

which, in terms strangely parallel to those used by Ssu-ma Ch'ien in his "Preface to the Chronological Table of the Three Dynasties" (SC 13), he describes the difficulties of the historian:

"Now at the very beginning, I make this declaration before all the world: let no one ever arrogantly contend that a sure and thorough knowledge of chronology is attainable. This every one will readily believe who ponders on the incontrovertible words of the Master to his disciples: 'It is not for you to know the times or the seasons, which the Father hath put in his own power' (Acts 1:7)." Shotwell, p. 356.

14. See Preface to SC 15.

15. In judging Ch'ien's labors, one might also keep in mind such incidents as that concerning Duke Hui of Ch'en who, set up by King P'ing of Ch'u five years after the state of Ch'en had been destroyed by King Ling of Ch'u, attempted to make it appear that his state had never gone out of existence by setting the date of his accession back five years (SC 36/15). This sort of "doctoring" of chronologies was hardly designed to make the work of the historian any easier.

16. Okazaki, Fumio, *Shiba Sen,* 24.

17. *Nien-erh-shih cha-chi* 1/4b.

18. *Mémoires historiques,* Intro., p. clxxiv.

19. Takeda Taijun, *Shiba Sen,* p. 124.

20. Pan Ku made one valuable addition to the chronological table form. His "Table of the Hundred Officials," HS 19, begins with a long description of officials and official titles from ancient times through the Former Han and then lists in the form of a graph the important offices of the Han government and the men who filled them. It is a source of invaluable information on this subject, and was the inspiration for similar treatises and tables in later histories. Pan Ku also made one addition to the tables which has proved a source of embarrassment to his admirers through the ages. This is his "Table of Ancient and Modern Men," HS 20, in which, after setting up nine lines representing nine grades of moral worth from Sage to Fool, he proceeds to classify all the famous men and women of Chinese history *down to the beginning of the Han.* This fact, that the table deals with a period entirely outside the scope of Pan Ku's history, and, contrary to its title, records nothing of "modern men," has dismayed critics who can only hope that it is not his composition at all. For a statistical study of the table and its significance, see Derk Bodde, "Types of Chinese Categorical Thinking," JAOS 59 (1939), 200–219.

21. *Mencius* IIIB, 10. Legge translates it as "an ancient and noble family."

22. He appears in five chapters, SC 31, 37, 42, 43, and 45.

23. Quoted in Takikawa VI, SC 47/2. I can find no biographical information on Liao Teng-t'ing.

24. Naitô, *Shigakushi,* 86–90.

25. Chen Shih-hsiang, "An Innovation in Chinese Biographical Writing," FEQ XIII (Nov. 1953), 49–62.

26. James R. Hightower, "Ch'ü Yüan Studies," *Silver Jubilee Volume of Zinbun-Kagaku-Kenkyusyo,* p. 197.

27. SC 61.

28. *Lü-shih ch'un-ch'iu* 12/6b and *Han-shih wai-chuan* 3/21a. Neither source includes the song which Ssu-ma Ch'ien quotes.

29. E.g., SC 74/17, the brief mention of various philosophers which concludes: "The world has many copies of their books and therefore I have not discussed their stories [*chuan*]."

30. Chen, *op. cit.,* p. 50.

31. See HS 27A/8a.

32. CCFL Sec. 1, 1/1b.

33. *Ch'un-ch'iu san-chuan* p. 306, note by an unidentified critic under the first entry concerning the princess, Duke Ch'eng 8. Although this principle, that length of narrative is directly related to the moral worth of the subject, is perhaps in general true of Chinese historiography, it should not be interpreted too literally. In his chapter on the lives of Lao Tzu, Chuang Tzu, Shen Pu-hai, and Han Fei Tzu (SC 63), for example, Ssu-ma Ch'ien devotes by far the largest amount of space to the last, though Han Fei Tzu receives in the "judgment" at the end of the chapter the severest criticism of all. Ch'ien in this case clearly did not have sufficient reliable material to write at length about the other men, while in the story of Han Fei Tzu he has devoted much space to copying in a portion of that philosopher's writings on persuasive speaking, not because he particularly admired him as a person, but, as he says, "only because I am moved by the fact that, though Han Fei Tzu wrote upon the 'Difficulties of Disputation,' he was not able to talk himself out of his own difficulties." It was not the worth of Han Fei Tzu, but the irony of this fact, that interested the historian.

34. See Henri Maspero, "Le roman historique dans la littérature chinoise de l'Antiquité," *Etudes historiques,* pp. 55–62.

35. Pan Ku followed the general form of Ssu-ma Ch'ien's postface, tracing the ancestry of his family, giving brief biographies of his father and himself, and closing with a table of contents of his history. But unfortunately he says less than Ch'ien about his motives and methods in compiling his work, instead filling his biography, somewhat immodestly, with the texts

of his own poems. Though these combination prefaces and autobiographies continued to be written by private historians, when the compilation of dynastic histories became an official duty carried out by groups of scholar-bureaucrats the practice unfortunately ceased. See Naitô, *Shigakushi,* pp. 188–89.

36. *Advancement of Learning,* Bk. II, Ch. IV.

37. The *Tso Commentary* has 87 such judgments, which frequently quote from the Classics to make their point. Some are clearly written after Confucius and discuss the *Spring and Autumn Annals* as he edited it, so that the phrase "The gentleman remarks" must refer not to Confucius but to the writer or compiler of the *Tso* itself. In addition the *Tso* includes a number of comments by historical persons of the day, which serve the same purpose of judging or pointing a moral. In some cases, particularly in his Chronological Tables, when Ssu-ma Ch'ien quotes these latter judgments he omits the name of the speaker and substitutes the conventional phrase "A gentleman remarks." The *Narratives from the States* contains 11 such judgments introduced by the same phrase; these are very short and do not cite the Classics. Ch'ien seems to have used none of these in his work. See Kamada Tadashi, "Concerning the *Shih chi* and *Tso chuan,*" *Memorial Volume in Honor of the Seventieth Birthday of Dr. Morohashi,* pp. 133–60.

38. See Cheng Hao-sheng, *op. cit.,* pp. 12–13 which summarizes the earlier theories and agrees with the last one mentioned. I shall not presume to decide which is correct, though the presence of the phrase "Your servant Ch'ien respectfully records" in the introduction to SC 17/7 would seem to indicate that Ch'ien in his original manuscript did not always refer to himself as "Grand Historian."

39. Liu Hsieh, in his *Wen-hsin tiao-lung* 2/8b, defines *tsan* as "to illuminate, to aid," but derives it from the *sung* or "ode of praise" form, and criticizes Ssu-ma Ch'ien as well as Pan Ku for using it for purposes of judgment. This is another example of how critics, by confusing the two historians, have blamed Ssu-ma Ch'ien for failing to conform to the implications of terminology he never used.

40. The *Shih chi* Table of Contents contains a few descriptions in four-character lines with occasional rhyme, e.g., those for the first eleven chapters. This same tendency toward four-character rhymed phrases may be seen in the brief prefaces which Yang Hsiung fixed to each chapter of his *Fa yen.* In the *Han shu,* Pan Ku put all of his Table of Contents in four-word rhymed lines. It is from this Table of Contents that the rhymed *tsan* form of later histories, such as the *Hou Han shu,* is derived.

41. "General Preface to the *T'ung chih*."

42. Ma Tuan-lin, "General Preface" to his *Wen-hsien t'ung-k'ao*. The Ch'ing historian Chang Hsüeh-ch'eng has given the fullest philosophical exposition of the advantages of the "continuous history" form. See his essays on the *Book of Documents*, the principle of continuity, and Cheng Ch'iao, *Wen-shih t'ung-i* 1, 4 & 5, and Lien-sheng Yang, "A Theory About the Titles of the Twenty-four Dynastic Histories," HJAS 10 (1947), 41–47.

V. THE THOUGHT OF SSU-MA CH'IEN

1. *Mo Tzu* Sec. 18, 5/7a. The same saying, in a slightly different version, appears in the *Book of Documents*, "Announcement on Wine" (*Chiu-kao*): "The ancients had a saying: 'Men need not mirror themselves in water; they may mirror themselves in the people.'" The concept of the mirror of history appears already in the *Book of Odes, Ta-ya*, "Decade of T'ang," "T'ang": "Yin, your mirror is not far; it is in the generation of the lord of Hsia," i.e., in the history of the preceding dynasty.

2. *Kuan Tzu* Sec. 2, 1/6b and CCFL Sec. 5, 3/10a.

3. *Chin shu* 60/5b.

4. Chavannes, *Mémoires historiques*, p. clxxxv, takes Ch'ien to task for applying the same criteria of historical judgment to materials dealing with later, well-documented ages, and those concerning the dim, legendary beginnings of Chinese history. The criticism, while not without basis, seems hardly just. It was Ch'ien's avowed objective to sift from these early accounts all that he considered fantastic and doubtful and extract the core of historical truth which he believed existed in them. It is hardly to be wondered at that he did not treat them solely as myths and attempt to evaluate them as such. It has been only in the last few centuries in the West that scholars have come to realize the mythical nature of the early parts of the Bible or Roman history and to begin to understand the nature and value of myth. This awareness of the nature of myth came about largely through the comparative study of the mythologies of a number of different peoples. (See Emery Neff, *The Poetry of History*, pp. 107–15.) Ssu-ma Ch'ien, familiar only with the literature and traditions of one country, his own, was in an even poorer position than the ancient Greeks, Romans, and Hebrews to appreciate the difference between myth and history. It is rather to his credit that he did attempt to make some distinction (even when, from our point of view, he should not have done so), between the believable and the purely fantastic. The famous example of this is his division of accounts of the legendary Yellow Emperor into two parts, the "historical"

ruler who appears in the "Basic Annals of the Five Emperors" (SC 1) and the "mythical" hero, focus of superstitious beliefs, who appears in the "Treatise on the Feng and Shan Sacrifices" (SC 28).

5. Lionel Pearson, "Real and Conventional Personalities in Greek History," *Journal of the History of Ideas,* XV (Jan. 1954), 136–45. The contrast between the Greek and Chinese attitudes toward history is especially striking in Thucydides, where the only event in earlier Greek history consistently referred to is the Persian War, and that is characterized as an event of "ancient times," though it occurred only some fifty years before (Bk. III, Ch. 4, p. 201, trans. by Rex Warner, *Penguin Classics,* 1954). When the Athenian representatives at Sparta begin a speech by declaring "There is no need to talk about what happened long ago" (Bk. I, Ch. 6, p. 53), we know that we are indeed in a different world from that of Ssu-ma Ch'ien and his countrymen. Had there been Chinese envoys at Sparta, they would undoubtedly have begun their address: "We have heard that in the time of emperors Yao and Shun. . . ."

6. Hightower, "Ch'ü Yüan Studies," p. 196.

7. Pearson, "Real and Conventional Personalities," p. 41.

8. *"Fu* on the Owl," SC 84/30.

9. The two terms were no doubt suggested by the passage in *Analects* VI, 16: "The Master said, 'When solid qualities are in excess of refinements, we have rusticity; when refinements are in excess of solid qualities, we have the manner of a clerk. When refinements and solid qualities are equally blended, we then have the man of virtue.' "

10. SC 47/68. Ch'ien has inserted the first sentence himself. The remainder is a quotation from *Analects* III, 14.

11. Benedetto Croce, *Theory and History of Historiography,* p. 194.

12. Such was the common Confucian view, which, while recognizing the existence of cycles of prosperity and decay, rigidly strove to exclude the idea that these were due primarily to any supernatural agency or inexorable fate. It may be noted, however, that the philosopher Wang Ch'ung of the Latter Han, though professing himself a Confucianist, pushed the idea of the organic growth and decay of society and the state to such an extreme that he flatly denied that human effort was of any use in attempting to avert or modify the direction of the times. "Whether the world is ordered or disordered," he declares, "depends upon the times, not upon the government. Whether the state is secure or in peril depends upon fate, not policy. A wise or an unwise ruler, an enlightened or an unenlightened administration can have no effect either way" (*Lun heng* 17/14b–15a).

It was largely because of this extreme fatalism that the philosophy of Wang Ch'ung was rejected by orthodox Confucianism.

13. See the beginning of SC 129/2, where Ch'ien ridicules Lao Tzu's idealization of the rustic simplicity of ancient times. On the interpretation of this passage, see J. J. L. Duyvendak's review of N. L. Swann, *Food and Money in Ancient China,* TP 40 (1951), 213–14.

14. *Hsün Tzu* Sec. 4, 2/17b. *Mencius* VIB, 2 also affirms the first part of the statement, that all men are capable of becoming sages like Yao and Shun. This was perhaps an old saying.

15. *Hsün Tzu* Sec. 3, 2/7b.

16. E.g., in SC 47/33–34 and SC 119/5 he uses the same phrases to describe the effects of the good government of Confucius and Tzu Ch'an respectively. Since both men belong to the same high moral category, it is only natural, according to the Chinese historian, that the results of their deeds should be described in identical words. For an excellent discussion of the uses of such stereotyped expressions in Chinese historical writing, see Hans Bielenstein, "The Restoration of the Han Dynasty," BMFEA 26 (1954), 61–67. Bielenstein's whole chapter on the historiography of the *Hou-Han-shu,* in my opinion, represents the most important contribution to the study of Chinese historiography to appear in a western language since Professor C. S. Gardener's pioneer work, *Traditional Chinese Historiography.*

17. *Tso* Duke Hsi twenty-third year.

18. The fact that right after the mention of "Dame Liu" in SC 8/4–5 we read of a "Dame Wang" who ran a wine shop in Kao-tsu's village would seem to indicate that the word "Dame" (*ao*) did not at this time carry a very high tone. This was probably not always true, however, for we find it used in SC 43/83 by the ministers of the queen dowager of Chao when addressing the queen personally.

19. Croce, *History as the Story of Liberty,* p. 27.

20. This essay is also found at the beginning of Chia I's *Hsin shu* with the sections arranged in a different order. One of the three sections is found in *Wen hsüan* 51.

21. The same point is made in the memorials of Chu-fu An and his friends in SC 112/15.

22. Introduction to Pan Ku's *Tien-yin, Wen hsüan* 48/21a.

23. This is no place to go into a comparative discussion of the role of fate and the supernatural in ancient western historiography. But it may be interesting here to note a few parallels to Ch'ien's remarks on fate in the

more famous historical works of Greece and Rome. None of these historians quoted were in any sense *dominated* in their historical outlook by a belief in the supernatural (as, for example, were Bede and the other medieval Christian historians). And yet all give evidence, directly or indirectly, that, like Ssu-ma Ch'ien and Pan Ku, they occasionally recognized the existence of superhuman forces working in history.

Herodotus: "Many things make it plain to me that the hand of God is active in human affairs." (Bk. IX, p. 591, trans. Aubrey de Selincourt, *Penguin Classics*, 1954.)

Thucydides, from a speech by Nicias: "Our enemies have had good fortune enough, and, if any of the gods was angry with us at our setting out, by this time we have been sufficiently punished. . . . So it is now reasonable for us to hope that the gods will be kinder to us, since by now we deserve their pity rather than their jealousy." (Bk. VII, Ch. 7, p. 481, trans. Michael Grant, *Penguin Classics*, 1954.)

Caesar, from a speech by Caesar himself: "The victory of which you boast so arrogantly and the surprisingly long time during which you have escaped punishment, are both due to the same cause. When the gods intend to make a man pay for his crimes, they generally allow him to enjoy moments of success and a long period of impunity, so that he may feel his reverse of fortune, when it eventually comes, all the more keenly." (*Conquest of Gaul* II, 1, p. 46, trans. S. A. Handford, *Penguin Classics*, 1951.)

Livy: "Jupiter frustrated their nefarious project" (Bk. IV, XLIII, p. 270); "Thereupon, contrary to the law of nations, the envoys seized their (the Gaul's) weapons, for the Fates were already urging Rome to its ruin." (Bk. V, XXXVI, p. 331, *History of Rome*, Vol. I, trans. Rev. Canon Roberts, *Everyman's Library*, 1926.)

Tacitus: "For it was not their fault; the cause was heaven's anger with Rome." (*Annals* XVI, 14, p. 376, trans. Michael Grant, *Penguin Classics*, 1956.)

24. On Ch'ien's economic thought, see Ojima Sukema, "The Laissez-faire Theory of Ssu-ma Ch'ien," *Kodai Shina kenkyū*, pp. 342–53, and Utsunomiya Kiyoyoshi, "A Study of the *Shih chi* Chapter on Merchandise and Prices," *Kandai shakai-keizaishi kenkyū*, pp. 166–202.

25. As a matter of fact, quite a good defense of Ch'ien's statement can be made on purely Confucian grounds. *Analects* IX, 1 states that benevolence was one of the things about which Confucius himself seldom spoke. And in *Li chi* Sec. 41, 59/14a, after describing eight attributes of benevolence, Confucius concludes that "even if the Confucianist has all these eight attributes in combination, he does not dare to speak of benevolence."

So the "talking of benevolence and righteousness" which Ch'ien criticizes would, by strict Confucian standards, be unbecoming in any man.

26. Here, as always, we must be careful not to judge Ch'ien solely on the basis of what he says in one chapter. Writing of the merchants and their race for profit in SC 129/7–8, he is so carried away, as it were, by his subject that he sees the profit motive everywhere. But in another chapter, writing in another mood (SC 74/2), he says:

"When I read the book of Mencius and come to where King Hui of Liang asked what would profit his country, I never fail to set the book aside with a sigh. Alas, I say to myself, profit is truly the root of disorder. Confucius seldom spoke of profit, for he wished to prevent disorder at its source. Therefore it is said, 'He who gives himself up to the search for profit in his actions will have many grievances.' From the Son of Heaven down to the common people, is there any difference in the corruption that comes from the love of profit?"

27. It is interesting to recall in this connection that, among Pan Ku's nine categories of men in his "Table of Ancient and Modern Men," HS 20, the lowest is not labeled "Evil Men" but simply "Fools."

28. *Hsün Tzu* Sec. 4, 2/16b.

29. Neff, *Poetry of History,* p. 4.

30. Cf. the discussion of the *Odes* by Chi Cha, SC 31/12.

31. The songs themselves are found in SC 2/40; at the beginning of his Treatise on Music, SC 24/2, Ch'ien remarks that he never reads them without weeping.

32. For a detailed discussion of these two songs see two articles by Yoshikawa Kôjirô, "Hsiang Yü's Song of Kai-hsia," *Journal of Chinese Literature* I (Oct. 1954), 1–18, and "Kao-tsu's Song of the Great Wind," *Journal of Chinese Literature* II (April 1955), 28–44.

33. *Mémoires historiques,* Intro., p. clx.

34. Pan Ku removed these speeches from the biography of Han Hsin in HS 34 and created a separate biography for K'uai T'ung. The change seems ill-advised, for K'uai T'ung never comes to life as a figure independent of the men he tricked to downfall, while the removal of the long temptations from the biography of Han Hsin weakens the picture of his repeated protestations of loyalty and the tragedy of his final submission to K'uai T'ung's persuasions.

35. See the note by Ku Yen-wu quoted in SC 30/44.

36. Arnold Toynbee, *Greek Civilization and Character,* p. xi.

37. H. G. Creel, *Confucius, the Man and the Myth,* p. 245.

38. Creel, *op. cit.,* p. 247.

39. *Fa yen* 7/2a.

40. Arthur Waley, *The Way and Its Power*, p. 108.

41. See the remarks of the Ming scholar Ch'en Jen-hsi, SC 47/2.

42. *Odes, hsiao-ya*, "Chü-hsia."

43. Lin Yutang, *The Wisdom of Confucius*, p. 100. My division of the biography into sections roughly follows that made by Lin Yutang in his translation, pp. 55–100.

44. This discussion of the biography of Confucius is adapted from my article in Japanese, "The *Shih chi* 'Hereditary House of Confucius' as Literature," *Journal of Chinese Literature* II (April 1955), 18–27.

45. Pan Piao's opinion is found in his discussion of the *Shih chi* in *Hou-Han-shu* 70A/4a (*lieh-chuan* 30A) and is repeated by Pan Ku in HS 62/25b.

46. In spite of its obvious drawbacks, this practice in Chinese histories of clarifying the language when quoting from older sources provides an invaluable aid in deciphering obscure passages. Sentences that are ambiguous or unintelligible in the *Shih chi* may often be understood by reference to Pan Ku's version of the passage, or even Ssu-ma Kuang's version. If an unintelligible sentence appears in identical form in the *Shih chi, Han shu*, and *Tzu-chih t'ung-chien*, one may be fairly certain that neither Pan Ku nor Ssu-ma Kuang understood the meaning clearly enough to know how to rewrite it.

47. The style of the *Tso Commentary* is notoriously bizarre and difficult, and one may be thankful that Ch'ien did not choose to quote from it verbatim. The Ch'ing critic Fang Pao mentions, for instance, the contrast between Ch'ien's version of the story of the assassination of Duke Hsiang of Ch'i in SC 32/15 and its original in the *Tso* Duke Chuang eighth year. "When we see the way The Grand Historian has augmented and improved it, we realize that the *Tso*'s narrative is as strange as though gods had written it and spirits set it forth." Quoted by Takikawa in SC 32/16.

48. Su Hsün, *Shih-lun* Pt. 3. This 3rd section is not found in his collected works, *Chia-yu-chi*, but is included in *T'ang-Sung pa-chia wen* 16.

49. See the remarks of Nagai Sekitoku and Ts'ui Shu quoted by Takikawa, SC 47/82.

50. Pan Ku, when he treated subjects already covered in the *Shih chi*, also added a few new facts and incidents to Ch'ien's accounts. But, as pointed out by Chao I, the fact that he added so little to Ch'ien's narrative, although he must have had access to some material that was not available to his predecessor, is proof of the excellence of Ch'ien's work and the high opinion Pan Ku held of it. See Chao I, *Nien-erh-shih cha-chi* 1 & 2.

51. See HHS 70A/5b. In spite of its shortcomings, however, the *Shih*

chi represents a great improvement in this respect over the *Tso*, which is so erratic in its use of names and titles that it is often necessary to refer to special explanatory tables compiled by later scholars to make sure of the identity of persons appearing in its narrative. Typically enough Ch'ien never even mentions his own alternate name or *tzu*, Tzu-ch'ang; it first appears when Yang Hsiung refers to him by it in *Fa yen* 7/2a. For some reason Pan Ku also fails to record Ch'ien's *tzu* in his biography of the historian.

52. Naitô, *Shigakushi*, pp. 160–62.

53. *Fa yen* 12/2a. The two interpretations discussed are those of Sung Hsien and Wu Pi quoted in *Fa-yen i-su* 18/9b–10a.

54. See the note quoted from his *K'ao-i* in *Tzu-chih t'ung-chien* 12/12b–13a.

55. *Mémoires historiques,* p. clxiii.

56. In his "appraisal" at the end of the biography of Yang Hsiung, HS 87/23b, Pan Ku remarks: "It is over forty years from the death of Hsiung till today." This is the only statement I find in all of Pan Ku's writing (excepting in material he quotes from his father) that would give so much as a clue to the relationship of the historian in time or space to his subject. Compare this with Ch'ien's frequent mentions of his personal experiences, the places he has visited, and his friends and associates as they relate to his narrative.

57. From the essay "Reading the *Shih chi,*" *Rai Sanyô zensho, Bunsho,* p. 115.

APPENDIX A

1. That is, the effects of their virtuous rule may still be discerned among the inhabitants of these places today, a typical example of Ch'ien's belief in the far-reaching and persistent influence of great men in history.

2. Perhaps only the *Book of Documents* is meant.

3. Duke Hsiang of Ch'in attacked the Jung barbarians in defense of the Chou king who had fled east to the city of Lo, and for this he was in 771 awarded the rank of feudal lord of the Chou (SC 5/12).

4. The *chih* was an altar used for sacrifices to Shang-ti, the Lord on High. The word "west," according to one theory, is added because Ch'in was in the west of China, but another theory, which identifies Shang-ti with the White Emperor, believes that it was used because west is the direction associated with this god in the five elements system. Cf. SC 5/12 and 28/8.

5. *Li chi* Sec. 5, 12/18a–b.

6. Meteor-like stones found in a place called Ch'en-tsang, which the Duke worshipped (SC 5/13 and 28/10).

7. The six lords of Chin were the Han, Wei, Chao, Fan, Chih, and Chung-hsing families. The first three eventually divided the state of Chin among themselves.

8. Son of T'ien Ch'ang.

9. The tallies broken and retained by the two parties of a contract.

10. Perhaps a reference to *Hsün Tzu* Sec. 2, 2/7b: "The ways of the hundred kings are the ways of later kings."

11. The capital of Wei. For this reason the state is referred to as Liang.

12. Wu-chi, son of King Chao of Wei, a famous and powerful warlord of the time. See his biography, SC 77.

13. A wise and virtuous minister of the Shang dynasty.

14. This remark has been the subject of much criticism by later scholars. Takikawa quotes some of their comments, two of which I give to show the nature of the objections:

Chiao Chou (d. 270 A. D.):

"I have heard it said that the so-called 'destruction of Heaven' means that there are wise men in the state who are not employed. If they were properly used, how could the state be destroyed? If Emperor Chou of the Shang had used his three virtuous ministers, the state of Chou would never have become ruler. How much more so in the case of the cruel and ruthless Ch'in!"

Liu Chih-chi (661–721):

"When one discusses cases of success or failure, he ought primarily to consider human affairs. To drag the Mandate of Heaven into the discussion only does violence to logic."

15. Cf. *Lao Tzu* 29: "The empire is a holy vessel"; *Chuang Tzu* Sec. 28, 9/18b: "The empire is a great vessel."

16. This story comes from *Chuang Tzu* Sec. 1, 1/9b.

17. Also from *Chuang Tzu* Sec. 28, 9/29a.

18. In Honan, Teng-feng Prefecture.

19. Praised by Confucius in *Analects* VIII, 1.

20. *Analects* V, 22.

21. *Ibid.*, VII, 14.

22. Literally, *i-shih,* meaning a song not included in the *Odes*. For this reason alone it would be suspect. The fact that it contradicts what Confucius has said about Po I confirms Ch'ien's assertion that one must be wary of material not found in the Classics.

23. The story of Po I and his brother appears in a number of early works such as *Chuang Tzu* 9; *Intrigues of the Warring States* 29 (Yen 1);

Lü-shih ch'un-ch'iu 12; and *Han-shih wai-chuan* 3. But none of these tells the whole story as Ch'ien relates it here, nor does any account include the poem attributed to them. So Ch'ien is here drawing either upon some lost text or upon popular tales concerning these men. The country of Ku-chu was supposedly a fief of the Yin dynasty and therefore Po I and his brother felt bound to support Yin against the invading Chou conquerors. Professor Kaizuka suggests that the whole legend, which is clearly anti-Chou in sentiment, reflects the resistance of the barbarian tribes who originally occupied the area of the state of Ch'i to the invasion of the Ch'i tribe of the west. See Kaizuka Shigeki, "The Problem of Fate in the Historiography of Ssu-ma Ch'ien," *Chûgoku kodai no kokoro* 132.

24. This section of the story is based on *Mencius* IVA, 13.

25. There are several different sites suggested for this mountain, but the actual location is immaterial here.

26. "He" in the song refers of course to King Wu of the Chou, who overthrew the Yin dynasty and set himself up as ruler.

27. *Lao Tzu* 79. See also the section of the *Book of Documents* called Ts'ai, now lost but quoted in the *Tso Commentary* Duke Hsi fifth yr.: "Bright Heaven is without favoritism: virtue is what it aids."

28. Cf. *Analects* VI and XI.

29. A notorious robber baron, subject of *Chuang Tzu* 9.

30. *Analects* XIV, 14.

31. *Ibid.,* VI, 12.

32. *Ibid.,* XV, 39.

33. *Ibid.,* VII, 11.

34. *Ibid.,* IX, 27.

35. This sentence is obscure and offers varying interpretations. The point of the paragraph is that, although some men may choose to do evil, the good man is forced by his own conscience to follow a course of virtue regardless of any hope of reward.

36. *Analects* XV, 19.

37. "*Fu* on the Owl," SC 84/32.

38. *Wen-yen Commentary* on the *Book of Changes,* first hexagram, *ch'ien.* Ch'ien does not quote verbatim. The original reads: "Things of the same voice answer each other; things of the same spirit seek each other out." There are two interpretations of the last phrase, "The sage arises and all creation becomes clear." The first, which I have followed, is that through the teachings and example of the sage, all things of creation become clear and understandable. The other is that all things of creation look up to, acknowledge, and admire the sage. Commentators on the *Shih chi* prefer the first interpretation.

39. At the end of *Shih chi* 95/35, Ch'ien gives examples of a number of humble workmen and officials of the beginning of the Han who, by "sticking to the horse's tail," i.e., becoming followers of Kao-tsu in his fight for control of the empire, eventually were able to rise to positions of leadership in the new government.

40. Literally, "a man of the blue clouds," i.e., a person in high position. Cf. SC 79/26, where Fan Chü is described as "rising above the clouds of the blue." Here the phrase has a moral connotation, i.e., a person of great virtue, a sage who can recognize other great men and give them the praise they deserve as Confucius did for Po I and Yen Hui.

41. I.e., the ruler of Ch'u fired the hatred of Wu Tzu-hsü, who eventually succeeded in turning Ch'u's rival, the state of Wu, against him.

42. When he was pursued and almost captured by his enemies from Ch'u.

43. The capital of Ch'u, where Tzu-hsü at last accomplished his revenge.

44. E.g., *Mencius* IIA, 3.

45. *Han shu* 30/44b lists a work in 31 sections attributed to Su Ch'in. Some commentators have attempted to identify this with the work known as *Kuei-ku Tzu,* asserting that the Master of Spirit Valley (Kuei-ku Tzu) was a pseudonym of Su Ch'in. Others believe that the Master of Spirit Valley was Su Ch'in's teacher. The book exists only in fragments today. See Ku Shih, *Han-shu i-wen-chih chiang-su* 152–53.

46. The Confucian philosopher Tung Chung-shu, friend and teacher of Ssu-ma Ch'ien.

47. Physician to the King of Ch'in. When Ching K'o attacked the King, the latter in his haste to escape was unable to draw his sword, but the physician struck Ching K'o with his medicine bag, distracting him long enough for the King to get out his sword and defend himself.

48. In 110 B. C., after performing the Feng Sacrifice at Mount T'ai, Emperor Wu journeyed east to the sea and then returned to the capital by way of the northern border route. Ch'ien accompanied him, and it is probably this trip that he is referring to here.

49. Some ancient text now lost. This is believed to have been the model for at least the name, if not the form, of the *Shih chi* "Basic Annals" section.

APPENDIX B

1. See note 9, p. 216.
2. See SC 9/22.
3. See HS 63/2a, biography of the prince.
4. See HS 66/4a, biography of Liu Ch'ü-li.

BIBLIOGRAPHY

Wherever possible I have tried to refer to Chinese works in terms of the divisions integral to the texts themselves, rather than by the use of page numbers, so that references may be easily located in any edition. Thus, for example, all references to the *Spring and Autumn Annals* and its commentaries are to the reigning duke and the reign year rather than to chapter and page. Where page numbers do occur the editions to which they refer will be found listed below. This bibliography does not of course represent all the works consulted, but only those actually cited in the text. The following abbreviations have been used.

BMFEA	*Bulletin of the Museum of Far Eastern Antiquities*	JCNBRAS	*Journal of the North China Branch of the Royal Asiatic Society*
CCFL	*Ch'un-ch'iu fan-lu,* by Tung Chung-shu	PNP	*Po-na-pen* edition
FEQ	*Far Eastern Quarterly*	SC	*Shih chi,* by Ssu-ma Ch'ien
HJAS	*Harvard Journal of Asiatic Studies*	SPPY	*Ssu-pu pei-yao* edition
		SPTK	*Ssu-pu ts'ung-kan* edition
HS	*Han shu,* by Pan Ku	TP	*T'oung Pao*
JAOS	*Journal of the American Oriental Society*	YCHP	*Yen-ching hsüeh-pao (Yenching Journal)*

I. PRIMARY CHINESE SOURCES

Analects—Lun yü.
Book of Changes—I ching, Ssu-pu ts'ung-kan (SPTK) ed.
Book of Documents—Shu ching.
Book of Odes—Shih ching.
Chia-yu-chi, Su Hsün (SPTK).
Chin shu, Fang Hsüan-ling and others, *Po-na-pen* (PNP) ed.
Ch'u tz'u (SPTK).
Chu-tzu yü-lei, ed. of 1603.
Chuang Tzu, also called *Nan-hua chen-ching* (SPTK).
Ch'un-ch'iu fan-lu, Tung Chung-shu (SPTK).
Ch'un-ch'iu san-chuan, Ssu-shu wu-ching III. Shanghai, 1914.
Ch'un-ch'iu-wei Han-han-tzu. In *Ku-wei-shu* 12, *Shou-shan-ko ts'ung-shu.*
Chung yung, The Doctrine of the Mean.

Fa yen, Yang Hsiung (SPTK).

Fa-yen i-su, Wang Jung-pao ed., 1933.

Han Fei Tzu (SPTK).

Han-shih wai-chuan, Han Ying (SPTK).

Han shu, Pan Ku: all references to *Han-shu pu-chu*, Wang Hsien-ch'ien. Ch'angsha, 1900.

Han-shu chu-chiao-pu, Chou Shou-ch'ang. In *Kuang-ya ts'ung-shu*.

Hou-Han-shu, Fan Yeh (PNP).

Hsiao ching, The Classic of Filial Piety.

Hsin shu, Chia I (SPTK).

Hsün Tzu (SPTK).

Huai-nan Tzu (SPTK).

I-wei t'ung-kua-yen, in *Wu-ying-tien chü-chen-pan ch'üan-shu* 1, 1899.

Intrigues of the Warring States—Chan-kuo-ts'e (SPTK).

Kao-shih-chuan, Huang-fu Mi, *Ssu-pu pei yao* (SPPY).

Ku-liang Commentary—Ku-liang-chuan, Fan Ning, commentator.

Kuan Tzu (SPTK).

K'uang-miu cheng-su, Yen Shih-ku, in *Ts'ung-shu chi-ch'eng*.

Kung-yang Commentary—Kung-yang-chuan, Ho Hsiu, commentator.

Lao Tzu, Tao-te-ching.

Li chi, in *Shih-san-ching chu-su*, ed. Jui Lin and others, 1871.

Lü-shih ch'un-ch'iu (SPTK).

Lun heng, Wang Ch'ung (SPTK).

Mencius—Meng Tzu.

Mo Tzu (SPTK).

Nien-erh-shih cha-chi, Chao I (SPPY).

Narratives from the States—Kuo yü (SPTK).

Ou-yang Wen-Chung-kung chi, Ou-yang Hsiu (SPTK).

Ping fa, Sun Wu (SPTK).

San-kuo-chih, Ch'en Shou (PNP).

Shang-chün-shu (SPTK).

Shih chi, Ssu-ma Ch'ien: all references to *Shiki kaichû kôshô*, Takikawa Kametarô. Tokyo, 1934.

Shih-chi p'ing-lin, Ling Chih-lung.

Shih t'ung, Liu Chih-chi (SPTK).

Shuo-wen chieh-tzu, Hsü Shen (SPTK).

Ta-Tai li-chi (SPTK).

T'ang-Sung pa-chia-wen.

Tso Commentary—Tso chuan, Tu Yü, commentator.

T'ung chih, Cheng Ch'iao.

Tzu-chih t'ung-chien, Ssu-ma Kuang. Commercial Press ed., 1917.
Wen-hsien t'ung-k'ao, Ma Tuan-lin.
Wen-hsin tiao-lung, Liu Hsieh (SPTK).
Wen hsüan, Liu-ch'en-chu Wen-hsüan (SPTK).
Wen-shih t'ung-i, Chang Hsüeh-ch'eng.
Yen-t'ieh-lun, Huan K'uan (SPTK).
Yen-tzu ch'un-ch'iu (SPTK).

II. SECONDARY CHINESE SOURCES

Cheng Hao-sheng, *Ssu-ma Ch'ien nien-p'u,* Shanghai, Commercial Press, 1931.
Ch'eng Chin-tsao, "Origins of the Form of the *Shih chi,*" YCHP 37, 95–120 (Dec. 1949).
Chi Chen-huai, *Ssu-ma Ch'ien.* Shanghai, People's Press, 1954.
Ch'ien Mu, "An Examination and Interpretation of the Title Tai Sze Kung," *Academic Review* I, 54–59 (June 1953).
Ch'ien Mu, "A Study of the Date of Birth of Ssu-ma Ch'ien," *Academic Review* I, 51–53 (June 1953).
Ku Shih, *Han shu i-wen-chih chiang-su,* Shanghai, Commercial Press, 1924. 2nd. ed.
Wang Kuo-wei, *T'ai-shih-kung hsing-nien k'ao.* In *Kuan-t'ang chi-lin* 11, *Hai-ning-wang chung-ch'üeh-kung i-shu ch'u-chi.*
Yü Chia-hsi, "On the Missing Chapters of Ssu-ma Ch'ien's Work *Shih chi,*" *Fu Jen Sinological Journal* XV, 1–91 (1947).

III. JAPANESE WORKS

Kaizuka Shigeki, *Chûgoku kodai no kokoro,* Kawade Series #69, Tokyo, 1951.
Kamada Tadashi, *"Shiki* to *Saden* ni tsuite," *Memorial Volume in Honor of the Seventieth Birthday of Dr. Morohashi,* 133–60. Tokyo, 1953.
Naitô Torajirô, *Shina jôkoshi.* Tokyo, 1944.
—— *Shina shigakushi.* Tokyo, 1948.
Ojima Sukema, *Kodai Shina kenkyû.* Tokyo, 1943.
Okazaki Fumio, *Shiba Sen* [Ssu-ma Ch'ien]. Tokyo, 1946.
Rai Sanyô, *Rai Sanyô zensho.* Tokyo, 1931.
Shigezawa Toshio, *Shû-Kan shisô kenkyû.* Tokyo, 1943.
Takeda Taijun, *Shiba Sen,* 3rd. ed., Sôgen Library A-82. Tokyo, 1951.
Utsunomiya Kiyoyoshi, *Kandai shakai keizaishi kenkyû.* Tokyo, 1955.

Watson, Burton, "The *Shih chi* 'Hereditary House of Confucius' as Literature," *Journal of Chinese Literature* II, 18–27 (April 1955).

Yoshikawa Kôjirô, "Hsiang Yü's Song of Kai-hsia," *Journal of Chinese Literature* I, 1–18 (Oct. 1954).

—— "Kao-tsu's Song of the Great Wind," *Journal of Chinese Literature* II, 28–44 (April 1955).

IV. WESTERN WORKS

Bacon, Francis, *Advancement of Learning* and *Novum Organum*. Rev. ed. New York, Willey Book Co., 1944.

Bielenstein, Hans, "An Interpretation of the Portents in the *Ts'ien-han-shu*," BMFEA 22, 127–43 (1950).

—— "The Restoration of the Han Dynasty," BMFEA 26, 1–209 (1954).

Bodde, Derk, "Types of Chinese Categorical Thinking," JAOS 59, 200–19 (1939).

Caesar, *Conquest of Gaul,* S. A. Handford trans., Penguin Classics (1951).

Chavannes, Edouard, *Les Mémoires historiques de Se-ma Ts'ien.* 6 vols. Paris, E. Leroux, 1895–1905.

—— *Le T'ai Chan: Essai de monographie d'un culte chinois.* Paris, E. Leroux, 1910.

Chen Shih-hsiang, "An Innovation in Chinese Biographical Writing," FEQ XIII, 44–62 (Nov. 1953).

Creel, Herrlee Glessner, *Confucius, The Man and the Myth.* New York, John Day, 1949.

—— *Studies in Early Chinese Culture.* Baltimore, 1937.

Croce, Benedetto, *History as the Story of Liberty.* London, Allen and Unwin, 1949; New York, Meridian Books, 1955.

—— *The Theory and History of Historiography,* Douglas Ainslee, trans. London, Harrap, 1921.

Dubs, Homer H. *The History of the Former Han by Pan Ku.* 2 vols. London, Waverly Press, 1939–44.

Duyvendak, J. J. L., Review of Nancy Lee Swann, *Food and Money in Ancient China,* TP 40, 210–16 (1951).

Forke, Alfred, trans., *Lun-heng.* 2 vols. London, Luzac and Co., 1907.

Gale, Esson M., trans. *Discourses on Salt and Iron* (ch. 1–19), Sinica Leidensia II. Leiden, 1931.

—— *Discourses on Salt and Iron* (ch. 20–28), JNCBRAS LXV, 73–110 (1934).

Herodotus, *The Histories,* Aubrey de Selincourt, trans., Penguin Classics, 1954.

Hightower, James Robert, "The *Fu* of T'ao Ch'ien," HJAS 17: 1/2, 169–230 (1954).

—— "Ch'ü Yüan Studies," Silver Jubilee Volume of the Zinbun-Kagaku-*Kenkyusya,* 192–223. Kyoto, 1954.

Hulsewé, A. F. P., *Remnants of Han Law.* Vol. I. Sinica Leidensia IX. Leiden, 1955.

Karlgren, Bernhard, *On the Nature and Authenticity of the Tso Chuan.* Göteborg, 1926.

Kennedy, George A., "Interpretation of the *Ch'un-ch'iu,*" JAOS 62, 40–48 (1942).

Kramers, R. P., *K'ung Tzu Chia Yü: The School Sayings of Confucius.* Sinica Leidensia VII. Leiden, 1950.

Lin Yutang, *The Wisdom of Confucius.* New York, Modern Library, 1938.

Livy, *History of Rome,* 6 vols. Rev. Canon Roberts, trans. Everyman's Library, 1926.

Maspero, Henri, *Etudes historiques.* Paris, 1950.

Murray, Gilbert, *Five Stages of Greek Religion.* London, Watts and Co., 1935; New York, Anchor Books, 1955.

Neff, Emery, *The Poetry of History.* New York, Columbia Univ. Press, 1947.

Nivison, David S., "The Problem of 'Knowledge' and 'Action' in Chinese Thought Since Wang Yang-ming." In: *Studies in Chinese Thought,* Arthur Wright, ed., 112–45. Chicago, 1953.

Pearson, Lionel, "Real and Conventional Personalities in Greek History," Journal of the History of Ideas XV, 136–45 (Jan. 1954).

Shotwell, James T., *The History of History.* New York, Columbia Univ. Press, 1939.

Soothill, William Edward, *The Hall of Light.* London, Lutterworth Press, 1951.

Soper, Alexander Coburn, "The 'Dome of Heaven' in Asia," *The Art Bulletin* XXIX, 225–48 (March 1947).

Tacitus, *Annals (Tacitus on Imperial Rome).* Michael Grant, trans. Penguin Classics, 1956.

Thucydides, *The Peloponnesian War.* Rex Warner, trans. Penguin Classics, 1954.

Tjan Tjoe Som, *Po-Hu T'ung.* 2 vols. Sinica Leidensia VI. Leiden, 1949.

Toynbee, Arnold, *Greek Civilization and Character*. London, 1924; New York, Mentor Books, 1953.

——— *Greek Historical Thought*. London, 1924; New York, Mentor Books, 1952.

Waley, Arthur, *The Way and Its Power*. London, Allen and Unwin, 1934.

——— *A Hundred and Seventy Chinese Poems*. New York, Knopf, 1929.

Yang Lien-sheng, "A Theory About the Titles of the Twenty-four Dynastic Histories," HJAS 10, 41–47 (1947).

——— "Toward a Study of Dynastic Configuration in Chinese History," HJAS 17:3/4, 329–45 (1954).

GLOSSARY

The following glossary does not attempt to include the characters for all the titles, place names, and personal names appearing in the text. Such a list would reach impossible proportions. Titles of rulers, names of states and cities, and other names that may be assumed to be familiar to students of Chinese history have been omitted. All terms and titles of officials cited in the text in Chinese have been included, however, as well as the characters for bibliographical references and the names of less well known persons and places.

1. *Chan-kuo-ts'e*   戰國策

2. *Chan-shih*   詹事

3. Chang Ao   張敖

4. Chang Ch'ien   張騫

5. Chang Erh   張耳

6. Chang Fu   張輔

7. Chang I   張儀

8. Chang Liang   張良

9. Chang Shou-chieh   張守節

10. Chang Ts'ang   張蒼

11. Chao Kao   趙高

12. Chao Liang   趙良

13. Chao Shê   趙奢

14. Chao T'an 趙談

15. Ch'ao Ts'o 鼂錯

16. Ch'en Jen-hsi 陳仁錫

17. Ch'en Shê 陳涉

18. *cheng* 正

19. Ch'eng Chin-tsao 程金造

20. Cheng Hao-Sheng, *Ssu-ma Ch'ien nien-p'u* 鄭鶴聲　司馬遷年譜

21. Cheng Hsüan 鄭玄

22. *ch'eng i chia chih yen* 成一家之言

23. "Ch'eng-min" 烝民

24. *cheng-shih* 正史

25. *chi* 吉

26. Ch'i (tribe) 姜

27. Chi Chen-huai 季鎮淮

28. *Chi-chuan* 集傳

29. *chi-hui* 忌諱

30. Chi Pu 季布

31. *chi-tung* 季冬

32. Chia I, *see Hsin shu*

33. *Chia-yu-chi*, Su Hsün 嘉祐集，蘇洵

34. Chiang Ch'ung 江充

35. Chiao Chou 譙周

36. *chien* (Superintendent) 監

37. *Chien* (Commentary) 箋

38. *chien* (mirror) 鑒

39. *chien* 儉, 檢

40. *ch'ien* 乾

41. Ch'ien Mu 錢穆

42. *chih* (altar) 時

43. *chih* (solid qualities) 質

44. *chih* (will; Treatise) 志

45. *ch'ih* 尺

46. Chih Chün 摰峻

47. *Chin shu*, Fang Hsüan-ling 晉書, 房玄齡

48. *Ching-chi-chih* 經籍志

49. Ching Chien 景監

50. Ching K'o 荆軻

51. *Chiu-kao* 酒誥

52. *Chou li* 周禮

53. Chou Po 周勃

54. Chu Chia 朱家

55. Chu-fu An 主父偃

56. *Ch'u-Han ch'un-ch'iu,* Lu Chia 楚漢春秋，陸賈

57. Chu Hsi 朱熹

58. "Chü-hsia" 車蓬

59. Ch'u Shao-sun 褚少孫

60. *Ch'u tz'u* 楚辭

61. *Chu-tzu yü-lei* 朱子語類

62. Ch'ü Yüan 屈原

63. *chuan* 傳

64. Chuang Tzu, *Nan-hua chen-ching* 莊子，南華眞經

65. *chüeh* 絶

66. *chüeh-ssu* 絶杞

67. *ch'un-ch'iu* 春秋

68. *Ch'un-ch'iu fan-lu,* Tung Chung-shu 春秋繁露，董仲舒

69. *Ch'un-ch'iu san-chuan, Ssu-shu wu-ching* 春秋三傳，四書五經

70. *Ch'un-ch'iu-wei Han-han-tzu, Ku-wei-shu, Shou-shan-ko ts'ung-shu* 春秋緯漢含孳，古微書，守山閣叢書

71. *Chün-tzu yüeh* 君子曰

72. *chung* (middle) 中

73. Chung 重

74. Ch'ung-erh 重耳

75. *chung-hsing* 中興

76. *Chung-shu-ling* 中書令

77. *Chung yung* 中庸

78. *Dainihonshi* 大日本史

79. *Erh-shih* 貳師

80. *Fa yen*, Yang Hsiung 法言，揚雄

81. *Fa-yen i-su, Wang Jung-pao* 法言義疏，汪榮寶

82. Fan Chü 范雎

83. Fang Pao 方苞

84. Feng Wang-sun 馮王孫

85. *fu* 賦

86. *fu-hsing* 復興

87. Fu Sheng 伏生

88. Han-ch'eng hsien 韓城縣

89. *Han Fei Tzu* 韓非子

90. Han Hsin 韓信

91. *Han-shih wai-chuan,* Han Ying   韓詩外傳, 韓嬰

92. *Han shu,* Pan Ku   漢書, 班固

93. *Han-shu chu-chiao-pu,* Chou Shou-ch'ang, *Kuang-ya ts'ung-shu*   漢書注校補, 周壽昌, 廣雅叢書

94. *Han-shu pu-chu,* Wang Hsien-ch'ien   漢書補注, 王先謙

95. Ho Ch'ü-ping   霍去病

96. *Hou Chih-pu-tsu-chai ts'ung-shu*   後知不足齋叢書

97. *Hou-Han-shu,* Fan Yeh   後漢書, 范曄

98. *Hsi-tz'u*   繫辭

99. Hsia-hou Ying   夏侯嬰

100. Hsia-yang   夏陽

101. Hsiang Liang   項梁

102. "Hsiang-po"   巷伯

103. Hsiang Yü   項羽

104. *Hsiao ching*   孝經

105. Hsiao Ho   蕭何

106. Hsien-wu Village, Mou-ling   顯武里, 茂陵

107. *Hsin shu,* Chia I   新書, 賈誼

108. Hsiu Fu   休甫

109. *hsiu-te* 修德

110. *hsiung* 凶

111. Hsü Yu 許由

112. "Hsüan-niao" 玄鳥

113. *Hsün Tzu* 筍子

114. *hu* 護

115. Hu Hai 胡亥

116. Hu Sui 壺遂

117. Hua-ch'ih 華池

118. *Huai-nan Tzu* 淮南子

119. *Huang-Lao* 黃老

120. *hui* 諱

121. *huo* 眵

122. *Huo-cheng* 火正

123. *I ching* 易經

124. *i-shih* 逸詩

125. *I-wei t'ung-kua-yen, Wu-ying-tien chü-chen-pan ch'üan-shu* 易緯通卦驗，武英殿聚珍版全書

126. Jang Chü 穰苴

127. Jen An, *tzu* Shao-ch'ing 任安，字少卿

128. *ju* 辱

129. Ju Shun 如淳

130. Kai Nieh 蓋聶

131. Kaizuka Shigeki, *Chûgoku kodai no kokoro* 貝塚茂樹, 中國古代の心

132. Kamada Tadashi, *"Shiki* to *Saden* ni tsuite" 鎌田正, 史記と左傳について

133. *K'ao-i* 考異

134. Kao-men 高門

135. *Kao-shih-chuan*, Huang-fu Mi 高士傳, 皇甫謐

136. *kao-shuo* 告朔

137. Kao Yu 高誘

138. *Ku-liang-chuan*, Fan Ning com. 穀梁傳, 范寧

139. Ku Shih, *Han-shu i-wen-chih chiang-su* 顧實, 漢書藝文志講疏

140. *ku-wen* 古文

141. Ku Yen-wu 顧炎武

142. K'uai T'ung 蒯通

143. Kuan Chung 管仲

144. Kuan Fu 灌夫

145. *Kuan Tzu* 管子

146. *K'uang-miu cheng-su,* Yen Shih-ku, *Ts'ung-shu chi-ch'eng* 匡謬正俗, 顏師古, 叢書集成

147. *Kuei-ku Tzu* 鬼谷子

148. *k'un* 坤

149. *kung* 功

150. K'ung An-kuo 孔安國

151. Kung-sun Hung 公孫弘

152. *K'ung-tzu chia-yü* 孔子家語

153. *k'ung-wen* 空文

154. *Kung-yang-chuan,* Ho Hsiu com. 公羊傳, 何休

155. *k'ung-yen* 空言

156. Kung-yü Tai 公玉帶

157. *Kuo-Ch'in-lun* 過秦論

158. Kuo Hsieh 郭解

159. *Kuo yü* 國語

160. *Lang-chung* 郎中

161. Lao Tzu, *Tao-te-ching* 老子, 道德經

162. Li 黎

163. *li* (rites) 禮

164. *Li chi, Shih-san-ching chu-su,* Jui Lin 　禮記, 十三經注疏, 瑞麟

165. Li I-ch'i 　酈食其

166. Li Kuang 　李廣

167. Li Kuang-li 　李廣利

168. Li Ling 　李陵

169. *Li sao* ("Encountering Sorrow") 　離騷

170. Li Ssu 　李斯

171. Li T'u, *tzu* Hsing-hsüeh 　李塗, 字性學

172. Liao Teng-t'ing 　廖登廷

173. *lieh-chuan* 　列傳

174. *Lieh-nü-chuan,* Liu Hsiang 　烈女傳, 劉向

175. Lien P'o 　廉頗

176. Liu An 　劉安

177. *Liu-ao* 　劉媼

178. Liu Chih-chi, *see Shih t'ung*

179. Liu Ch'ü-li 　劉屈氂

180. Liu Hsiang, *see Lieh-nü-chuan*

181. Liu Hsin 　劉歆

182. Lu Chung-lien 　魯仲連

183. Lü Hsiang 呂向

184. *Lü-shih ch'un-ch'iu*, Lü Pu-wei 呂氏春秋, 呂不韋

185. Lüan Pu 欒布

186. *lun* 論

187. *Lun heng*, Wang Ch'ung 論衡, 王充

188. *Lun yü* 論語

189. Lung-men 龍門

190. Master Hsü 徐生

191. Master Huang 黃子, 黃生

192. Master Yüan Ku 轅固生

193. Meng T'ien 蒙恬

194. *Meng Tzu* 孟子

195. *ming* 命

196. *Ming-shan* 名山

197. *Ming t'ang* 明堂

198. *Mo Tzu* 墨子

199. Naitô Torajirô, *Shina jôkoshi; Shina shigakushi* 內藤虎次郎, 支那上古史; 支那史學史

200. *Nan-cheng* 南正

201. *Nei-shih* 內史

202. *Nien-erh-shih cha-chi,* Chao I　　廿二史劄記，趙翼

203. Ojima Sukema, *Kodai Shina*　　小島祐馬
　　　kenkyū　　古代支那研究

204. Okazaki Fumio, *Shiba Sen*　　岡崎文夫，司馬遷

205. *Ou-yang Wen-chung-kung*　　歐陽文忠公集，
　　　chi, Ou-yang Hsiu　　歐陽脩

206. Pan Piao　　班彪

207. Pao Sheng-chih　　暴勝之

208. Pao Shu　　鮑叔

209. *pei*　　悲

210. *Pei-cheng*　　北正

211. *Pei shih-pu-yü fu*　　悲士不遇賦

212. *pen-chi*　　本紀

213. P'eng Yüeh　　彭越

214. *piao*　　表

215. *p'ien*　　篇

216. *pien-nien*　　編年

217. *p'ing*　　評

218. *Ping fa,* Sun Wu　　兵法，孫武

219. *po*　　搏

220. Po Ch'i　　白起

221. Po I & Shu Ch'i   伯夷，叔齊

222. *Po-na-pen* (PNP)   百衲本

223. *Po-shih*   博士

224. *Po-wu-chih*   博物志

225. *pu-jen*   不忍

226. P'u Shih   卜式

227. *pu-yung*   不用

228. Rai Sanyô, *Rai Sanyô zensho*   賴山陽全書

229. *San-kuo-chih*, Ch'en Shou   三國志，陳壽

230. Sang Hung-yang   桑弘羊

231. *sha*   殺

232. *Shang-chün-shu*, Shang Yang   商君書，商鞅

233. *Shang-ti*   上帝

234. Shen Pu-hai   申不害

235. "Sheng-min"   生民

236. Shigezawa Toshio, *Shû-Kan shisô kenkyû*   重澤俊郎，周漢思想研究

237. *shih* (assassinate)   弒

238. *shih* (deeds)   事

239. *shih* (historian)   史

240. *shih* (lesser nobility)   士

241. *Shih-che* 使者

242. *Shih-chi p'ing-lin*, Ling Chih-lung 史記評林, 凌稚隆

243. *shih-chia* 世家

244. *Shih ching* 詩經

245. *Shih-chung* 侍中

246. *Shih pen* 世本

247. *Shih t'ung*, Liu Chih-chi 史通, 劉知幾

248. *Shiki kaichû kôshô*, Takikawa Kametarô 史記會注考證, 瀧川龜太郎

249. *shu* (Treatise) 書

250. *shu* (transmit) 述

251. *Shu ching* 書經

252. Shu-sun T'ung 叔孫通

253. *Shuo-wen chieh-tzu*, Hsü Shen 說文解字, 許慎

254. *ssu-hao* 四皓

255. *Ssu-k'u ch'üan-shu tsung-mu* 四庫全書總目

256. Ssu-ma Ang 司馬卬

257. Ssu-ma Ch'ang 司馬昌

258. Ssu-ma Chen 司馬貞

259. Ssu-ma Ch'ien, *tzu* Tzu-ch'ang 司馬遷, 字子長

260. Ssu-ma Chin or Ch'i 司馬靳, 靳

261. Ssu-ma Hsi 司馬喜

262. Ssu-ma Hsiang-ju 司馬相如

263. Ssu-ma K'uai-wai 司馬蒯聵

264. Ssu-ma I 司馬懿

265. Ssu-ma T'an 司馬談

266. Ssu-ma Ts'o 司馬錯

267. Ssu-ma Wu-tse 司馬無澤, 毋擇

268. Ssu-ma Yen 司馬炎

269. *Ssu-pu pei-yao* (SPPY) 四部備要

270. *Ssu-pu ts'ung-k'an* (SPTK) 四部叢刊

271. Su Ch'in 蘇秦

272. *Su-wang miao-lun* 素王妙論

273. Sui Hui *or* Shih Hui 隨會, 士會

274. *sung* 頌

275. Sung Hsien 宋咸

276. *Ta-Tai li-chi* 大戴禮記

277. *T'ai-hsüan-ching* 太玄經

278. *T'ai-kung* 太公

279. *T'ai-shih-kung* 太史公

280. *T'ai-shih-ling* 太史令

281. Takeda Taijun, *Shiba Sen* 武田泰淳，司馬遷

282. T'ang Tu 唐都

283. *T'ang-Sung pa-chia wen* 唐宋八家文

284. *te* 德

285. *ti-chi* 帝紀

286. *t'ien* 天

287. *t'ien-hsia-chih-hsiao* 天下之笑

288. T'ien Jen 田仁

289. *t'ien-ming* 天命

290. *Tien-yin* 典引

291. *to* 多

292. Tou Ying 竇嬰

293. *Ts'ai* 蔡

294. Ts'ai Tse 蔡澤

295. *tsan* 讚

296. Ts'ao Ts'an 曹參

297. *tse* 澤

298. *tso* 作

299. Tso Ch'iu-ming 左丘明

300. *Tso chuan*, Tu Yü com.　　左傳，杜預

301. Tsou Yen　　鄒衍

302. Ts'ui Shih, *Shih-chi t'an-yüan*　　崔適，史記探源

303. *ts'un*　　寸

304. *Tu-shih tsung-p'ing*　　讀史總評

305. *tuan-tai-shih*　　斷代史

306. *t'ung*　　統

307. *T'ung chih*, Cheng Ch'iao　　通志，鄭樵

308. Tung Chung-shu, *see Ch'un-ch'iu fan-lu*

309. Tung-fang So　　東方朔

310. *t'ung-shih*　　通史

311. *Tzu-chih t'ung-chien*, Ssu-ma Kuang　　資治通鑑，司馬光

312. *Tz'u-shih*　　刺史

313. Utsunomiya Kiyoyoshi, *Kandai shakai keizaishi kenkyû*　　宇都宮清吉，漢代社會經濟史研究

314. Wang Kuo-wei, *T'ai-shih-kung hsing-nien k'ao, Kuan-t'ang chi-lin, Hai-ning-wang Chung-ch'üeh-kung i-shu ch'u-chi*　　王國維，太史公行年考，觀堂集林，海寧王忠慤公遺書初集

315. *Wang-ming-lun* 　王命論

316. Wang Su 　王肅

317. Wei Ch'ing 　衛青

318. *wei-tz'u* 　微辭

319. *wen* 　文

320. *Wen-hsien t'ung-k'ao*, Ma Tuan-lin 　文獻通考，馬端臨

321. *Wen-hsin tiao-lung*, Liu Hsieh 　文心雕龍，劉勰

322. *Wen hsüan, Liu-ch'en-chu* 　文選，六臣注

323. *Wen-shih t'ung-i*, Chang Hsüeh-ch'eng 　文史通義，章學誠

324. *Wen-yen* 　文言

325. Wu Ch'en 　武臣

326. Wu-ch'iu Shou-wang 　吾丘壽王

327. Wu Pei 　伍被

328. Wu Pi 　吳祕

329. *wu-shang* 　誣上

330. *Wu-ta-fu* 　五大夫

331. Wu Tzu-hsü 　伍子胥

332. Yang Ho, *tzu* Shu-yüan 　揚何，字叔元

333. Yang Hsiung, *see Fa yen*

334. Yang Yün 楊惲

335. *yen* 言

336. *Yen-t'ieh-lun*, Huan K'uan 鹽鐵論, 桓寬

337. *Yen-tzu ch'un-ch'iu* 晏子春秋

338. Yen Ying 晏嬰

339. *yin-yüeh* 隱約

340. Ying Shao 應劭

341. Yoshikawa Kôjirô 吉川幸次郎

342. Yü Chia-hsi 余嘉錫

343. *Yü pen-chi* 禹本紀

344. *Yü-shih ch'un-ch'iu*, Yü Ch'ing 虞氏春秋, 虞卿

345. *yu-shui* 遊說

346. Yüan Ang, *tzu* Ssu 袁盎, 字絲

347. *yüeh* 樂

348. Yung Ch'ü 雍渠

INDEX

Cheng, Prince, 99

Cheng Ch'iao, 134, 222, *n.* 14; critical opinions on Ssu-ma Ch'ien, 134, on Pan Ku, 134; quoted, 93

Ch'eng Chin-tsao, 225, *n.* 1

Cheng Hao-sheng, 41

Cheng Hsüan, 227, *n.* 10

"Cheng-min" (*Odes, Ta-ya* section), quoted, 69

Ch'eng T'ang, King, 5

Ch'en Shê, 22, 24; "Hereditary House" of, 118, 119-20; quoted, 119-20

Chen Shih-hsiang, 124; quoted, 121, 122

Chi (fortune), 136

Ch'i, Grand Historian of, 80

Ch'i, Lady, 167

Chia I, 140-41, 149, 203, *n.* 87; quoted, 20, 189

Chiang Ch'ung, 195

Chia Sheng, 56

Chi Chen-huai, 95-96

Chieh, 5

Chien (to look at, to observe), 136

Chi-hui (words of avoidance), 94

"Ch'in Chronicle," 113

Ch'in dynasty, 6, 8, 9, 25-27, 42, 56, 68, 74, 99, 110, 111, 114, 119, 184-86; Confucianist opposition to, 25-26; destruction of Chou chronicles, 113; downfall of, 149, view of Chia I on, 149, view of Pan Ku on, 149, Emperor Ming's criticism of Ssu-ma Ch'ien's view on, 150

Chinese historiography, beginnings of, 70-99

Chinese history: origins of, 67-68; sources of, 70-75

Ching, Duke, 80

Ching, Emperor, 29-30, 35, 120, 145

Ching Chien, 59

Chi Pu, 64, 96, 192-93, 219, *n.* 134

Chou, Duke of, 14, 49

Chou, Emperor, 5, 218, *n.* 128

Chou dynasty, 5, 6, 9, 13-15, 17-26 *passim,* 35, 42, 53, 55, 70-71, 74, 75, 110, 111, 113, 114, 117-18, 119, 127; literature of, 14-15; Han attitude towards, 25; humanism of, 135

Chou li (*Rites of Chou*), 70

Chou Po, Marquis of Chiang, 64, 219, *n.* 132

Chou Shou-ch'ang, quoted, 194, 196, 198

"Chronological Canons" (Eusebius), 227, *n.* 13

"Chronological Table of the Six States, Preface to" (Ssu-ma Ch'ien), quoted, 184-86

"Chronological Table of the Three Dynasties" (Ssu-ma Ch'ien), 111; quoted, 86; Preface to, quoted, 184

"Chronological Tables" (Ssu-ma Ch'ien): form, 112-14; as source for facts not to be found elsewhere in the *Shih chi,* 113-14; value of, 113-14; praised by Chao I, 113-14; relationships, spatial and temporal, in, 114; introductory essays to, 114-15; Pan Ku's addition, to, 228, *n.* 20

Chronologies, "doctoring" of, 228, *n.* 15

Ch'u, 9, 43

Chuan, given meaning of "biography" by Ssu-ma Ch'ien, 122; additional meaning implied by Ssu-ma Ch'ien, 122-24

Ch'üan Barbarians, 93

Chuang, Duke of Ch'i, 80

Chuang, Duke of Wei, 9

Chuang Tzu, 138-39; quoted, 20, 238, *n.* 15

Chuan Hsü, 42, 68, 110

Chu Chia, 64, 96

Chüeh-ssu (the cutting off of the sacrifices), 7

Ch'u-Han ch'un-ch'iu (Lu Chia), 68, 220, *n.* 145, 224, *n.* 40

Chu Hsi, 222, *n.* 14

Ch'un-ch'iu (Spring and Autumn), 103; *see also* Spring and Autumn Annals

Ch'un-ch'iu fan-lu (Tung Chung-shu), 211, *n.* 65, 222, *n.* 16

Chung, *Nan-cheng,* 42, 202, *n.* 3

Ch'ung-erh, 125, 144

Chung Tzu-ch'i, 58, 215, *n.* 101

Chung yung, quoted, 225, *n.* 42

Ch'u Shao-sun, 16, 110, 194, 195, 196, 198, 226, *n.* 9, 227, *n.* 10; quoted, 146

Chü-shih, 64

Ch'ü Yüan, 23, 25, 54, 65; quoted, 215, *n.* 99

Classic of Filial Piety, 208, *n.* 54

Classic of Hills and Seas, 193

Classics, Confucian, *see* Confucian classics

Collected Ritual, see Li chi

Collected Ritual of Tai the Elder, see Ta-tai li-chi

Commentaries, as philosophical works, 163; word-by-word interpretation in, 222, *n.* 14; *see also titles of specific commentaries*

Comprehensive Mirror for the Aid of Government, see Tzu-chih t'ung-chien